THE IRISH BOOK IN THE
TWENTIETH CENTURY

THE IRISH BOOK
IN THE
TWENTIETH CENTURY

Editor

CLARE HUTTON

IRISH ACADEMIC PRESS
DUBLIN • PORTLAND, OR

First published in 2004 by
IRISH ACADEMIC PRESS
44, Northumberland Road, Dublin 4, Ireland

and in the United States of America by
IRISH ACADEMIC PRESS
c/o ISBS, 5824 N.E. Hassalo Street, Portland
Oregon 97213-3644

Website: www.iap.ie

Copyright collection © 2004 Irish Academic Press
Copyright chapters © 2004 contributors

British Library Cataloguing in Publication Data

ISBN 0-7165-2780-4 (cloth)
ISBN 0-7165-3335-9 (paper)

Library of Congress Cataloging-in-Publication Data

Typeset by FiSH Books, London
Printed by Betaprint Ltd., Dublin

Contents

Acknowledgements

Book history is a highly collaborative enterprise and would not be possible but for the archivists and librarians who locate, maintain and make available unpublished materials. In this regard, and for providing us with research assistance, the editor and contributors would like to thank Mike Bott of the University of Reading Library, Noel Kissane of the National Library of Ireland, Steve Enniss of the Woodruff Library at Emory University, and Thomas Staley of the Harry Ransom Humanities Research Center, Austin. Staff at the Royal Irish Academy, the University College Dublin Archives, the British Library, the University of Kansas Library, the Berg Collection of the New York Public Library, and the Houghton Library of Harvard University have also been unfailingly helpful.

Two libraries deserve particular thanks, for this book began life at an exhibition on 'Irish Writing and English Reading', expertly mounted from the collections of the University of London Library and the Library of Trinity College Dublin, by Julia Walworth and Emma Robinson in London and Charles Benson and Bill Simpson in London. Thanks are also due to Bill McCormack, organiser of the London University conference on 'The Irish Book in the Twentieth Century', and to Warwick Gould, Director of the Institute of English Studies, where the conference took place. I am deeply grateful to them both for their scholarly generosity and guidance.

This volume has been long in the making, and I should like to express my personal thanks to the contributors for the care taken in transforming their conference papers into finished essays, and for their patience and understanding. Others who attended the conference, including Edward Barrington, Helen Carr, Roy Foster, Andrew Gibson, Hilary Laurie, Derek Mahon, Alastair McCleery, Jean Paul Pittion, Eileen Reilly, and Colin Smythe did much to make it a lively and stimulating occasion. Thanks too to my husband, Grant Lamond, for his unfailing support, willingness to read and discuss ideas, good humour and good cooking.

Unpublished writings of W. B. Yeats and Elizabeth Yeats appear by permission of Michael B. Yeats (through A. P. Watt, Ltd.) and Oxford University Press. Unpublished writings of Samuel Beckett appear by permission of Edward Beckett. Unpublished writings of Francis Stuart appear by permission of Paul Durcan. The permission to quote from the archives of Thomas Kinsella, Michael Longley, Derek Mahon, Liam Miller and Paul Muldoon at Emory University is gratefully acknowledged. Every effort has been made to establish contact with the holders of original copyrights; in cases where this has not been possible, I hope this general acknowledgement will be taken as sufficient.

Notes on the Contributors

Michael Adams is publisher at Four Courts Press. From 1974 to 1996 he ran Irish Academic Press; prior to that he worked at Irish University Press (1968–72) and Scepter Publishers, Dublin, (*c*.1959–68). He is the author of *Censorship: The Irish Experience* (1968) and of some books of popular theology. He translates from Spanish.

Nicola Gordon Bowe is Senior Lecturer in Art and Design History at the National College of Art and Design (National University of Ireland). She has published and lectured widely on the applied and decorative arts, with special attention to the Arts and Crafts Movement in Ireland, and Twentieth Century Irish stained glass. Her publications include *Harry Clarke: His Graphic Art* (1983) and *The Arts and Crafts Movements in Dublin and Edinburgh, 1885–1925* (1998). She is currently working on a critical biography of Wilhelmina M. Geddes.

Stephen Enniss is Curator of Literary Collections at the Robert W. Woodruff Library of Emory University. He has directed the rapid growth of the Library's literary collections, including the acquisition of a string of major literary archives, among them the papers of poet and novelist James Dickey, the archives of many of Ireland's leading contemporary poets, and the papers of the late poet laureate of England, Ted Hughes. He has recently received a Leverhulme Fellowship to conduct research in London towards a critical study of the contemporary Irish poet Derek Mahon.

Clare Hutton is an AHRB Research Fellow at the Institute of English Studies, University of London. She is currently editing volume 5 of the Oxford *History of the Irish Book* (1891–2000). She is also working on a monograph that examines the sociology of reading and publishing in Ireland during the Literary Revival.

Ruth Ling is a Visiting Research Fellow at the Institute of English Studies, University of London. She has published articles on MacNeice and Kinsella, and has recently completed a book-length study of Longley entitled *The Papery House: The Making of Michael Longley's Poems*.

Anne McCartney is a British Academy Research Fellow at the University of Ulster in Coleraine. She has research interests in modern Irish fiction and is currently completing editorial work on volume 4 of the *Oxford History of the Irish Book* (1800–1891). She is the author of *Francis Stuart, Face to Face: A Critical Study* (Belfast, 2000).

W. J. McCormack was Professor of Literary History at Goldsmiths College, University of London, until his early retirement in 2002. His most recent publications are *Roger Casement in Death: Haunting the Free State* (Dublin, 2002) and *The Silence of Barbara Synge* (forthcoming). He is contemplating a biography of Oliver Goldsmith.

Colleen McKenna is Lecturer in Education and Professional Development at University College London. She has completed a doctorate (London, 2000) on 'Presences and Absences in Seamus Heaney's Place of Writing', and an article on 'Reading Yeats Through the Eyes of Seamus Heaney', *Yeats Annual*, 13 (1998).

Niall Ó Ciosáin is Lecturer in the Department of History, National University of Ireland, Galway. He is the author of *Print and Popular Culture in Ireland, 1750–1850* (1997). His current research concerns the relationship between state institutions and local populations in early nineteenth-century Ireland.

Siobhán Ó Rafferty has been Librarian at the Royal Irish Academy since 1997. She is currently working on contributions to the Oxford *History of the Irish Book*. She is also editing a series of papers to celebrate the Royal Society of Antiquaries' 150th anniversary year.

John Pilling is Professor of English and European Literature at the University of Reading, and Co-Director of the Beckett International Foundation. His publications include *Beckett before Godot* (1997) and (as editor) *The Ideal Core of the Onion: Reading Beckett Archives* (1992) and *Beckett's 'Dream' Notebook* (1999).

D. C. Rose is Jim O'Beirne Research Scholar at Goldsmiths College, London and the Editor of *The Oscholars*, a journal of Wilde studies. He is currently completing a doctoral thesis on the cultural and social background to Wilde's periods of residence in Paris.

Anne Tannahill joined Blackstaff Press as an editor in 1976 and has been Managing Director since 1980. She attended Queen's University Belfast as a mature student in the 1970s, graduating with a BA (Hons) and MA in English Language and Literature. She is past president of Clé: The Irish Publishers' Association, and has served as a governor of the Linen Hall Library and as a member of the Broadcasting Councils for both BBC Northern Ireland and RTÉ.

Derval Tubridy is a lecturer in English at Goldsmiths College, University of London. She has published a monograph on *Thomas Kinsella: The Peppercanister Poems*, and a number of articles on Kinsella and Samuel Beckett.

List of Illustrations

Introduction

Clare Hutton

This book is the first of its kind. It applies a 'history of the book' approach to Ireland's twentieth-century literary and cultural history. As that century itself recedes into history, it seems a particularly apt moment to introduce such a book. Many Irish scholars are currently engaged in research for a multi-volume 'History of the Irish Book' which will examine Ireland's written and printed heritage over a period of 1,500 years. And just over one hundred years ago, in 1903, Elizabeth Yeats, the poet's younger sister, issued the first publication of the Dun Emer Press, a private press which was founded in order to expand the horizons of W. B. Yeats's 'literary principality' and to revive printing 'as an art'.[1] 'Ireland after Parnell', Yeats's epoch-making account of the beginnings of the Literary Revival, suggests why such a venture was necessary:

> Irish literature had fallen into contempt; no educated man ever bought an Irish book; in Dublin Professor Dowden, the one man of letters with an international influence, was accustomed to say that he knew an Irish book by its smell, because he had once seen some books whose binding had been fastened together by rotten glue.[2]

Throughout the 1890s, Yeats worked tirelessly to perfect his idea of the aesthetic book and became, in his own words, increasingly 'opinionated' and 'crotchety over this question of design'.[3] He came to regret that many of his compatriots 'felt it inappropriate to publish an Irish book that had not harp and shamrock and green cover.'[4] The tradition which the Yeatses inaugurated – a tradition of combining standards of excellence in typographical design with standards of literary excellence – was of considerable significance for the development of Irish cultural publishing during the opening decades of the century, and has been continued by enterprises such as Liam Miller's Dolmen Press (1951–1987) and Peter Fallon's Gallery Press (est. 1970).

But this book is not a celebration of Dun Emer. Nor does it attempt a detailed survey of the Dun Emer legacy. Instead, it puts that legacy in a broader perspective by examining several different aspects of Irish book history in the twentieth century, a period of sustaining cultural interest owing to the cultural revival of the 1900s and the 'Northern Revival' of more recent decades. *The Irish Book in the Twentieth Century* began life at a conference held in London University in 1999 to mark the opening of an exhibition on 'Irish Writing and English Reading' which had been mounted from the collections of the University of London Library and the Library of Trinity College Dublin. Those who delivered papers at the conference were understandably keen to celebrate the richness of the exhibition.

But the conference also extended the parameters of the exhibition by examining more abstract topics such as censorship, and the role that Irish editors have played in London publishing houses. The occasion revealed a growing interdisciplinary interest in book history and topics such as the history of negotiations between Irish authors and publishers in Ireland, Britain and further afield; the role which publishers have played in the service of Irish culture; the role that books have played in the formation of twentieth-century Irish society; the role that the Irish government has played in the creation and suppression of Irish books; and the aesthetic qualities of prominent Irish books.

'Histoire du livre' has been well established as a field of French intellectual history since 1952 when Lucien Febvre, the co-founder of *Annales* and one of the foremost historians of his generation, described the work of Henri-Jean Martin as 'l'histoire du livre, *terra incognita*'. As Ian Willison points out, this prepared the way for the leadership of the French in the field of the history of the book, which was subsequently established in 1958 by Febvre and Martin's *L'Apparition du Livre*, a work which explored the changes that the invention of the printed book brought about in society, their causes and effects.[5] Following the lead set by Febvre and Martin, French scholars collaborated on a multi-volume *Histoire de l'édition française* (1982–98) which examined all aspects of the history of production, publication and distribution, from the stage of authorship, to the impact of books on readers, and ultimately, on society. Scholars in the English-speaking world have tended to combine this kind of *annaliste* cultural history with the concerns of more traditional bibliographical approaches. This is certainly true of the essays gathered here, which are concerned with the history of individual books and publishing houses, and the role of the book in history.

The broad range of methodologies that book historians draw upon has much to offer scholars in the field of Irish studies. For, as D. F. McKenzie saw, book history opens up the possibility of a more comprehensive reconstruction of cultural history.

> Bibliography as such knows no canon. The ephemera of broadsides, notices, images, tracts – all the physically slight, evanescent, occasional, uncanonical, but prolific missives of commercial impositions, entertainment, radical protest, and state power – are also enrolled as testimony to the dense and complex nature of any culture served by print and the complexity of its construction.[6]

This is not to suggest that the 'book history' approach is a panacea for all methodological ills. While the approach is valuable to the extent that it can give weight to the many different and dissonant elements of Irish culture, it depends on researchers being interested in a comprehensive view and, crucially, on the survival of archives, which depends on institutions and individuals deeming that the material is worth preservation. It is also true that not all individuals and communities, even those of the recent past, leave significant written records. For instance, as Niall Ó Ciosáin observes in his essay on 'Innovation and Reception in

Irish Language Publishing, 1880–1920', the corpus of printed material available to literate Irish speakers remained small because norms had yet to be established in printed Irish and no institution, political or religious, had given its support to a form of written Irish. Native speakers generally came from the poorest socio-economic background and those who survived the Famine often emigrated. The bibliographical heritage of the Irish language in the nineteenth century is therefore full of gaps and silences. Nevertheless – and despite the methodological difficulties which it poses – this heritage, and the story of the way in which the status of the Irish language was transformed by the cultural revival of the early twentieth century is an extremely important and highly distinctive part of the history of the Irish book. O Ciosáin's essay, the first in this collection, is therefore particularly welcome. It explores the sudden increase in Irish language printing during the Irish cultural revival in the late nineteenth and early twentieth centuries and shows how the practice and assumptions of revivalist printing tended to marginalise existing readers of Irish in *Gaeltacht* areas.

Though it may only be a problem of terminology, another problematic aspect of book history is the emphasis it gives to the printed book. As Roger Chartier has noted, 'not all texts are necessarily given in book form' and not all books are necessarily printed.[7] In the absence of a culturally sympathetic native book publishing industry, Irish authors have often turned to pamphlets, periodicals, newspapers and self-publication: these less formal (and often interim) forms of publication have played an extremely important role in the developing textual culture of twentieth-century Ireland. Under the imprint of the Peppercanister Press, Thomas Kinsella has been issuing volumes of his own poetry since 1972: the interpretive significance of this venture in self-publication is explored here by Derval Tubridy. Another means by which literary authors can control the dissemination of their works is by cultivating publishers and editors who are sympathetic to their intentions. This was clearly the aim of W. B. Yeats when he became involved in the negotiations that led to the foundation of Maunsel and Company, the subject of my own contribution to this book. Maunsel is one of the publishing houses noted for its 'Arts and Crafts' design standards in Nicola Gordon Bowe's essay, 'The Book in the Irish Arts and Crafts Movement', which shows the lengths to which authors were prepared to go to achieve excellence in Celtic design. But the relationship between an author's intentions and the publisher's realisation of those intentions can go badly awry, and Stephen Enniss's essay on 'Derek Mahon and the Literary Marketplace' examines a case in point. In 1987 Mahon asked to be released from all contractual obligations to Oxford University Press: his *Poems 1962–1978* was riddled with typographical errors and the reprinting of unrevised texts had only served to make the situation worse. Indeed he regarded 'that awful Brown Book' as a kind of artistic theft that froze the further development of his poems in time and he wanted to take steps to remove his work from the public sphere. In this Mahon shares something with Samuel Beckett who was 'only interested in those I like having copies' of *Echo's Bones* (Paris, 1935), his first volume of poetry. As John Pilling notes in his essay on the composition and publishing history of Beckett's early poetry, by early 1936

– a few months after the publication of the volume – it was becoming painfully clear that there were not many who reciprocated by liking the poems.

The history and significance of literary publishing is a particular strength of this collection. Colleen McKenna's essay, 'Seamus Heaney and the Book as Expressive Form', explores the way in which *Sweeney's Flight* (1992) reworks Heaney's earlier *Sweeney Astray* (1983), while Ruth Ling's piece examines the composition history and ordering of Michael Longley's first volume, *No Continuing City* (1969). Anne McCartney's piece surveys Francis Stuart's publishing history and argues that the tribulations of that history mirror those of the Irish publishing industry. It is a history that suggests the importance of 'little magazines' to the Literary Revival, the limitations of the Irish market for novels, and the need which many twentieth-century Irish authors have had for British and American publishers and readers. In '*Salome*: A Text Unveiled', David Rose looks at the production and dissemination of Oscar Wilde's play, a text which has been rewritten, translated and even made into an opera. Through that process, the meaning of *Salome* has been transformed for new readers and audiences and, arguably, the meaning of the text now lies amidst the totality of those rereadings. W. J. McCormack's essay on 'Censorship: Some Uncomfortable Revisions' rereads the riots that accompanied the first performances of Synge's *Playboy of the Western World* in 1907. McCormack takes issue with the notion that censorship in Ireland originated in the 1920s and argues that a reconsideration of the *Playboy* riots suggests a longer history, and a more complex figuration of hostilities and alliances.

This book concludes with reflections by two individuals who have extensive experience of working in the publishing business. Anne Tannahill describes the history of the Blackstaff Press and Michael Adams discusses 'The World of Irish University Press', which went bankrupt in 1974. But his 'Gazetteer' of 'the people of IUP and where they went' shows how this was not the end but a beginning for late twentieth-century Irish publishing. Many of those who had trained and worked at IUP have gone on to distinguished careers as publishers since that collapse. These pieces serve as a vivid reminder of the value of being told the story of Irish publishing at first hand. Though undoubtedly a story 'complete with missing parts' (in Beckett's memorable phrase) let us hope that others will follow suit and write it all down.

Chapter 1

Creating an Audience:
Innovation and Reception in Irish Language
Publishing, 1880–1920

Niall Ó Ciosáin

One of the more remarkable features of book history in twentieth-century Ireland is the sudden increase of printing in the Irish language at the turn of the century. Production in Irish went through a change in order of magnitude, from perhaps two or three books per decade in the late nineteenth century to ten or twenty per year thereafter. There is as yet no statistical study of this area, but the trend can be illustrated in a graph showing production of Irish-language periodicals in the same period. Before 1895, the only periodical published in Ireland was *Irisleabhar na Gaeilge*, founded in 1882, although *An Gaodhal*, founded in New York in the same year for an emigrant readership, had subscribers in Ireland. By 1920, nine weekly or monthly titles had appeared.[1] (See Fig. 1.1) This printed production was centred in Dublin, and associated with the language revival movement. The Gaelic League was the principal publisher, although commercial houses such as M. H. Gill, James Duffy, and Browne and Nolan were also involved.[2] (There were some publications outside Dublin, but these tended to be printed in Dublin. One example is *Clann Uisnigh* by J. P. Craig, published in 1909 in Derry by D. G. Craig, but printed in Dublin by J. Falconer.)

One of the most striking features of this published corpus is its novelty and innovation. The Irish language movement was self-consciously and deliberately attempting to create a new literature, a new print culture and a new readership. The texts produced were of all kinds, with new fiction and drama, autobiography and memoir, retellings of myths and legends, children's literature, history, poetry and mathematics all being published. It also encouraged new writing and new writers. The Gaelic League's annual cultural festival, *An tOireachtas*, featured competitions for short stories and plays, and the winning entries were usually published.

These publications were accompanied by substantial debates about the possible forms of a print culture in Irish.[3] In the realm of typography, a choice had to be made between using roman type and gaelic type. The vast majority of books in the early twentieth century used Gaelic type, chosen probably as a sign of the distinctiveness of gaelic culture. This meant that a printing trade which had functioned almost exclusively in English needed to procure new fonts, the best-known of which was commissioned from Figgins of London in 1897, and used for *An Claidheamh Soluis* and other Gaelic League publications.[4] Orthography was also an issue, with spelling systems of varying degrees of complexity being proposed and discussed. The spectrum of possibilities can be illustrated by *Fiche Duan* ('Twenty Poems'), published in 1919 by Shán Ó Cuív partly to illustrate the

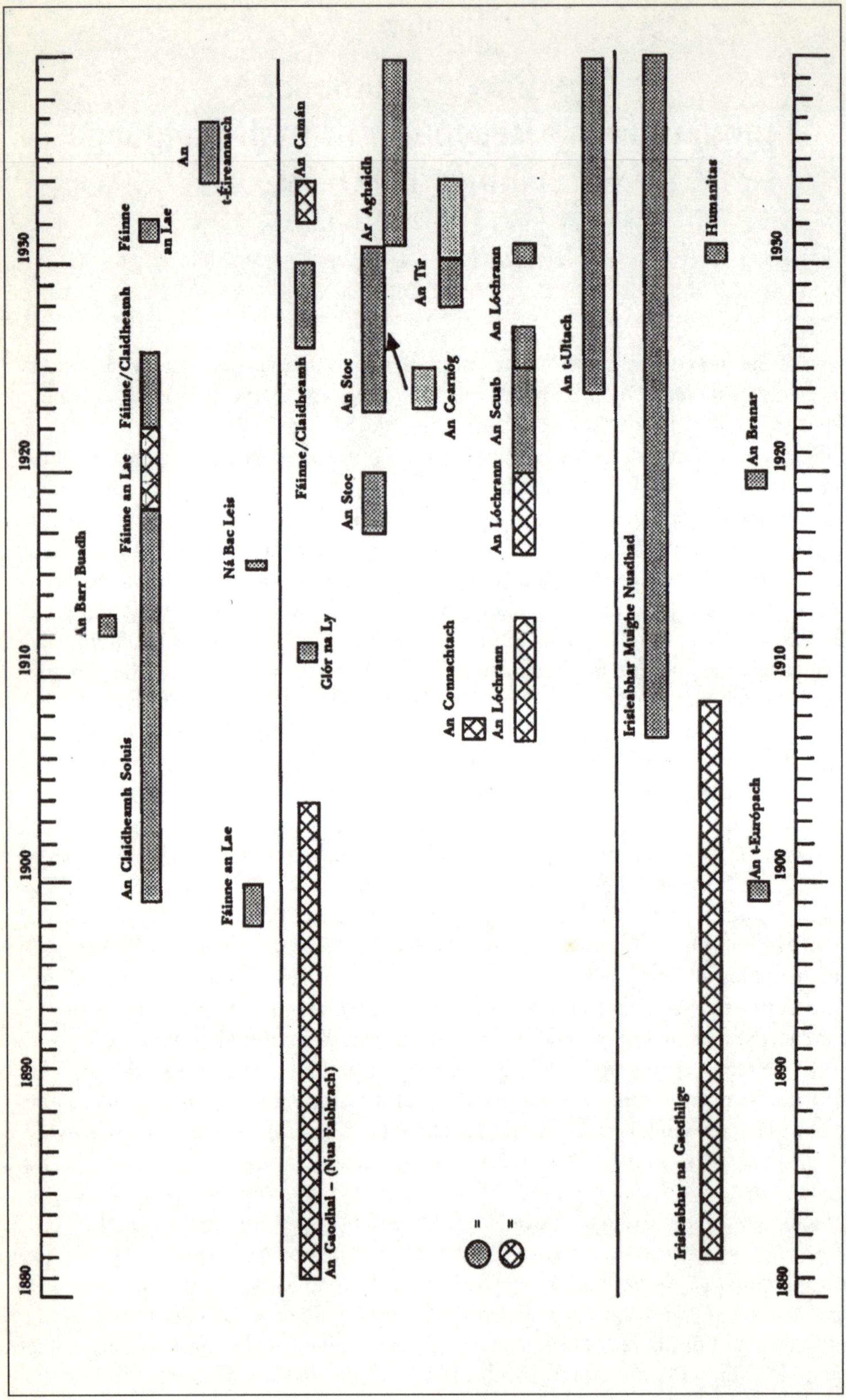

Figure 1.1 Newspapers and periodicals printed in Irish, 1880–1937. (By kind permission of An Clóchomar)

merits of his own simplified spelling. The book contains on facing pages the same poems printed in gaelic font and complex spelling, and in roman font with simplified spelling.[5] (See Fig. 1.2.)

More extensive debate took place over the forms of language to be used. Some urged that writing and publishing in Irish should base itself on the last national linguistic norm that had existed, that of educated and professional writing of the seventeenth and eighteenth centuries, exemplified particularly by Geoffrey Keating's *Foras Feasa ar Éirinn*, written in the early seventeenth century. Others felt that it should adopt the contemporary spoken vernacular, referred to as '*caint na ndaoine*' ('the speech of the people'), which contained at least three separate regional dialects. According to one of the principal exponents of this view, the Revd Peter O'Leary, 'to build up a literature without laying its foundations on the living speech of the people is like starting to build your house with the chimney'.[6] The success of O'Leary's novella, *Séadna*, written in contemporary Munster Irish, is generally held to have settled the issue in favour of the vernacular.

It was not simply the norms and forms of print culture in Irish that had to be debated and created, but also its readership. The Irish language movement in the early twentieth century was predominantly a revival movement, and its texts as much as its language classes were designed to create a literate public. The principal mechanism for the creation of such a public was the educational system, and the Gaelic League concentrated much of its energy on having Irish accepted as a subject in State schools and examinations. The pedagogic emphasis is also striking in its publications. Primers and other teaching texts, particularly the more elementary kind, were the most

Seán Ó Dige.

Níor ġéilleas riaṁ do ráiḋtiḃ
  Fileaḋ, fáiḋ, ná draoi,
Go ḃfuair an Ḃulcán gránda
  Ḃénus ḃreáġ mar ṁnaoi,
Nó go ḃfeaca péarla an ḃáin-ċnis
  Le toil a cáirde gaoil
Gan roga ná malairt áruis
  I ḃfoċair Ṡeáin Uí Ḋige.

Ní ġéillim nać sprid náiṁdeać,
  Do ṫáṫuig dlúiṫ an dís.
A ċuspóir ṗeacaiḋ, a Ṁámoin,
  'Na measc, mo náire, ḃís!
"Mopso Nysa datur"—
  Is fíor an ráiḋteaċt í
Ó fuair an stuaire d'áḋḃar
  Fear mar Ṡeán Ó Dige.

Dá mba fear mar ċác mé
  'S gur ṁait mar ċéard liom í,
Do ṫroidfinn seal mar Ṁárs di
  'S do ġráḋfainn í óm' ċroiḋe;
Ó 'sé do ḃreoiḋ 'is do ċráiḋ mé,
  Is d'ḟág mé taṁ gan ḃríġ.
Ar gcearṫlín sneaċta ṁná ḃeiṫ
  'Na tráill ag Seán Ó Dige.

Piaras Mac Gearailt.

SHÁN Ó DÍ.

Níor ghéleas ryav do ráitiv
  Fili, fáig ná dry,
Go vuer an Vulcán grána
  Vénus vreá mar vny,
Nú go veaca péarla an váin-chnish
  Le toil a cáirdi guíl
Gan rou ná maluirt áruish
  A vochuir Cheáin I Ghí.

Ní ghélim nách sbrid nâideach
  Do háhig dlúh an dísh
A chuspóir feaca, a Vámuin
  'Na mease, mo náiri, vísh!
Mopso Nysa datur—
  Is fíor an ráiteacht í
O fuer an sdueri d'ávar
  Fear mar Cheán O Dí.

Dá ma fear mar chách mi
  'S gur vah mar cheárd lium í
Do hroiting sheal mar Várs di
  'S do ghráhing í óm chry;
O 'shé do vreóig 's do chráig mi,
  Is d'ág mi tâv gan vrí,
Ar geartlín shneachda vná veh
  'Na tráil ig Shán O Dí.

PIARAS MAC GEARUILT.

Figure 1.2 Shán Ó Cuív, *Fiche Duan*, 1919.

frequently printed and were the best sellers. In October and November 1900, for example, 7,562 copies of the first volume of O'Growney's Irish manual, the most widely used primer, were sold, along with only 254 copies of the fifth volume.[7] The pedagogic emphasis was more fundamental than this, however, and in most cases, even when literary texts were published they were thought of and presented as educational. Editions of eighteenth-century poetry such as those by Father Patrick Dineen contain introductions and extensive glossaries, all in English.

The educational system was not the only public or official sphere in which revivalists attempted to have writing or print in Irish recognised. They also aimed at establishing it in public spaces such as shopfronts, or having it recognised by State agencies such as the Post Office. In 1905, two hundred members of the Gaelic League tried to post parcels with addresses written in Irish in the General Post Office in Dublin. To assist them in this endeavour they had a League publication from the same year, *Post-sheanchas* ('post-lore'), an extensive guide to addressing letters in Irish. This involved not simply supplying the Irish originals of, or equivalents to, placenames in English, but an alternative division of space, since counties were ignored in favour of older regions. Thus 'Tinahely, Co. Wicklow' became *'Tigh na hÉille, Gabhail Raghnaill'*, but 'Newtownmountkennedy, Co. Wicklow' became *'Baile Ó gCearnaigh, Críoch Bhranach'*.[8]

The strategies of the authors and editors of the Irish texts therefore envisaged the creation of a literate culture which would be entirely new. Its reading public, consisting principally of learners of the language, but also of those who spoke Irish in *Gaeltacht* areas, would also be a new creation. Underlying this was an analysis which assumed that there was no literate or print culture in Irish, and that the culture of Irish-speakers, of the *Gaeltacht*, was overwhelmingly oral or even exclusively illiterate. The formulation of the debate over forms of language in terms of an opposition between seventeenth- and eighteenth-century scribes and *'caint na ndaoine'*, between a literate past and an oral present, between writing and speech, is revealing. This assumption was also shared by critics of the language movement, who were dismissive of attempts to foster a crude peasant tongue, a 'kitchen Kaffir', in the words of the London *Morning Post*.[9]

The assumption that Irish-language culture was entirely oral also underlies most historical accounts. O'Leary's magisterial survey of the debates surrounding writing in Irish in the early twentieth century begins:

> Many of the leading writers of the Gaelic Revival never read a book in the Irish Language in their formative years. Some had not even imagined that such a thing was possible. Looking back on the language movement and his own involvment in it, one of the most prolific pioneers of modern Gaelic prose...(Séamus Ó Dubhghaill) recalled 'I myself never laid eyes on a book in Irish until I was twenty [i.e. 1875]'.

According to Eoghan Ó hAnluain's introduction to twentieth-century writing in Irish in *The Field Day Anthology*, 'the notion of literary composition no longer existed in the Irish-speaking areas [in 1900], although the tradition of storytelling still flourished'.[10] F. S. L. Lyons, describing the people of Co. Roscommon during Douglas

Hyde's youth, maintained that 'because they were unlettered, they had preserved much of the oral tradition of the west of Ireland'. There is room for scepticism here, about both the description – Roscommon had a developed primary school system during most of the nineteenth century – and the implied incompatibility between literacy and an oral tradition.[11]

These assumptions about literacy and orality are, however, not untypical of the primitivism through which western areas of Ireland were perceived, and which was shared by proponents and opponents of cultural nationalism, as well as many commentators on it. Thus E. M. Forster, in an introduction to Maurice O'Sullivan's *Twenty Years A-growing*, refers to the Blasket islanders in the early twentieth century as living in a 'neolithic' civilisation, despite the presence of state schools, market-oriented fishing, and regular receipt of letters and money from kin living thousands of miles away.[12]

As regards printed production in Irish in the later nineteenth century, the diagnosis has some validity, as total output was very small. There were some academic editions of old texts, whose readership consisted primarily of specialists. For a more popular audience there was some Catholic devotional material, including the *Pious Miscellany* of Tadhg Gaelach Ó Súilleabháin, which had had some twenty editions between 1800 and 1845, and which was reprinted in 1858 and 1868 (apparently in two different editions in the latter year). There was also some Protestant religious printing, including a New Testament in 1858 and the Book of Common Prayer in 1856 and 1861. Various collections of poetry were printed by John O'Daly, including the *Irish Language Miscellany* and *Poets and Poetry of Munster*, which had four editions between 1850 and 1900. No periodical in Irish appeared before *An Gaodhal* and *Irisleabhar na Gaeilge* in 1882.[13] The level of printed production was therefore sparse indeed between 1850 and 1900, both absolutely and relative to either the period 1800–50 or after 1900.

In this, Ireland is in striking contrast to other Celtic language areas. The greatest difference is with Wales, where the period was probably the high point of printed production in Welsh (although precise quantification is difficult – the main biblio-graphic tool, *Libri Walliae*, stops in 1820).[14] There had been in fact a far greater printed production in Welsh for some centuries before 1900. The background to the strength of printing in Welsh was the early success of the Protestant Reformation in Wales. This established Welsh as a printed language by the late sixteenth century, when there were bibles in Welsh in all churches and many houses, along with prayer books and other religious texts. In the eighteenth century, the Methodist religious revival took place overwhelmingly in Welsh and was accompanied by a substantial printed literature in that language, consolidating the link between the vernacular, literacy and print. The nineteenth century was the 'golden age' of printing in Welsh, with over 10,000 items being printed, many in print runs of tens of thousands. Book production concentrated overwhelmingly on the religious sphere, and many preachers were involved in printing and publishing. A substantial newspaper and periodical press also developed, also mainly religious in content but less so than books. In 1866, there were an estimated eight weeklies, twenty-five monthlies and five quarterlies in production, with a total circulation of 120,000. This was as true of north Wales as of the industrialised south. In 1900, there were six Welsh-language papers in Caernarvon and three in Bangor, as well as five other shorter lived papers in Caernarvon in the second half of the nineteenth century.[15]

A similar pattern is evident in Brittany, where a high point of production was reached in the later decades of the nineteenth century. The background here was also religious, notably a series of intense Jesuit missions during the seventeenth century which were accompanied by the production and dissemination of printed religious literature in Breton. By the late eighteenth century the print literacy created by religious campaigns had created a market for secular material also, and towards the end of the nineteenth century Breton print literacy had become allied with the politics of anti-republican, anti-secularist Catholicism. The peaks of production were in the 1860s and the years 1900–19, and roughly half of the titles in every decade from 1820 to 1920 were religious. (See Fig. 1.3). The most characteristic form of printed religious text was the cantique, a type of hymn or religious song. New cantiques continued to be produced between about 1870 and 1940, with a peak at the turn of the century; many of these texts refer to contemporary political, social or religious events.[16] (See Fig. 1.4).

Compared with Welsh or Breton, print culture was less well established in Scottish Gaelic. The first substantial productions, almost exclusively religious, came with an evangelical revival in the late eighteenth century. During the nineteenth century, a series of religious revivals and controversies in the Highlands, particularly the Great Disruption of 1843 which led to the foundation of the Free Presbyterian Church, took place in Gaelic, and were accompanied by the printing of religious texts. As a result, printing in Gaelic was increasing during the second half of the nineteenth century, and new productions were accompanied by the continued reprinting of the most successful older texts. The *Laoidhe Spioradail* or 'Spiritual Lays' of Dugald Buchanan, which first appeared in 1767, had new editions every three or four years after 1850, while Peter Grant's *Nuadh Dhain Spioradail* ('New Spiritual Poems') of 1818 had nine editions between 1857 and 1889.[17]

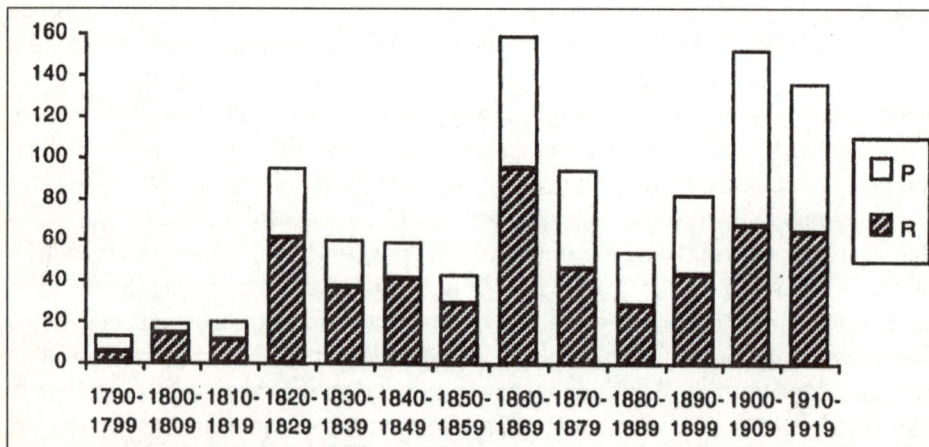

Figure 1.3 Works printed in Breton, 1790–1919. (By kind permission of Presses Universitaires de Rennes)

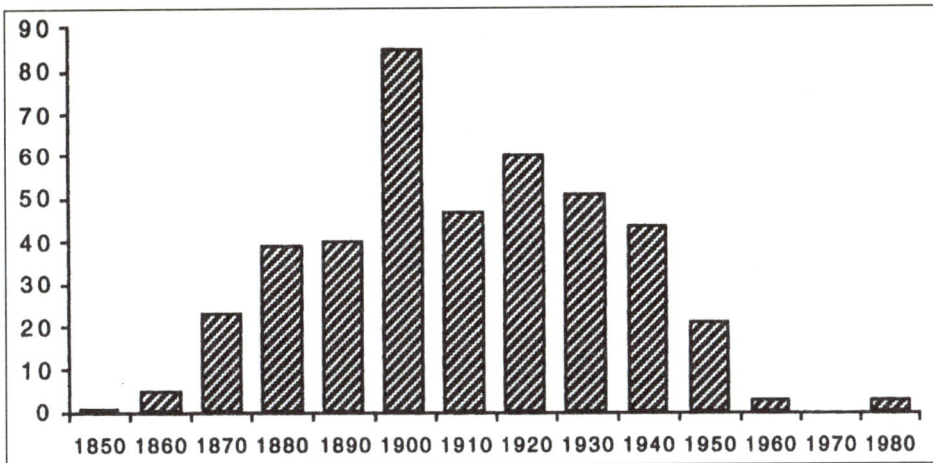

Figure 1.4 Cantiques printed in Breton, 1850–1989. (By kind permission of Presses Universitaires de Rennes)

In Wales, Brittany and Scotland, the success of a vernacular print culture in the late nineteenth century was based on Churches that adopted the vernacular for catechesis and as part of a wider cultural position which differentiated them from other denominations or from a central state. In Ireland, by contrast, this was not the case, and the Catholic Church, to which the vast majority of Irish speakers belonged, did not see Irish as part of its identity, and in most areas, the link between religion and literacy in the vernacular was never firmly established. Before the eighteenth century, the Catholic Church in Ireland was insufficiently organised and insufficiently affluent to create such a print culture, and by the end of that century, when restrictions on organisation and practice had been lifted and the Church was becoming more prosperous, its clergy was recruited mainly from anglophone parts of the country.[18]

There were, however, three or four million Irish speakers in 1800 and a religious literacy in Irish did exist in some areas, notably in east Munster. Printed production for that market was actually increasing, with dozens of editions of catechisms being printed between about 1760 and 1845, mainly in Cork and Limerick, and, to a lesser extent, Clonmel. These were accompanied by some translations and the *Pious Miscellany* of Tadhg Gaelach Ó Súilleabháin, a collection of devotional songs, which had about twenty editions between 1800 and 1845.[19] While these productions were supported, and often instigated, by individual members of the Catholic clergy and hierarchy, support for vernacular religious literacy and print culture by the Church as an institution was weak, and was further diminished in reaction to the activities of a series of Protestant evangelical organisations in the early nineteenth century, known collectively as the 'Second Reformation' or the 'Protestant Crusade'. Some of these organisations concentrated on missionary activity in Irish, establishing schools to teach reading in Irish and distributing bibles and tracts printed in Irish. Although they had some early success, the principal long-term effect of these efforts was to increase sectarian tension: consequently, because of the association of printing in Irish with Protestant evangelism, the Catholic Church became even less well-disposed to Irish than before. Indeed the 'Devotional

Revolution' of the nineteenth century – the consolidation of orthodox Catholic belief and practice against less orthodox local forms – was also to a large extent a displacement of religion in Irish by religion in English. As a result, in the later nineteenth century, when Protestant evangelical organisations were far less active, the Catholic Church did not encourage practice in Irish and many or most of the clergy remained hostile to print in Irish, particularly in *Gaeltacht* areas. The high point of vernacular printed production in Wales, Brittany and Highland Scotland was therefore not matched in Ireland.[20]

Print culture, therefore, was less developed in Irish than in the other Celtic languages, particularly Welsh and Breton, during the nineteenth century. Print culture is not coterminous with written culture, however. Manuscripts in Irish continued to be produced throughout the century, and the all-time high point of production was probably in the early nineteenth century. In Munster, this was a continuation of the rich eighteenth-century tradition, as documented for Co. Cork by Ó Conchúir. In Connaught, by contrast, as Cullen has shown, manuscript production is mainly a creation of the early nineteenth century, linked to the growth of schooling and literacy in English. As a result, Connaught manuscripts, which contain contemporary compositions such as those of Anthony Raftery as well as older material, are heavily influenced by English-language literacy, often being written in school copy books and using roman letters and phonetic spelling.[21]

Later scholars and revivalists such as Douglas Hyde tended to ignore or play down the existence of these manuscripts, which they regarded as being of little worth. Hyde's edition of Raftery's poems, for instance, presented them as having been collected orally for the most part, even though in some instances he had consulted more manuscript versions than oral. Moreover, Hyde did not keep accounts of the manuscripts he had been lent and did not copy them completely. Such attitudes have tended to obscure the existence of a literate and literary subculture in east Connaught in the late nineteenth century, a culture whose products were valued sufficiently for them to be taken abroad, to the United States in particular, when their owners emigrated.[22]

They have also misled later historians, not only political historians such as Lyons who had no familiarity with sources in Irish, but even as learned and sophisticated a commentator as Joep Leerssen, who can read Irish, but who nevertheless describes Irish speakers as being 'pauperised into virtual illiteracy' in the early nineteenth century, precisely the point when Connaught literacy was forming.[23] In this context, it is important to ask what exactly constitutes literacy in Irish. Some estimates suggest that perhaps twenty or fifty people were literate in Irish in the whole country in 1900. There may well have been no more who could competently transcribe a manuscript from the seventeenth or eighteenth century. However, most literacy in an unofficial language will consist of reading ability only, and the number of those who could read Irish was more likely to be measured in hundreds or even thousands. Moreover, where texts in phonetic spelling were being produced, Irish speakers literate in English would have been able to read them. By the late nineteenth century, literacy in English was a mass phenomenon, even in western areas, and the potential readership for such texts was greater than has generally been assumed.

The forms of literacy in Irish in the nineteenth century, therefore, owed a certain amount to English-language models. This is clearest in those texts that used phonetic spelling, but it is also felt in those that used Irish orthography but roman typeface, as was the case with the vast majority of the printed output. In this respect, the type of written or print culture later developed by revivalists was not ideal for native speakers of Irish. It may have privileged *'caint na ndaoine'* over elaborate written norms, but it also settled on gaelic typeface rather than the roman which people had been used to. This can be illustrated by a booklet of 1899 which reprinted 'Aighneas an Pheacaig Leis an mBás', a religious poem that had circulated widely in print in the mid-nineteenth century, mainly in east Munster. The booklet is exceptional in that it was printed in Waterford rather than Dublin, and was not published under the auspices of the Gaelic League. Roman type was used, according to the editor, 'partly for economic motives, but mainly on the desire to accommodate the older generation of Irish readers... which, half a century since, learned to read the 'Aighneas' in roman characters'.[24] This suggests that the practice as well as the assumptions of revivalist printing could well have marginalised existing readers of Irish in *Gaeltacht* areas.

As well as distinguishing between reading and writing, as above, it is also worth making a distinction between two styles of reading. These are 'intensive' reading, where a few texts are read repeatedly, and 'extensive' reading, where new texts are read, often only once.[25] The former was still the more common in rural areas throughout Europe in the nineteenth century, and reading in Irish in rural areas was no exception, with religious texts in particular being read repeatedly in ritual contexts such as funeral wakes. There existed therefore the possibility of a print culture or subculture without a continuous and substantial supply of printed material. Copies of the *Pious Miscellany*, for example, last printed in 1868, continued to be possessed and read at the end of the century in houses as far apart as counties Waterford, Kerry, Limerick, (west) Galway and (north) Donegal. Séamus Ó Dubhghaill, quoted earlier by O'Leary as not remembering seeing a book in Irish until he was twenty in Kerry, immediately goes on to say, 'I would hear tell of certain people who had 'Tadhg Gaodhlach' [i.e. the *Pious Miscellany*] and who were able to read it. Those who could read Tadhg Gaodhlach had a great reputation.' Protestant texts also formed part of this culture. Seamus Fenton, a school inspector who was born in Iveragh, Co. Kerry in 1874, recalled that 'the first book I ever read in the Irish language was one containing the alphabet and extracts from the Protestant Bible; it was distributed to the tenants by the mother of [the land agent]. The sentences were badly graded, but the language was faultless.'[26]

There was, therefore, a print culture in Irish-speaking areas at the end of the nineteenth century, even if it was dwarfed by those of Wales and Brittany. Moreover, nineteenth-century manuscripts frequently copied from printed books in Irish, and ultimately came to resemble them. There were manuscripts copied from printed books such as Charlotte Brooke's *Reliques of Irish Poetry* and the *Pious Miscellany*, manuscripts with illustrations copied from books, and manuscripts with parallel texts, with verse in Irish written in gaelic letters and translations in English written in roman letters.[27] This suggests that too great a distinction should not be made between manuscript and print as far as reception and use are concerned. It also suggests that the demand for printed material in Irish was not being met by the production of what was in the late nineteenth century a monoglot anglophone printing trade. In other words, the paucity of print in Irish after 1850 compared to the period 1820–40 may be due as much to the rapid centralisation of the print trade in Dublin (and the consequent demise of many of the Munster firms which had printed in Irish) as to a drop in demand.[28]

From this perspective, the printing projects of the language revival look less innovative. While they certainly had the aim of teaching Irish and creating a reading public *ab ovo* in urban areas, there was also a pre-existing readership in some rural areas whose existence has been obscured by the rhetoric and assumptions of the revival itself. This argument can be supported by looking at the reaction to an earlier printing enterprise, that of John O'Daly, who began publishing poetry in Irish, with translations, in the mid 1840s. Printed in Dublin, these were intended for a broad public, and initially appeared in instalments costing a penny each. The contemporary press without exception assumed them to be language primers rather than being intended for Irish speakers and readers. Reviewing the first volume of *Reliques of Irish Jacobite Poetry*, published in 1844, the *Wexford Independent* 'agree[d] with our excellent contemporary the *Drogheda Argus* in thinking they may be rendered subservient to a further purpose, and would afford the most valuable help in learning the language for the first time'; the *Belfast Vindicator* 'rejoice[d] in any effort to assist in diffusing a knowledge of the language and therefore warmly recommend the songs, now in the course of publication by Mr. O'Daly, to the patronage of all true-hearted Irishmen. Even those who cannot read them should buy them.' Even the *Kerry Examiner*'s notice was prefaced by the admission that 'of the language of our forefathers we blush to say we are ignorant'. In other words, at a time when there were perhaps three million Irish speakers, and a reading public which over the previous thirty or forty years had purchased tens of thousands of printed books and produced hundreds of manuscripts, the press assumed that the publication of a small volume of eighteenth-century verse, most of which would have been familiar to that same reading public, was principally revivalist and pedagogic, and more or less ignored its main potential customers.[29] Moreover, publishers in Irish during the nineteenth century had also dealt with most of the problems of language and presentation faced by revivalists: what typeface to use, gaelic or roman, what form of language, learned or colloquial, what spelling, whether 'correct' or phonetic, and so on.[30]

In conclusion, therefore, while it is the innovatory and quantitative aspects of twentieth-century publishing in Irish that are most striking initially, and that may well constitute its lasting impact, they present a misleading picture of that publishing enterprise and its readership in its wider contemporary context. Because many revivalists believed themselves to be creating a readership in a language that was exclusively oral, this has tended to obscure the fact that there was a pre-existing literate culture and readership, albeit a small one. While the Gaelic League did of course create readers among the urban anglophone middle classes, it also had a major impact in some Irish-speaking rural areas. It was particularly influential in those areas with such a pre-existing literate culture, such as west Co. Cork, where its books were bought and its literary competitions entered.[31] Revivalists also believed themselves to be creating the forms of a written language, but the debates over norms of language within Irish-language printing at the turn of the century likewise create a false impression. Norms needed to be established in printed Irish, not because Irish speakers were all illiterate, but because no institution, political or religious, had given its support to a form of written Irish, as Churches had done in other Celtic language areas.

Chapter 2

The Book in the Irish Arts and Crafts Movement

Nicola Gordon Bowe

Though many books are printed in Ireland, book printing as an art has been little practised here since the eighteenth century.

The first prospectus of the Dun Emer Press, 1903[1]

Our Celtic books mean to me not in the end books but in the end a more passionate kind of life – a present revery 'calling up a new age, calling to mind the queens that were imagined long ago'.

W. B. Yeats to the Duchess of Sutherland, *c*. 20 December 1903[2]

By the 1880s in Ireland, the desire for political autonomy and cultural identity had been so fuelled by antiquarian and literary research, as well as national zeal, that a new visual imagery began to emerge. In Ireland, no less than in other countries seeking an evocation of a real and mythical past on which to pin hopes for future independence, romantic nationalism was closely bound to an Arts and Crafts ideology. The aspect of Irish art that came closest to the literary and language revivals, and that had the greatest support, was applied art. Revivalism in general perceived that 'the great need of modern Ireland is to be reunited with its past' through 'the general intellectual cultivation of the country' and the encouragement of 'the element of national individuality'.[3] Pioneering illustrated books describing hitherto unheeded, specifically Irish, antiquarian masterpieces, provided clear evidence of a rich treasury of Celtic ornament. Notable examples include Margaret Stokes's vividly decorated illuminations to Samuel Ferguson's poem, 'The Cromlech on Howth' (1861), the topographical artist Henry O'Neill's fine volume, *The Fine Arts and Civilisation of Ancient Ireland* (1863) and Eugene O'Curry's scholarly *On the Manners and Customs of the Ancient Irish* (1873).[4] They consolidated the theatrically romantic sentiment of an earlier publishing landmark in Irish visual culture, Daniel Maclise's illustrated Longman edition of Thomas Moore's *Irish Melodies* (1845). For Maclise, Moore was 'the great champion of Celtic civilization, and the poet of Ireland's tragic past'. Moore and Maclise transformed their vision of Irish legend into an unusually successful Romantic synthesis of word and text where, in Moore's words, 'an Irish pencil has lent its aid to an Irish pen in rendering due honour to our country's ancient harp'.[5]

The succeeding generation was 'profoundly affected' by Standish O'Grady. Variously described by his peers as 'the father of the Literary Revival in Ireland' and 'the Irish Ruskin', his two-volume *History of Ireland* ('The Heroic Period' (1878) and 'Cuchulain and His Contemporaries' (1880)) 'with its artistic enchantment' drew 'many an ardent spirit to the romantic age of Ireland'.[6] The writer, artist, visionary and reformer, George 'Æ' Russell, spoke for many when he declared himself 'proud of this great prose-poet of ours, whose work has been to later writers not as the morning star, but as the dawn itself...When I close my eyes, and brood in memory over the books which most profoundly affected me, I find none excited my imagination more than Standish O'Grady's epical narrative of Cuchulain.'[7] Indeed, through O'Grady's writings,

> the submerged river of national culture rose up again, a shining torrent and I realised...that the greatest spiritual evil one nation could inflict on another was to cut off from it the story of the national soul...[w]hatever is Irish in me he kindled to life.[8]

Æ also acknowledged that Patrick Pearse's love of Cuchulain was 'for the Cuchulain whom O'Grady discovered or invented'.[9] Similarly, W. B. Yeats avowed that 'here was a man whose rage was a swan-song over all that he had held most dear, and to whom for that very reason every Irish imaginative writer owed a portion of his soul'.[10] Alice Milligan, the Ulster poet and patriot, imagined that he had been self-educated 'in the reading-room of the Royal Irish Academy':

> Surely insight came to him, not from the manuscripts and pages of O'Curry and the others, but more subtly from the torques and mins of gold, the leathern targes and wooden methers, the spearheads and bronze sword-blades, which were housed there in Dawson Street before the Kildare Street Museum was built.

She too, as an Academy reader, had been lured there by the Keeper of the Treasures up to the gold room 'to see a man from Enniskillen unpacking a saintly shrine that had been fished up from the bottom of Lough Erne.'[11]

The National Museum of Ireland's first Keeper of Irish Antiquities, George Coffey (1857–1916), was to play a major role in the early years of the Arts and Crafts Society of Ireland. He also executed the earliest extant book bindings that can be said to display a true Arts and Crafts ideology. Initially trained as an engineer, he became an 'ardent Nationalist', committed Parnellite and the honorary secretary of the Dublin Working Men's Clubs.[12] He was also a founder member of the National Literary Society and a pioneering antiquarian who became Professor of Archaeology at the Royal Hibernian Academy. In 1888, he was the only Irish person to exhibit at the first exhibition of the English Arts and Crafts Exhibition Society in London, where his three embossed leather bindings, bound in calf by James Sherrin and sewn by Mary Anne O'Hare, were adapted from the 'Early Irish'. They are contemporary with Margaret Stokes's authoritative two-part educational volume, *Early Christian Art in Ireland* (London, 1887), which clearly illustrates intricately interlaced book shrines, an obvious source for their competent design. Blind-tooled on tan calf leather, his bindings for Samuel Ferguson's *Lays of the Western Gael*, Thomas Davis's *National and Historic Ballads, Songs and Poems* , Katharine Tynan's *Shamrocks* and an anthology entitled *The Spirit of the Nation* (see Fig. 2.1) also appear to be modelled on the enclosed whorls embossed on the back cover of a George Allen edition of John Ruskin's *Praeterita* (1886). Although not 'finished' in a technical sense (being neither decorated, coloured nor gilded), these bindings demonstrate that Coffey was carefully following every step necessary in the procedure of 'forwarding', as laid down subsequently in T. J. Cobden-Sanderson's classic Arts and Crafts essay on 'Bookbinding'.[13] Coffey served on the editorial sub-committee that organised the first exhibition of the Arts and Crafts Society of Ireland in 1895, where he displayed a symmetrically tooled leather-bound volume of a work entitled *Parables of Our Lord*. Thereafter, his interests in design became increasingly scholarly and educational.

Figure 2.1 George Coffey, *The Spirit of the Nation; or Ballads and Songs by the Writers of 'The Nation'* (Dublin, n.d.), blind-tooled calf leather binding, *c*.1888. (Private collection, Ireland.)

The Irish Society was founded, in 1894, on the crest of a wave of 'new hope and interests ... a setting free of the imagination ... in those first years after Parnell's death'.[14] The previous year had seen Douglas Hyde's momentous founding of the Gaelic League and in 1894 Horace Plunkett founded the Irish Agricultural Organisation Society. Five years later the new Department of Agriculture and Technical Instruction began its seminal encouragement of Irish arts and industries. Inspired by the heroic example of William Morris and his followers, by the revelations of past Irish literary and artistic skills compared with present declining ones, and by philanthropic aspirations to provide remunerative aesthetic and industrial employment to a largely impoverished nation, 'a few enthusiastic pioneers, ... amateurs and connoisseurs weary of the time-worn conventions of the

Irish designer'[15] had become swept up in the climate of romantic nationalist optimism which had been gathering momentum throughout the nineteenth century.[16] Spurred on by the obvious need to counteract the steady decline of traditional skilled craftsmanship and to encourage the growth and employment of Irish industrial skills, they set about organising an ambitious programme aimed at reviving individually identifiable, functional yet imaginative work. The Irish Arts and Crafts Society aspired to quality and originality. It aimed to improve the artistic level of the craftsman's work; to make the workman less of a machine and more of a designer; to credit everyone involved in the design and execution of what they had made; to encourage architecturally-related craftsmanship, and to revive vanished skills while introducing those needed for modern Ireland. They sought restraint, the suppression of unnecessary detail, the formal expression of the nature of the materials used, and the enhancement of daily life by useful, well-made, beautiful artefacts. T. W. Rolleston, a key figure in the early years of the Irish Arts and Crafts Society, and a trenchant and articulate critic, insisted that good work should be devoid of plagiarism. It should emulate but never copy the simple refinement of Celtic art:

> The age of tradition and authority is past – in their stead the individual has emerged, bringing all things to the test of his own personality. What new forms art and life may take in future generations we know not, but this, at any rate is the age of the individual, and the central art of the time will be done by workers of strong artistic personality who will work to please themselves, to assert themselves, and not to assert their Irishism or Frenchism, or Germanism, or whatever else may have come to them from the past. The infinite realm of nature and thought is theirs . . . Don't imitate; don't conceal the qualities of your material. Study arts of the past, above all those of your own land, but remember that you do not live in the times of Brian Boru, but of Mr. Edison.[17]

Because the Society became the principal focus for progressive Irish design during the first quarter of the twentieth century, with a committed policy of encouraging high standards of handcrafted, skilled and original (yet nationally informed) achievement, it is impossible to write of the Arts and Crafts movement without tracing its ideals and exhibitions. Reference is made here to its journals, reports and, where possible, exhibited items. Many of these have not yet come to light, many have disappeared and most are in private, often family, collections.

On the Executive, General Management and Retrospective Irish Craftsmanship Committees for the Society's first exhibition was Sir Edward Sullivan, Bt., a skilled amateur bookbinder of singular erudition, Irish but based in London.[18] Doubtless he was responsible for inviting the leading English Arts and Crafts bookbinders, T. J. Cobden-Sanderson and Sydney Cockerell to collaborate with the architect Halsey Ricardo in preparing an exemplary loan exhibition representing a range of 141 of the best pieces of English Arts and Crafts work as a feature of the Society's first exhibition. In a parallel exemplary exhibition, showing retrospectively the best of Irish art-craftsmanship past, Sullivan lent some of the fine eighteenth- and nineteenth-century Dublin bindings that were a speciality of his own superlative collection, while the forty-four tooled and onlaid bindings that he designed and contributed to the main Irish Arts and Crafts exhibition were among the few contemporary exhibits singled out for critical praise. Like his admired contemporary and fellow lawyer, Cobden-Sanderson, Sullivan had taught himself the skills of finishing (i.e. decorating with gold-tooling, painting, inlay and onlay) by decorating old bindings, but he was committed to encouraging strong artistic spirit and 'original design'. The rich variety of imaginative floral, dot and geometric 'carpet' designs with which he decorated his consummately crafted morocco book bindings,[19] conformed with Cobden-Sanderson's definition of a 'well-bound beautiful book':

> Neither of one type, or finished so that its highest praise is that 'had it been made by a machine it could not have been made better'. It is individual; it is pleasant to feel, to handle and to see; it is the original work of an original mind working in freedom simultaneously with hand and heart and brain to produce a thing of use, which all time shall agree ever more and more also to call 'a thing of beauty'.[20]

Sullivan's carefully instructive exhortation on 'Irish Bookbinding, and how it may be Improved' was published as a special appendix to the Society's published report of the first exhibition:

> Excellent work was turned out by Irish binders fifty and a hundred years ago. Why should not our modern craftsmen do as good?...One thing alone is wanting – an artistic spirit strong enough to shake itself free from beaten lines and worn-out conceptions, and capable of leaving its impress and character on the work it takes in hand...The combinations of ornament are simply endless which may be effected with, say a flower, a bud, a leaf, a dot, and a couple of gouges. Then, again, we might fall back on the many exquisite forms of Celtic design supplied by our national manuscripts...how rarely one sees a binding of recent date Irish or from abroad, on which this obvious form of pattern has been successfully used![21]

He followed up this advice in his exquisite decoration on a pale green crushed morocco binding by Marcus Ward of Belfast, containing an album of views of Irish scenery, made for presentation by the Irish Tourist Association to the Queen. Sullivan collaborated with his fellow Arts and Crafts Society member, the architect Richard Caulfield Orpen, in adapting drawings from the recently documented Hiberno-Romanesque church at Rahan, Co. Offaly for what he believed was 'the first attempt to work out a Celtic pattern of any complexity in gold tooling on the cover of a book'.[22] His recommendation of the 'exquisite design and detail' of 'purely Celtic...ornamentation' in ancient Irish architecture as a rich source for contemporary design was published in the Society's report of their second exhibition, where the album was a major feature. Examples of Sullivan's work – signed in gold-tooling with his tiny upper-case signature, 'E. S. Aurifex', and occasionally his monogram – include bound volumes of all shapes and sizes, blank books, albums, miniature volumes, blotters, a jewel box, a manicure case and a mirror case.[23] A representative example of his work is his binding for an edited volume of *Dublin Verses by Members of Trinity College* (including Douglas Hyde, Standish O'Grady, T. W. Rolleston, Sir William Wilde and his son Oscar), published in London and Dublin in 1895 (Fig. 2.2). He designed his own pressmark *c.*1903 on becoming a member of the London dilettante circle, Ye Sette of Odd Volumes with the pseudonym His Oddship Brother 'Bookbinder' (Fig. 2.3).

Figure 2.2 *Dublin Verses by Members of Trinity College*, (ed.) [H. A.] Hinkson, published London: Elkin Mathews, and Dublin: Hodges, Figgis & Co., 1895; inscribed 'E. S. Aurifex' tooled in beige on front cover. Contemporary green (faded to brown) morocco binding, gilt-tooled, with an onlaid and hand-painted daisy and shamrock border with circular corner ornaments surrounding a similar oval centrepiece on the upper cover; the lower cover with gilt-tooled floral spray opposing the repeated centrepiece, the spine gilt-tooled and hand-painted similarly.

Figure 2.3 Sir Edward Sullivan, Bt., the binder's own pressmark as His Oddship Brother 'Bookbinder', member of Ye Sette of Odd Volumes, London *c.*1903, reproduced in his illustrated pamphlet *Decorative Book-Binding in Ireland*. (Letchworth: Arden Press, 1914).

Sullivan's detailed studies of the renowned great eighteenth-century folio volumes of Ireland's Parliamentary records provided him with a formal basis for his own free-style interpretations. Thomas Lange has documented that Sullivan made pencil rubbings and detailed records of 208 of the bindings he had 'finished' by tooling and onlaying between 1896 and 1926, while stating that he may well have been responsible for double that amount.[24] Sullivan also continued to write, for example on 'Design in Gold-Tooled Bookbinding' in *The Studio* magazine in 1904, the same year as the third exhibition of the Arts and Crafts Society of Ireland, on whose Executive Committee he served. He firmly believed bookbinding to be

> in no sense inferior to the finest work we know in pottery, wood-carving, metal-chasing, or any of the textile crafts whose very excellence makes it a matter of extreme difficulty to determine the boundary line which really separates Craft from Art.[25]

Nobody could match the skill and scholarly ingenuity of Sir Edward Sullivan's bindings in successive Arts and Crafts exhibitions, but several embroidered book covers were singled out for praise ('where nature is not too closely imitated') in the 1901 report on the Society's second exhibition of 1899, notably Alice Jacob's dramatic whiplashed triskel for *Moore's Irish Melodies*. Jacob, a skilled and versatile textile designer, who had been appointed to teach ornament and design classes at the Dublin Metropolitan School of Art in 1898, would subsequently instruct her students in leatherwork, and include her own blind-tooled, embossed leather book cover for Alice Milligan's *Hero Lays* in the Society's fifth exhibition of 1917. Although Richard Caulfield Orpen's black and white graphic work drawn expressly for reproduction (i.e. the headpiece of the Society's exhibition catalogue (Fig. 2.4) and another for The Royal Society of Irish Art Needlework), had been a feature of the first exhibition, it was not until their 1917 exhibition that the Society's attempts to improve the visual, textual, typographic and illustrative nature of printed material became generally discernible, for example in a number of bookplates by John Vinycomb of Belfast, which were designed to be mechanically printed.

Figure 2.4 Richard Caulfield Orpen, headpiece for The Arts and Crafts Society of Ireland, pen and ink drawing for reproduction, 1895, printed in the Society's first *Journal and Proceedings*, 1896. (National Library of Ireland.)

One of the earliest ephemeral publications to incorporate a concerted editorial policy of integrating commissioned artwork and literature with a striking cover appeared in Dublin in December 1897: 'A Celtic Christmas' was the first of a series of twelve special annual literary supplements issued (until 1908) by *The Irish Homestead*, the weekly support journal of the Irish Agricultural Organization Society. Initially edited by T. P. Gill, a seminal figure in the Irish industrial revival, its richly varied, often visionary visual and literary content was announced by large format, earthily coloured cover designs (initially by C. F. Core, and later, more evocatively, by Pamela Colman Smith between 1904 and 1908) and reflected the interest of Æ, an employee of the IAOS and subsequent editor of the *Homestead* from 1905. Its 1905 cover by Colman Smith, printed on matt terracotta coloured paper in black, illustrates the Pre-Raphaelite personification of Ireland guarding cottage industries throughout the land, while watching over trade on the Irish sea (Fig. 2.5). The magazine's editorial aim to evoke practical and national aspiration by representing the economic along with the spiritual resulted in specially drawn illustrations by Æ, Jack and Mary Cottenham Yeats, Beatrice Elvery, Sarah Purser, Constance Gore-Booth and John Campbell. Its verse and prose included contributions by the major Irish Literary Revival figures. Its seasonal covers, decorative layout and synthesis of words and images by young, contemporary, romantic nationalist poets, writers and artists, exponents of 'modern Celtic design', emulated the four issues of Patrick Geddes's short-lived Celtic 'Northern Seasonal', *Evergreen* (1895–7), finely printed and published in Edinburgh between 1895 and 1897. Irish contributors to the Scots journal included Standish O'Grady and Douglas Hyde.[26]

Figure 2.5 Pamela Colman Smith, cover design for 'A Celtic Christmas', the Christmas number of *The Irish Homestead*, the weekly support journal of the Irish Agricultural Organization Society, 1905. (Private collection.)

Other short-lived, fundamentally literary reviews flourished in Ireland during the first decade or so of the twentieth century, but few incorporated contemporary, specially commissioned artwork as an intrinsic part of their design and literary content. Exceptions include *The Irish Builder and Engineer*, revamped in 1899 under the enlightened editorship of R. M. Butler, with graphics by R. C. Orpen, the short-lived *Uladh* (in Ulster), *The Shanachie* (published by Maunsel & Co.),[27] Patrick Pearse's school magazine, *An Macaomh*, the Belfast-based *An Craob Ruad*, *Bean na-h-Eireann* (with Constance Markievicz's titlepiece) and *Sláinte*, the Journal of the Women's National Health Association of Ireland, also produced by Maunsel. It was not until 1911–14 that *The Irish Architect and Craftsman*, a weekly 'Journal of Architecture, Allied Arts and Crafts, and The Official Organ of the Arts and Crafts Society of Ireland', included striking artwork by P. O. Reeves, who had produced the first catalogue cover and headpiece of graphic strength and originality for the Society's fourth exhibition in 1910 (see Fig. 2.12).

The catalogue of the Society's third, much smaller and more specifically Irish exhibition, held in Dublin in 1904, while of no particular typographic interest, referred to sections on bookbinding and 'the various Processes of Book Illustration'.[28] 'Confined to the best examples of the living art industries of Ireland', it reflected the successful educational steering of the Department of Agriculture and Technical Instruction (for example, at the Dublin Metropolitan School from 1900, at the Glasgow 1901 International and Cork 1902 Exhibitions, and at the 1904 St Louis World's Fair), and the literary activities of W. B. Yeats and his colleagues.[29] Inspired by the English Arts and Crafts movement, and by *The Cuchulain Saga* (1898), a popular anthology written by Eleanor Hull, founder of the Irish Texts Society, and her fellow Gaelic League and Irish Literary Society member in London, the carpet designer Evelyn Gleeson had returned to Dublin in 1902 to establish her Morrisian Dun Emer Guild.[30] She was joined by Yeats's sisters, Lily, who ran an embroidery workshop, and Elizabeth, who had followed the advice of Emery Walker, Morris's advisor, by setting up a fifty-year-old Albion handpress, and selecting 'a good eighteenth century fount of type which is not eccentric in form, or difficult to read', using 'crisp, thin, lightly toned mouldmade', untrimmed paper 'made of linen rags . . . without bleaching chemicals at the Saggart Mill, in the county Dublin'.[31] The ideals of the Press were issued as one of the many ephemeral flyers and small prospectuses that were a hallmark of private presses of this period (Fig. 2.6).

Elizabeth Yeats exhibited with the Irish Arts and Crafts Society the first three Dun Emer Press books she and the girls she trained[32] had hand-printed in a clear, simple format that became the hallmark of the eleven books she published at Dun Emer and then, after 1908, under her Cuala Press imprint ('founded resolutely in the Morris tradition'):[33] black ink, unleaded fourteen-point Caslon Old Style type, often red ink for her distinctive typographical colophons and some headings and notes, small quarto format, wide margins, a natural Irish linen spine binding (in a style similar to the quarter holland style favoured by contemporary English private presses) by Galwey & Co., Dublin, in between paper-covered boards with a printed paper label on the front. The sixty-two books she published over thirty-seven years

THE DUN EMER PRESS

THOUGH many books are printed in Ireland, book printing as an art has been little practised here since the eighteenth century. The Dun Emer Press has been founded in the hope of reviving this beautiful craft.

A good eighteenth century fount of type which is not eccentric in form, or difficult to read has been cast, and the paper has been made of linen rags and without bleaching chemicals, at the Saggart Mill in the county Dublin. The pages are printed at a Hand Press by Miss E. C. Yeats, and simplicity is aimed at in their composition.

The first book printed has been 'In the Seven Woods' a new volume of poems, chiefly of the Irish Heroic Age, by W. B. Yeats. The edition is limited to 325 copies, and the book will not be republished in this form. It is now ready, price ten shillings and six pence a copy payable in advance. The next book will be 'The Nuts of Knowledge' a book of new and old lyrical poems by A. E. The price will be seven shillings and sixpence a copy. Subscribers names will be received by Miss E. C. Yeats at the Dun Emer Press, Dundrum, Co. Dublin.

Other books are in preparation, an Irish prose story by Mr G. Bernard Shaw; Dr Hyde's famous translations of the Love Songs of Connacht; some translations by Lady Gregory of heroic and mediaeval Irish poems; and a book on speaking to the Psaltery, with music, and a description of the art by Mr Arnold Dolmetsch and others. Other books will be announced shortly.

Figure 2.6 Elizabeth Yeats, early prospectus of the Dun Emer Press, 1903. (Collection of Dr Patrick Kelly, on loan to Trinity College Dublin.)

were 'the only offshoot from the Doves Press to survive in the original ideal form as handcraft, producing books as [W. R.] Lethaby had wanted, "made by a human being for a human being"'.[34] Her first book, *In the Seven Woods: Being Poems Chiefly of the Irish Heroic Age* by W. B. Yeats, reflected her brother's active editorial and design interest in the Press[35] and was originally to include a device of the legendary Emer's eponymous fortress designed by Emery Walker (Fig. 2.7a). This crumbling stone tower device was abandoned after the proof stage of *In the Seven Woods*; in 1907, Yeats invited Elinor Monsell, whose striking design of Queen Maeve poised with her wolfhound had become the National Theatre's emblem, to design a pressmark depicting Emer, the wife of the legendary hero Cuchulain, languishing beside a tree (Fig. 2.7b). The Press's second book featured Æ's circular device, 'The Sword of Light', in his anthology, *The Nuts of Knowledge, Lyrical Poems Old and New*. The third, Douglas Hyde's translations of Gaelic poetry, *The Love Songs of Connacht*, demonstrated the growing national interest in Ireland's own, long-ignored vernacular traditions, as pursued by the National Literary Society and the Gaelic League.[36] Elizabeth Yeats's books were exhibited first with the imprint of Dun Emer and, from July 1908, after the Yeats's schism with Evelyn Gleeson, with that of Cuala at all the Irish Arts and Crafts and Gaelic League exhibitions in Ireland and abroad. She also exhibited bookplates which, with calendars, hand-coloured prints, illustrated verses, pamphlets and his periodical, *A Broadside*, designed, illustrated and produced by her younger brother, the artist Jack Yeats, would subsequently expand the scope of the Press.

Figure 2.7a Emery Walker, the first pressmark for the Dun Emer Press, eventually unused except on the proof of the colophon page for W. B.Yeats, *In the Seven Woods* (Dublin, 1903). (Collection Dr Patrick Kelly, on loan to Trinity College Dublin.)

Figure 2.7b Elinor Monsell, pressmark commissioned by W. B. Yeats for the Dun Emer Press, 1907. (Reproduced in Liam Miller, *The Dun Emer Press, later the Cuala Press* (Dublin, 1973).)

In 1904, a bindery was inaugurated at Dun Emer by Norah Fitzpatrick from Belfast. Two of her Dun Emer Press volumes, bound in blue morocco and simply tooled, were exhibited at the Society's third exhibition beside work by two fellow Belfast designer-craftsmen: bound albums designed by John Vinycomb and verses illuminated and inscribed by Charles Braithwaite.[37] Mary Galway Houston, similarly from Ulster (Coleraine in Co. Derry), a versatile student and 'most admirable Irish designer in metal'[38] who had studied at the Dublin Metropolitan School from 1890 until 1896, was responsible for the four finely tooled leatherwork medallions depicting damsels engaged in the Arts on the cover of an album designed, decorated and illuminated by staff and students of the Dublin School of Art, for presentation to the retiring headmaster James Brenan. After successfully competing and exhibiting her delicate, low-relief leather and metalwork in Dublin and London, where she moved in 1896, Houston had exhibited drawings and a binding in the first and second Irish Arts and Crafts exhibitions; in 1898, acclaim for her swirling, figural, exquisitely modelled leather book cover for a Kelmscott *Chaucer* and her 1899 *Ruba'iyat of Omar Khayya'm*[39] led to her bookbindings being featured in *The Studio's* special winter issue, *Modern Bookbindings and their Designers* (1899–1900) and in an article devoted to her by the *Magazine of Art*.[40]

The elaborate, mediaevally-inspired illuminated calligraphy on vellum by Charles Braithwaite, an influential Arts and Crafts Lethaby-trained teacher in Belfast, was singled out at the Irish 1904 and successive Irish and English Arts and Crafts exhibitions. W. R. Lethaby (1857–1921), architect and designer, was co-founder of the English Arts and Crafts Exhibition Society in 1887, co-director, then principal of the new Central School of Arts and Crafts in London (1900–12) and first Professor of Ornament and Design at the Royal College of Art (1900–18). His educational influence was seminal in Ireland, not least for his Artistic Crafts Series of Technical Handbooks. 1906 saw two Ulster brothers, Joseph and John Campbell, who had been collaborating since 1904 on *The Songs of Uladh* (Ulster), a collection of folk songs, then on the literary periodical *Uladh*, each illustrating separate small, but important publications. Maunsel & Co. of Dublin published *The Rushlight*, 'on the Feast of Brigid of the Candles', a small, artistically printed volume of Seosamh MacCathmhaoil's folk poetry, ripe with allusions to Gaelic sagas, powerfully illustrated in heavy black lines. On the title page, he describes himself as *'ceann-maor'* ('big-head'), the Irish version of his name, which he abandoned 'when he heard a woman asking for the poems of Seo-sam MacCatwail'[41] (Fig. 2.8). And W. & G. Baird of Dublin and Belfast published a set of six small booklets, printed on card bound with ribbon, each reproducing a poem from Ethna Carbery's *Songs from the Four Winds of Eirinn*, set to music by Charlotte Milligan Fox[42] and evocatively illustrated in line and colour by Seaghan Mac Cathmhaoil (John Campbell)[43] (Fig. 2.9). That year Maunsel published twelve illustrations John Campbell had drawn for his own *Calendar of the Saints: Patric*, as well as a frontispiece he drew for the first issue (spring 1906) of their newly established 'Irish Miscellany Illustrated', *The Shanachie*, while the Gaelic League published two cover designs and frontispieces he had drawn for Irish-language books by Patrick Pearse.

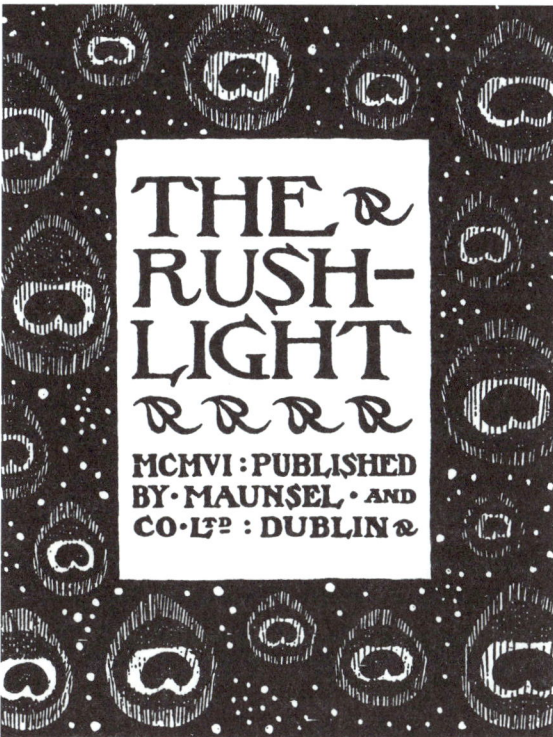

Figure 2.8 Joseph Campbell (*'ceann-maor'*), title page design for *The Rushlight* (Dublin, 1906). (Private collection.)

Figure 2.9 John Campbell (Seaghan Mac Cathmhaoil), illustration for 'The Green Woods of Truagh', from Ethna Carbery, *Songs from the Four Winds of Eirinn* (Dublin, 1906). (Private collection.)

The striking cover design of *The Shanachie* (Fig. 2.10) was drawn by Beatrice Elvery, a clever and versatile Arts and Crafts sculptor, graphic and stained glass artist,[44] whose simply-outlined cover design anticipated her bold cover and line illustrations for *Iosagan agus Sgealta Eile* (Dublin, 1907). This was a small Gaelic League edition of four further short stories by Patrick Pearse which had appeared in *An Claidheamh Soluis* during the previous two years; its cheap brown paper cover with simple, blocked-in colours was deliberately aimed at a wide, romantically nationalist readership. Her boldly linear, narrative 'nursery-style' Cuala prints and strong, black and white illustrations for Violet Russell's *Heroes of the Dawn*, first published by Maunsel & Co. in 1913, were successful in transporting children and adults alike into a homely land of enchanted innocence.

Figure 2.10 Beatrice Elvery, cover design for *The Shanachie*, 1907. (Private collection.)

At the fourth Arts and Crafts Society of Ireland exhibition, held in Dublin in 1910, John Campbell showed fifteen examples of his graphic work, along with graphic work by fellow northerners Vinycomb and Braithwaite, while among Elvery's exhibits was a painted panel, *The Mountain Singer*, incorporated into a leather binding by Eleanor Kelly for the Dun Emer Guild. Kelly had taken over the Guild's bindery *c.*1908 from Norah Fitzpatrick, while also working independently, for example on what sounds like a unique (and, sadly, unillustrated or further documented) essay at the time, a binding in peat for a copy of the poet and writer Padraic Colum's book, *The Land*. This Kelly had exhibited in the Arts and Crafts Society's subsection of the Home Industries exhibit at Dublin's 1907 Irish International Exhibition, along with leather bindings for Sir Horace Plunkett's *Ireland in the New Century*, Æ's *Homeward Songs by the Way*, Moira O'Neill's *Songs of the Glens of Antrim*, two volumes on *The 1798 Irish Rebellion*, and a sixteenth-century 'Old Irish Catechism', whose design was based on a contemporary sixteenth-century pattern.[45] However, by 1910, at the Arts and Crafts exhibition, Kelly's reproduction of a sixteenth-century binding, two morocco-bound illustrated books, *The Hen* and *Omar Khayyam*, and a blue morocco-bound church missal tooled with a design from the Cross of Cong, were exhibited by the Dun Emer Guild. Among the few other bindings at the 1907 Dublin show were two embroidered book covers by ladies from the Royal Irish

School of Art Needlework, a leather binding made by Kathleen Fox under Alice Jacob, and six enamelled panels made as book covers in Oswald Reeves's flourishing metalwork classes set up in 1903 at the Dublin Art School. A smaller number of embroidered, modelled or embossed leather covers made by students from both these schools also featured in the 1910 Irish Arts and Crafts exhibition. The following year, on the occasion of Queen Mary's 1911 visit to Ireland, Eleanor Kelly combined a blue morocco, gold-inlaid Celtic binding with a 'wreath of May blossoms, entwined with shamrocks, encircling the Royal Crown' with the Royal Irish School of Art Needlework's cover of 'Irish white poplin sprinkled with gold shamrocks' and Tudor roses for a series of presentation volumes containing the signatures of 165,000 'Women of Ireland' (Fig. 2.11).[46]

Figure 2.11 Photograph of commemorative album book cover presented to HM the Queen, 1911, embroidered by the Royal Irish School of Art Needlework, Dublin, on 'dust-coloured' damask, 'flowered all over with Tudor roses in silk and metal-gold, silver, copper and aluminium'. Signed by 165,000 Irishwomen on the occasion of Queen Mary's visit to Dublin in June 1911. (Private collection.)

The Society's fourth exhibition was deliberately smaller, more selective, regionally based and now centred around the newly formed Guild of Irish Art-Workers, led by Oswald Reeves, who designed its refreshingly bold catalogue cover and Foreword headpiece (Fig. 2.12). He had also become responsible for the graphics and thoughtful design reports in *The Irish Architect and Craftsman*

Figure 2.12 P. O. Reeves, headpiece for catalogue of the fourth exhibition of the Arts and Crafts Society of Ireland, Dublin, 1910. (Collection the National Library of Ireland.)

(1911–14) while continuing to execute his own designs for enamelling and metalwork.[47] These included *A Double Star*, an exquisite silver and *basse-taille* enamel slipcase cover, enclosing a delicately bound green leather book inscribed 'Days to be Remembered' (1909), and an icon of the Irish industries revival he had made in 1908 for presentation to Sir Horace Plunkett, retiring Vice-President of the Department of Agriculture and Technical Instruction. This was a presentation album, bound in silver, whose repoussé silver cover was set with an enamelled panel on which was enamelled a full-length, book-bearing figure personifying the Spirit of Instruction, bordered by smaller panels symbolising Agriculture, Fishing, Science, Industry, Handicraft and Harvest. He exhibited the Plunkett album at the 1908 Royal Academy in London, and both books at the 1910 ACSI exhibition.[48] The metalworking and design skills Reeves had learned in Birmingham, at the Royal College of Art and with Alexander Fisher in London, and the calligraphy through Edward Johnston's seminal Central School teaching were already influencing a new, motivated generation of art students in Dublin. Similarly, at the Dublin Art School's annual summer schools they could avail of the skills of George Atkinson, typographer, printmaker and graphic artist, trained directly by Johnston in London.[49] Illustrations by students of the Dublin School, featuring the picturesque fancy dress 'Irish Industries' costumes worn at a St Patrick's Eve Pageant held in 1909 had been reproduced in a souvenir booklet entitled Irish Industries Pageant (Dublin, 1909), published by Maunsel & Co. that year. The pageant celebrated the recent progress of Irish industries and the adoption of the protective Irish trademark since 1906.

By 1917, a number of individual, skilled and imaginative talents had clearly emerged, mostly trained at the Dublin Metropolitan School. In the field of book production, Harry Clarke, who designed the striking, idiosyncratically decadent cover for the Arts and Crafts Society's fifth catalogue, was eminent. Finely printed by George Roberts in a new 7 × 9 format on handmade paper in bold black Caslon, with Clarke's initial foreword letter in red, the catalogue reflects the optimistic and energetic support the Society could now expect from committed, well trained and often versatile practitioners as well as enlightened patrons, expressing a more clearly perceived national design ideology. For the first time, an exhibition, consisting of 260 exclusively Irish artefacts, would travel to Cork and Belfast from Dublin. Sir John O'Connell, a prominent Dublin solicitor, subsequently ordained, who belonged to a circle of Dublin professionals, all strong supporters of the new generation of Irish Arts and Crafts practitioners, wrote the foreword to the catalogue. Responsible for the building and furnishing of the Celtic Revival showpiece, the Honan Hostel Chapel in Cork (completed 1917), he justified the importance of holding the exhibition during such precarious times – a year after the Easter Rising and during the First World War. He was in no doubt that the exhibition displayed 'the high degree of excellence...in stained-glass, embroidery, book-binding, printing and enamelling work' visible in Ireland at the time in what amounted to 'a renaissance in Irish craft work'.[50]

Harry Clarke's exhibits included his designs for the catalogue cover and its initial letter design, a bookplate and original and reproduced book illustrations.[51] Elizabeth Yeats's Cuala Press exhibits included eleven hand-printed books. Eleanor Kelly showed three morocco-bound, inlaid and tooled books: one a red-and gold-tooled *Mass Book of the Dead* for the newly built Honan Chapel in Cork, inscribed with an illuminated frontispiece by Joseph Tierney, one of several illuminators exhibiting; another in grey morocco was set with jewels, like her earlier binding for Rabindranath Tagore's *Gitanjali* c.1913, with W. B. Yeats's introduction (Fig. 2.13);[52] the third in green levant morocco with inlay and gold-tooling. George Roberts exhibited three books, notably 'one of the most beautifully printed books ever published by Maunsel & Co.', Joseph Campbell's twenty-one chunky, velvety black designs and twenty-one poems, *Earth of Cualann*, in a limited edition of 500, printed in hand-set type by Roberts on a handmade 'paper which should...bring a printer of the present day to his knees in adoration'.[53] Other book-related exhibits included four original drawings by Jack Yeats for Maunsel's 1912 edition of his *Life in the West of Ireland*, and assorted 'decorative drawings',[54] lithographs, engravings, bookplates and illuminated pages by a medley of exhibitors.

There were only to be two more major Arts and Crafts Society of Ireland exhibitions, in 1921 and 1925. By then the passionate aspirations of two generations had succumbed to mellow age, to disillusionment and emigration after the Civil War, or to the pressures of work, fuelled by war memorials and the national self-confidence of the new, increasingly conservative Irish Free State. The cover of the sixth exhibition catalogue, printed by Maunsel & Roberts in the same format as its predecessor, featured a darkly sombre, expressionist linocut design depicting

Figure 2.13 Eleanor Kelly, binding for Rabindranath Tagore's *Gitanjali*, (London, 1913), with an introduction by W. B. Yeats. Contemporary olive green goatskin with Islamic-style centrepieces in blue and green, gold-tooled and set with a garnet, *c.*1914. Boxed in cigar box covered with hand-printed Japanese papers. (Private collection.)

artworkers paying homage to elders depicted as Irish Romanesque effigies by Wilhelmina Geddes. Trained in Belfast but based in Dublin since 1912, she, like Harry Clarke, worked as readily (but not as frequently) in graphics as in stained glass.[55] For the sixth exhibition, a selective all-Ireland representation, the Society took a firm stand by banning 'copies and reproductions', particularly of the widely plagiarised *Ardagh Chalice* and *Book of Kells*, and had enough exhibits of an improved standard and clearly defined process that it was able to classify them according to medium.[56] 'Bookbinding' included works by Eleanor Kelly and Harry Clarke, whose graphic design classes (1918–23) at the Dublin Metropolitan School were already captivating aspiring illustrators (and imitators). He exhibited his gilded vellum design for Harraps's recent publication of his illustrations to *The Years at the Spring* (1920), an anthology of recent poetry, and eight colour and eight black and white illustrations intended for reproduction. Colm O'Lochlain, co-founder of The Craftworkers' Guild in Dublin, showed bookbinding specimens and examples of printing from his recently established Candle Press;[57] and William Pender exhibited 'Richly Tooled and Inlaid' bindings with silk doublures in 'Crimson Crushed' and in 'Olive Cape Levant', in 'Old Rose Seal' and in 'Soft Green Morocco' for copies of Morris's *Life and Death of Jason*, Herrick's *Poems*, Keats's *Poems* and a French nineteenth-century binding manual.[58]

The 'Printed Books and Printing' category included Elizabeth Yeats's hand-printed edition of Lady Gregory's *Kiltartan Poetry Book*, *Further Letters of John Butler Yeats* selected by Lennox Robinson, and her brother's *Two Plays for Dancers*, as well as three replicable volumes by Colm O'Lochlain. In the 'Enamels' section, only Kathleen Bridle's panel entitled *Inspiration* was intended as a book cover, as was the Belfast Irish Decorative Art Association designer Eva McKee's incised and modelled leatherwork.[59] *The Studio* critic considered 'the worst work' in the exhibition to be 'in the section devoted to illumination, the art in which the ancient Irish were pre-eminent. One or two pieces there ... are downright bad, and most ... indifferent.'[60] Perhaps in response to this, a year later, Art O'Murnaghan, who never exhibited with the Arts and Crafts Society of Ireland, completed an illuminated page in black and red ink entitled *Eire*, illustrating 'The Vision of Brigid', which had been conceived over three years as 'the most beautiful and most representative design I could create' for 'the idea' of 'the Name of my Country'.[61]

By 1925, when the seventh and final Irish Arts and Crafts Society exhibition was held, many exhibitors had participated in the national *Aonach Tailteann*, an extensive revivalist fair held the previous year at the Royal Dublin Society in emulation of a seventh-century BC Irish olympiad celebrating the best native achievements in memory of the legendary druidic queen Tailte. At this, Colm O'Lochlain had won a bronze medal for his bookbinding, and Harry Clarke, who was by now acting as art editor for Seumas O'Sullivan's newly established *Dublin Magazine*, was awarded a silver medal for his book illustrations. Under his influence the 'Drawings for Black and White for Reproduction' section at the Arts and Crafts Society exhibition was bigger than before, and included works by Austin Molloy, his Art School colleague, who had designed the somewhat art deco catalogue cover and its foreword's initial letter. Fresh names join those of Eleanor Kelly, Colm O'Lochlain, the Cuala Press and Harry Clarke in the 'Book-binding', 'Decorative Engraving and Lithography', 'Decorative Drawing for Reproduction', 'Block Printing', 'Writing and Illuminating' and 'Printing' categories. The most unusual books in the exhibition, both illustrated by Harry Clarke, were exhibited by Maunsel and Roberts: the eight-volume *Ireland's Memorial Records, 1914–1918* of 1923, privately printed and engraved on handmade paper in a limited edition of 100 copies with folio holland-backed boards and doublures by Oswald Reeves, bound and tooled by William Pender (Fig. 2.14); and *The History of a Great House: The Origins of John Jameson Whiskey, Containing some interesting observations thereon together with the Causes of its Present Scarcity* (1924).

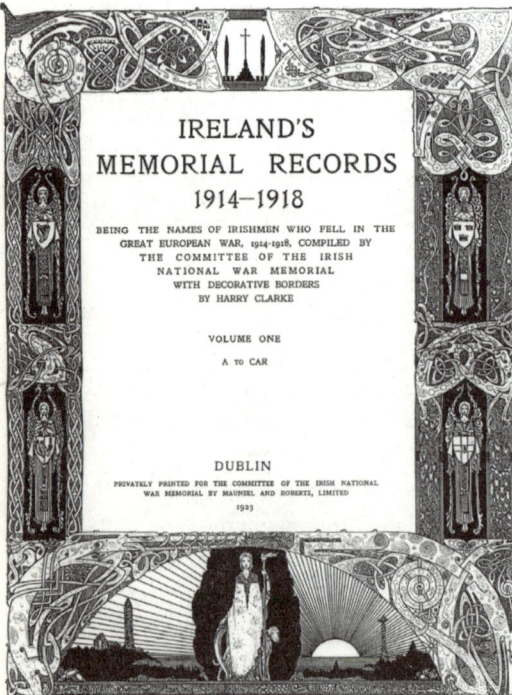

Figure 2.14 Harry Clarke, title page design for *Ireland's Memorial Records, 1914–1918,* privately printed by Maunsel and Roberts for the Committee of the Irish National War Memorial (Dublin, 1923). This limited edition of 100 copies also contains eight repeated decorated borders by Clarke, engraved on handmade paper, with folio holland-backed boards and doublures by P. O. Reeves; each of the eight volumes in each set were bound and tooled by William Pender. (Collection of National College of Art and Design, Dublin.)

The legacy of the Arts and Crafts movement can be seen as having fundamentally affected those arts connected with the book in Ireland. Its ideals were maintained by various presses, notably Cuala, whose values and example would be nobly upheld by its principal champion, Liam Miller, through his Dolmen Press, founded in 1951.

Chapter 3

'Yogibogeybox in Dawson Chambers': The Beginnings of Maunsel and Company

Clare Hutton

Maunsel and Co. = Geo. Roberts and Maunsel Hone. From what I learn Roberts is the person Hone being an Oxford insipid. I called to see Hone: he was in Belfast. I met Roberts in the street and smoothed him down standing him a drink (I took lithia). He is very self-important.

James Joyce to his brother Stanislaus, 4 August 1909

I have been very unwell for some time or I would have written to you sooner about our project for my book on Aran. It has been suggested that the new publishing house in Dublin – Maunsel & Co – should bring it out, and I have thought it best to agree for several reasons. One or two of my plays have made me very unpopular with a section of our Irish Catholic public and I feel it will be a great advantage to me to have this book printed and published in Dublin on Irish paper – small matters that are nevertheless thought a good deal of over here.

J.M. Synge to his publisher, Elkin Mathews, 11 November 1905[1]

INTRODUCTION

The Dublin publishing firm of Maunsel and Company, which was founded in 1905, emerged at a key moment in the Irish Literary Revival, and did much to promote the literature of that movement and the thinking behind the more general cultural revival and political upheavals that took place in Ireland in the period preceding the foundation of the Irish Free State in 1922. The firm did not publish much work by Yeats, the originator and most important writer of the Literary Revival, but it did publish many of the plays which were first performed at the Abbey Theatre, several volumes of poetry (which Yeats derided as 'the Twilight School'), and the *Collected Works* of both J. M. Synge and Patrick Pearse.[2] Ironically, the firm is perhaps best known now for failing to publish Joyce's *Dubliners*, which it finally refused in September 1912 (after issuing a contract in August 1909) on the grounds that it questioned the sex life of Edward VII ('a bit of a rake' who was 'fond of his glass of grog') and contained references to 'going concerns … mentioned by actual name'.[3] This essay, which is part of a wider project on the publishing and reception history of the Literary Revival, describes the cultural context of Maunsel's achievements and the way in which the firm was founded. My aim in so doing is to facilitate a deeper understanding of the cultural and literary history of the Revival period.

Figure 3.1 The Irish trademark.

CULTURAL CONTEXT

Maunsel was founded in a period when many Irish nationalists were becoming more aware of the need to 'de-anglicise' the Irish economy by rejecting imported British products and insisting on Irish ones instead. A small token of the burgeoning sense of national identity can be found in the *'déanta i nEirinn'* (made in Ireland) trademark which began to appear on many Irish products from the end of 1906, including books printed and published within Ireland (see Fig. 3.1).[4] Irish authors who wished to earn a living from writing – who were, on the whole, crucially dependent on the support of British publishers and readers – began to desire publication in Ireland, 'on Irish paper', as a means of displaying their cultural commitment to Ireland's economy and nationhood and influencing their reception by Irish readers, as the epigraph from Synge suggests. The foundation of Maunsel in 1905 may also be seen as part of a more general revival in the Irish publishing industry, a revival which was led by the example of the Dun Emer Press, a private press established in Dublin in 1903 by Elizabeth Corbet Yeats (1868–1940), the younger sister of the poet, who issued first editions of his work through the Press and edited all of the other titles (a position which allowed him the freedom to define his aesthetic, create a context in which his works could be appreciated and fulfill an obligation to his family). Inspired by the British private presses, notably William Morris's Kelmscott Press and T. J. Cobden-Sanderson's Doves Press, Elizabeth Yeats printed Dun Emer books on a handpress in Caslon Old Face, 'a good eighteenth-century fount of type', which is, as the first prospectus of the Dun Emer Press boasted, 'not eccentric in form or difficult to read'.[5] The books were printed on all-rag mouldmade paper, which had been specially prepared – 'without bleaching chemicals' – at Swiftbrook Paper Mills in Saggart, Co. Dublin.[6] These books were both beautiful and expensive (usually 10s 6d) and, as Elizabeth Yeats told P. S. O'Hegarty (once described as 'the only one of the old Yeats–Joyce–Dunsany–Gogarty crowd who not only walked down

Sackville Street but also collected first editions'), they were intended for 'people who really want something rather exclusive and are ready to pay for it'.[7] Some of Maunsel's publications – for instance the de luxe edition of *The Aran Islands* which was co-published with Elkin Mathews in 1907 (Fig. 3.2) – made excellent use of the 'Arts and Crafts' style of book production that had been so successfully deployed by Dun Emer. As D. F. McKenzie argued, the 'highly conscious deployment' of book art resources (i.e. typography, binding, paper and illustrations) makes it quite impossible to divorce the 'substance of the text' from the 'physical form of its presentation':

> The book itself is an expressive means. To the eye its pages offer an aggregation of meanings both verbal and typographic for translation to the ear;... its shape in the hand speaks to us from the past... Its total form is itself a significant historical statement.[8]

The 'Arts and Crafts' style of book production afforded both Dun Emer and Maunsel the opportunity to set a distance between their own books and the many cheap and badly printed books that were issued by other Irish publishing houses during this period. It liberated Irish authors and readers 'from bad paper made from one knows not what refuse, from evil-smelling gum, from covers of emerald green'[9] and suggested an allegiance between the Literary Revival and two more sophisticated contexts – the Arts and Crafts movement of the 1880s and 1890s, and the world of avant-garde literary publication in London during the same period – the contexts in which W. B. Yeats had formulated many of his ideas about book design.

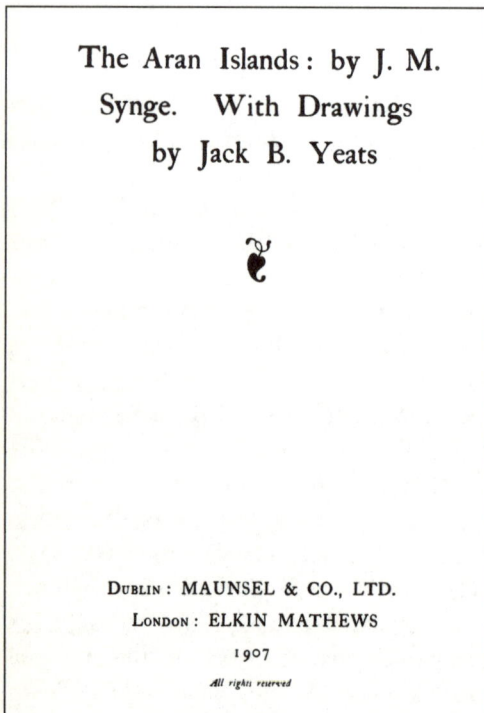

The Aran Islands : by J. M.
Synge.   With Drawings
by Jack B. Yeats

DUBLIN : MAUNSEL & CO., LTD.
LONDON : ELKIN MATHEWS
1907

Figure 3.2 The title page of *The Aran Islands* (1907). This work was actually printed in Edinburgh, not in Dublin on 'Irish paper'.

BEGINNINGS

Some of London's newer literary publishers – such as A. H. Bullen, Elkin Mathews and T. Fisher Unwin – had served the developing careers of Irish authors such as Yeats and Wilde relatively well in the 1890s. But when the Irish theatre movement began in the early 1900s the need for a commercial publishing house in Dublin with interests in the new literature, particularly the drama, was more acutely felt. In part Maunsel and Company evolved to serve that need. In July 1904 George Roberts (1873–1953), who was the secretary to the Irish National Theatre Society (INTS), decided to set up in publishing, with James Sullivan Starkey (1879–1958), a poet and editor who was sometimes known by the Irish form of his name, Seumas O'Sullivan.[10] It is not clear how they planned to finance their business. But they started to publish books from 27 Dawson Chambers, one of a group of offices at 12 Dawson Street, under the imprint 'Whaley and Company'.[11] In itself this name suggests something about the intellectual and cultural pedigree of those who were involved with the new enterprise, namely the close association between literary and esoteric interests in Dublin at the time. The name 'Whaley' was borrowed from Charles Weekes (1867–1946), a friend of Yeats and George William Russell (Æ) who had become interested in the Theosophical Society in the early part of the 1890s, though he had resisted the temptations of actual membership.[12] Weekes set up as a publisher in Dublin in 1894 in order to publish a collection of Æ's poetry, *Homeward Songs by the Way*.[13] This was followed by two further volumes by two other theosophical friends: John Eglinton's *Two Essays on the Remnant* (1894) and Charles Johnston's *From the Upanishads* (1896). Inevitably, these books did not bring in much money for Weekes and as a result he decided to move to London and try his hand in business there. By 1911, he had established himself as secretary and legal advisor to the British Electrical and Allied Manufacturers' Association, a practical world that was far removed from his earlier interests in poetry and theosophy.[14] As young men Roberts and O'Sullivan shared Weekes's interests. They both wrote poetry, were interested in publishing and were members of Æ's Hermetic Society, which also happened to meet at Dawson Chambers. In the Library episode of *Ulysses*, an episode which may be read as a 'designed assault on the foundations of revivalism', Joyce ruthlessly parodies the nature of their 'Hermetic' meetings ('Yogibogeybox in Dawson Chambers'), their admiration for Æ ('The faithful hermetists await the light, ripe for chelaship, ringroundabout him'), and the amateurish and rather cynical nature of their negotiations as publishers ('George Roberts is doing the commercial part. Longworth will give it a good puff in the *Express*... We are becoming important, it seems.')[15] Roberts later claimed that he could not even 'attempt' to define the purposes of Æ's Hermetic Society;[16] nevertheless his membership suggests the relationship between literature and a general interest in mysticism and theosophy, which was characteristic of his circle.

The foundation of Whaley and Company coincided with the opening, on 27 December 1904, of the Abbey Theatre, a permanent home for the INTS, paid for by Annie Horniman. Roberts was involved in both enterprises. From December

1903 he was paid a salary of £1 per week for acting as secretary to the INTS, a position which brought him into close contact with actors, playwrights, printers, publishers and newspaper editors.[17] This was clearly an extremely busy and exciting period for Roberts, who played parts in some of the performances put on by the INTS, including Dan Burke in J. M. Synge's *The Shadow of the Glen*, Timmy in the same author's *The Well of the Saints*, and Murrough in Lady Gregory's *Kincora* (see Fig. 3.3).[18] In his role as secretary Roberts also made arrangements, late in 1904 or early in 1905, for the publication of the first three volumes of the Abbey Theatre Series, a series of plays which were performed at the new theatre.[19] These were J. M. Synge's *The Well of the Saints*, Lady Gregory's *Kincora*, and Padraic Colum's *The Land*. Priced at one shilling and sold in the theatre and at booksellers, these plays were all published in 1905 by the Abbey Theatre, not Whaley and Company.[20] Later in the same year they were reissued by Maunsel and Company.

Figure 3.3 George Roberts as Murrough in Lady Gregory's *Kincora* (1905).

Further impetus to the fledgling enterprise of Whaley and Company was given by A. H. Bullen, one of Yeats's publishers.[21] Bullen came from an Irish family; his father, George Bullen (1816–1894), the Keeper of Early Printed Books at the British Museum, was from Clonakilty in Cork. He considered setting up as a publisher in Dublin in December 1901 and July 1904 but had abandoned these plans by 17 August 1904 when he told Yeats that he had started the Shakespeare Head Press in Stratford-upon-Avon, a venture inspired by a dream in which he had visited Shakespeare's birthplace.[22] But although Bullen was reluctant to invest further capital in a new venture, he told Yeats that he 'might be of some service' to Roberts and O'Sullivan 'by buying editions for the English markets'.[23] Late in 1904, probably in November, Bullen agreed to buy 100 copies of Seumas O'Sullivan's *The Twilight People* from Whaley and Company for the English market.[24] Other Whaley titles included *The Mask of Apollo* by Æ (which was co-published in London by Macmillan), a reissue of Bullen's 1897 edition of *The Flight of the Eagle* by Standish O'Grady, and a book of verse in English and Irish called *Blátha Fraoich* ('Heather Blossoms') by Níall MacGiolla Bhrigde. Despite the mediocrity of these titles, Yeats was supportive of Whaley and Company. He knew that his position as an 'Irish poet, looking to my own people for my ultimate best audience' would be strengthened by the foundation of a Dublin-based commercial publishing house which was supportive of the literary and cultural revival.[25] In December 1904 he urged Bullen to let Roberts become Bullen's agent in Dublin because he 'had an instinct' – he must have heard rumours – that if Bullen did not do so, 'some other man would get his toes into your boots'.[26] At the same time, Bullen also agreed to transfer some copies of the sheets from two volumes of his own series of 'Plays for an Irish Theatre' to the Abbey Theatre Series, an arrangement which gave Roberts a strong hand in the negotiations that subsequently led to the foundation of Maunsel.

Of all the negotiations that took place between Bullen and Whaley and Company, the most significant were those that resulted in the sale in Ireland of a three-shilling edition of three of Yeats's prose works, *The Secret Rose*, *The Celtic Twilight*, and *Ideas of Good and Evil*. The Dublin editions of these books appeared under the Maunsel imprint in the autumn of 1905 but it is clear that the arrangements for their reissue in Dublin had first been made with Whaley.[27] The title page of each of these Dublin editions consisted of a cancel with the words 'for sale in Ireland only' printed on the verso, bound with the sheets from Bullen's edition.[28] Yeats had wished for a popular edition of his writings 'with an Irish printer's name & the name of some Irish publishing house side by side with your own [i.e. Bullen's] on the title page', but this particular arrangement was hardly the realisation of that ambition.[29] In effect Bullen was using the Dublin market to dispose of copies of Yeats's prose works because he found them difficult to sell in Britain. Yeats was particularly annoyed that the revised edition of *The Celtic Twilight* (1902), which his father had described as 'an immortal book', was sold by Maunsel in Ireland for three shillings, a substantial reduction on the original price of six shillings:

I can not see any reason why it should be sold at remainder prices. It is complete, I do not want to change it in any way, and your collected edition being so much more expensive would hardly make the cheaper volume unnecessary.[30]

There were, however, only 400 copies of *The Celtic Twilight* sold at this price. Bullen may have placated Yeats through normal royalty payments or he may have argued that Yeats could not hope to become popular in Ireland if his works were only published in expensive editions. Whatever the case, these arrangements are a testimony to a close level of cooperation between Bullen, Roberts and Yeats and to Yeats's authority within the context of the new venture in Irish publishing.

Charles Weekes does not appear to have been as supportive of the Irish venture as A. H. Bullen. According to Frances-Jane French, Weekes demanded that Roberts and O'Sullivan change the name of their imprint, when he realised what was going on.[31] Although he had not published any titles under the Whaley imprint since 1896 he had yet to relinquish his own plans for his career in publishing. This intervention from Weekes – combined with the realisation that their publishing business needed to be put on a firmer financial footing – led Roberts and O'Sullivan to begin the negotiations that resulted in the foundation of Maunsel and Company, 'Maunsel' being a modification of the middle name of a new director, Joseph Maunsell Hone (1882–1959). The name 'Maunsel' (pronounced to rhyme with 'cancel') was clearly accepted because it suggested that the new publishing concern was a well-connected and worthy Protestant enterprise. Roberts and O'Sullivan were trying to suggest the same sort of thing when they picked on 'Whaley', which had originally been chosen by Charles Weekes to honour the memory of 'Buck' Whaley (1766–1800), the notorious Irish politician and aristocrat, from whom Weekes claimed to be descended. The negotiations that established Maunsel were being discussed in early January, before Yeats left Dublin.[32] The new firm was registered with the Companies Office in London in the summer of 1905.[33] Both Roberts and O'Sullivan had a strong hand to play in their negotiations with Hone: they had arranged a number of publications under the Whaley imprint; they had arranged to co-publish some titles with A. H. Bullen; and Roberts had arranged for the publication of the first six volumes of the Abbey Theatre Series. Nevertheless, it is clear from surviving correspondence that there was a degree of bad feeling between the individuals associated with the new company.

Hone, a young man of 23 'with about £1000 to venture', had been discovered by Æ.[34] According to A. H. Bullen, Hone had 'a thorough dislike' of Roberts:

Evidently he would be glad to back out of the arrangement if he could find a decent excuse; but he stands in some fear of Æ…for Russell wants eventually to thrust Roberts on him as a partner…Hone's alarm at the prospect is tempered with disgust.[35]

Roberts did not have any capital to offer and Hone regarded him as a 'social inferior'.[36] Both men were Protestant but Hone came from a distinguished

Ascendancy background whereas Roberts's origins were more obscure. Never one to resist the opportunity to become involved in awkward business negotiations, Yeats tried to persuade Roberts to accept Hone's offer and take a position as manager:

> I think that if I were in your position I would be satisfied with the three years guarantee [of your present income] & a share of the profits from the second year. A share of the profits given in this way is substantially a partnership but without risk in case of bankruptcy. If you became a partner in this business you would practically risk all you have.[37]

Yeats did not want Æ to be involved: 'there is no use mincing words in this matter. Russell will never make a successful publishing firm.'[38] In Æ's place, Yeats cajoled Stephen Gwynn into serving as Maunsel's 'literary advisor'. He wrote to Bullen to explain why:

> Russell had drawn up a scheme by which Hone, Roberts and Starkey [i.e. Seumas O'Sullivan] were to start publishing; Starkey nominal literary adviser, Russell real one. I knew that this arrangement was impossible... Hone's money would be lost and enterprise discouraged. I tried to find out if Hone would throw in his lot with you. Roberts' impression was that he would not. I succeeded however in getting Stephen Gwynn to take up with Hone and arrange a practicable scheme. Gwynn has of course plenty of publishing experience. He is the literary advisor & Hone will I believe act on his advice... All I could do was to see that this new ship was properly manned.[39]

At the close of negotiations, probably in June 1905, Stephen Gwynn, Joseph Hone and George Roberts were made directors. Hone contributed £2,000 which enabled Maunsel to commence business.[40] The other directors contributed their expertise. Apart from editing the Tower Press Booklets, Seumas O'Sullivan did not become formally involved. Nor did Æ. When Maunsel was being set up, Russell was fully employed by Sir Horace Plunkett's Irish Agricultural Organisation Society, a position which he maintained after he became the editor of *The Irish Homestead* in August 1905. He had resigned his Vice-Presidency of the INTS in April 1904, after disagreements with Yeats about play selection.[41] Given these factors, it seems likely that Russell did not want to become involved in something as controversial and time-consuming as publishing.

Yeats's reasons for not wanting Æ to be involved with Maunsel and Company were related, primarily, to aesthetic concerns. Describing his reaction to *New Songs*, Æ's edition of lyric verse by Padraic Colum, Eva Gore-Booth, Thomas Keohler, Alice Milligan, Susan Mitchell, Seumas O'Sullivan, George Roberts and Ella Young, Yeats noted that:

> the dominant mood in many of them is one I have faught in my self and put down... an exageration of sentiment & sentimental beauty which I have come to think unmanly.[42]

Russell could not become a director of Maunsel because Russell had 'great influence over Starkie and would get all the bad poets in Dublin printed', that is the poets of *New Songs*.[43] Unfortunately, as Yeats was to learn, stopping Æ from becoming a director of Maunsel did not save the company from the poets of the 'Twilight School'. With the exception of George Roberts (who never published a collection of his own poetry), Maunsel published new works by all of the poets who had appeared in *New Songs*.[44] These writers valued the 'transcendental quality' of Æ's work, saw him as a 'most prominent figure' and gathered around him to 'get courage, fresh hope and inspiration'.[45]

As is often the case with small publishing companies, the books published by Maunsel strongly reflected the interests of its directors. Of the three directors who formed the company in 1905, George Roberts, a Protestant who was born in Castlewellan, Co. Down in January 1873, was the most important. Roberts really ran the company throughout its existence – between 1905 and 1920 as Maunsel, and from December 1920 until 1925 as Maunsel and Roberts. Unfortunately, little is known about Roberts's early life, where he was educated, and how (or indeed whether) he received any formal training as a printer. His father, Oliver Goldsmith Roberts, was the manager of Murland's Linen Mill at Castlewellan until about 1883, when he moved to London, intending to trade independently. When he died in 1886 the family moved to Belfast.[46] It was there whilst working in a book shop in 1899 that Roberts made the acquaintance of James Cousins. Discovering their mutual interest in theosophy, the work of Æ and the Irish Literary Revival, the two men became friends. Cousins found Roberts a position with his own employers, who ran a coal and shipping office and Roberts moved to Dublin on 1 January 1900.[47] Between taking up this position and starting in publishing in 1904, Roberts worked as a commercial representative for an underwear firm in Dublin. This led A. H. Bullen to refer to him as the 'ex-Knight of the Garter' and Joyce to quip that the 'playboy shift' was 'pinched as swag / From Maunsel's manager's travelling-bag'.[48]

In the early 1900s Roberts was associated with most of the principal cultural interest groups of Dublin at the time. In addition to Æ's Dublin Hermetic Society, he was, for a brief period, a member of the Gaelic League. When his plans to introduce George Moore to the branch were rejected by the teacher, 'a middle-aged buxom woman from the Aran Islands' who 'threw up her arms in horror' at the prospect, Roberts 'fled ignominiously' never to return to the League again.[49] It seems probable that Roberts could not speak or write the Irish language, although Maunsel made a significant, if slight, contribution to the development of Irish-language printing. Roberts gained considerable insight into the development of the Irish Literary Revival through his involvement with the Irish National Dramatic Society (later the INTS) which was formally constituted on 9 August 1902. He was instrumental in the formation of the society, as he recalled in his memoirs:

> It occurred to me that instead of continuing to give performances under the auspices of societies with other objects, it would be much better for those interested in Irish drama to form a society whose object would be

solely to develop drama in Ireland. I talked this over with AE and Cousins, who thought the Fays would be interested in my scheme and accordingly introduced me. I found the Fay brothers most anxious to work on these lines and I met the members of their company to discuss ways and means.

We met in a little hall at the back of a tobacconist's shop in High Street... Being full of confidence and the assurance of youth, the fact that the offers of subscriptions amongst ourselves totalled something under £5 did not dismay us, and the Irish National Dramatic Society was founded then and there.[50]

Máire Garvey, whom Roberts married in 1910, was also a member of the Society from 1902.[51] As secretary to the INTS, Roberts was obviously well placed to enter into the business of publishing. However, he does not appear to have had any formal training in the business before he became a director of Maunsel, nor does he appear to have been quick to learn from his mistakes. It is also true that his relationship with Yeats, an important relationship given Yeats's power in the Irish literary world by this time, disimproved towards the end of 1905 when Yeats put his plan for eliminating democracy in the INTS into action. There were two elements to this plan: the incorporation of the INTS (to limit its liability and raise further capital), and the issue of contracts to the actors, an act that made them professional employees rather than fellow members of an enthusiastic amateur group. According to Murphy, Roberts was the 'most outspoken' opponent of these developments, which completely altered the nature of the INTS.[52] Together with Frank Walker, Máire Nic Shiubhlaigh, Fred Ryan, Padraic Colum and Máire Garvey, Roberts left the INTS in December 1905.[53] With Maunsel being managed by Roberts and Máire Nic Shiubhlaigh working at Dun Emer and, worse still, Æ a regular visitor to both establishments, it is little wonder that Yeats thought that his difficulties as coordinator of the revival in Irish literary publishing were akin to his difficulties in the Irish theatre. As he explained to his friend Katharine Tynan: 'It is really all one dispute', the dispute between a determined professional with a keen view of his own aesthetic objectives and a group of enthusiastic amateurs with varying levels of ability.[54]

CONCLUSION

Given the level of fractiousness and bad humour that beset Maunsel in these early months, it is remarkable that the firm went on to achieve such prominence and success as a publisher. By 1915, in the esteemed view of *The Irish Book Lover*, Maunsel had achieved 'the one thing which those acquainted with social conditions in the Irish capital would have said could not be done'; they had established a market in Ireland for Irish books.[55] Roberts drew on the services of the best printing firms of the era, and from 1910 he printed a number of Maunsel's titles himself and achieved very high standards of typographical excellence. Unfortunately, his excellence as a producer of books did not stretch to other essential elements in the publishing business. Although Maunsel published an impressive range of material, Roberts was not a reliably good judge of quality and sometimes failed to read manuscripts because he believed that he could depend upon the opinions of Æ. He was also financially reckless. Most significantly, he argued with virtually all of his most successful authors, including John St. John Greer Ervine (regarding the contents of his book on Carson), Lady Gregory (over the payment of royalties), Joyce (regarding the publication of *Dubliners*), Seán O'Casey (regarding payment for his book on the Citizen Army), and Yeats and the executors of J. M. Synge (regarding the contents of the *Collected Works of J. M. Synge*). As Padraic Colum noted: 'There are people who study how to win friends and influence people; George Roberts knew how to lose friends and alienate people.'[56] When the firm's enlarged premises at 96 Middle Abbey Street were devastated during the Rising of Easter 1916, John Quinn told Lady Gregory that he wished that Roberts, whom he regarded as a 'little redheaded ruffian', 'had got effectively shot in the rebellion' which he believed 'would have been a good thing for Irish writers and Irish letters'.[57]

Chapter 4
Early Science and Learned Publication

Siobhán Ó Rafferty

In order to show the way in which science has played an important role in shaping contemporary Ireland, this essay examines scientific publication and the role of the learned societies in Ireland from an early date to the beginnings of the twentieth century.

Scientific publication in Ireland preceded the advent of printing. From an early stage scientific matters were being written about and promulgated in manuscript form. Apart from early mentions of birds, and animals, and allusions to the weather and the landscape, David Cabot has drawn attention to the fact that Giraldus Cambrensis' *Topographia Hibernica* (1185) deals with Ireland under the three themes – position and topography, wonder and miracles, and the inhabitants of the country.[1] This early example, though it is in many respects unreliable, serves as an example of the later approaches to surveying the Irish landscape, of which more later. Another science which was of interest to the early Irish was astronomy, and several astronomical tracts in Irish survive.

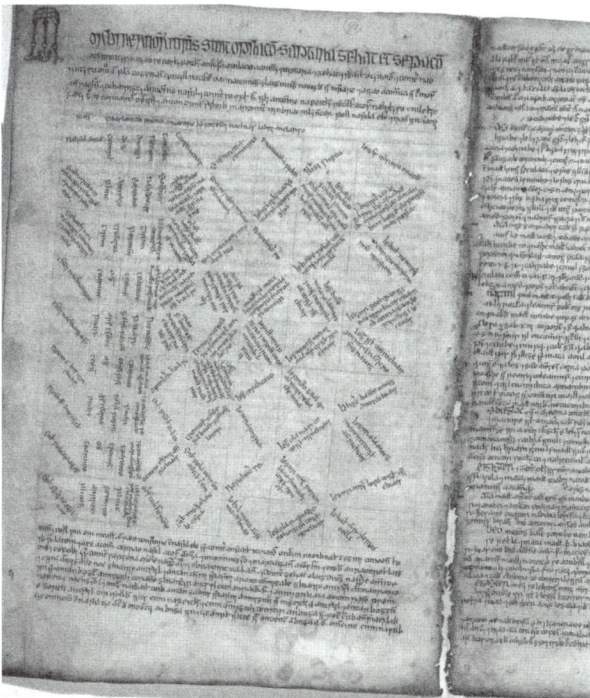

Figure 4.1 *Book of the O'Lees*, RIA Ms 23.P.10(ii), p.48 'morbi nervorum visus…' fifteenth-century translation of Latin text on medicine. This page illustrates the practice of using a table as a quick guide to the description of a particular disease, the name and cures for the disease and so on. The facing page would contain fuller information regarding the disease in question. (Photograph reproduced by kind permission of the Royal Irish Academy.)

I should particularly like to draw attention here to the existence of medical works in the Irish language, and in manuscript format. Medicine played an important role in mediaeval Ireland and physicians were held in great esteem. The *laoi*, or physician (hence the English surname Lee) was usually a member of a medical family attached to one of the great Irish families, just as were the *brehons*, law-givers, *filí*, poets, and *geinealaí*, genealogists. The Irish physicians were unique in Europe in that they wrote their medical works in this vernacular, and they translated mainstream continental and British medical texts into Irish. Irish was the language of higher learning. Many of these medical texts survive: at the Royal Irish Academy there are thirty-three, at Trinity College Dublin there are twenty-eight; the National Library of Scotland holds twenty-two, the National Library of Ireland holds ten and the British Library has nine. They date from the fifteenth century to the eighteenth, thus they well overlap the print era. According to Dr Aoibheann Nic Dhonnchadha of the Dublin Institute of Advanced Studies, who is the Irish expert in this field, the Irish medical texts were, and are, important for the plant lore contained therein, Irish doctors being seen as the main repository of botanical knowledge.[2] They were held in the highest esteem in Europe. The continuing importance of botany, medicine and the Irish language can be attested to in several different areas of science.

THE SEVENTEENTH CENTURY

The seventeenth century marks the beginning of real scientific discussion and research in Ireland. Various societies were formed which promoted scientific investigation and collaboration across a range of disciplines. These societies were the precursors of the Royal Dublin Society, the Royal Irish Academy and other eighteenth- and nineteenth-century associations that operated on a grander scale and were, for the most part, to endure up to the present time. Before discussing the Dublin Philosophical Society and some of the publications for which it was either directly or indirectly responsible, I should like to make reference to a publication entitled *Ireland's naturall history, being a true and ample description of its situation, greatness, shape, and nature...*[3] This book, which was published by Samuel Hartlib in London in 1652, was intended 'for the common good of Ireland, and more especially, for the benefit of the adventurers and planters therein'. In a dedication to Oliver Cromwell, Hartlib expresses his hope that Ireland will shortly be replanted with adventurers, 'exiled Bohemians and other Protestants', and those 'well affected out of the Low Countries'. He continues: 'To further the settlement thereof, the *Naturall History* of that Countrie will not bee unfit, but very subservient.'[4] The author, Gerard Boate (1604–49), was a Dutch physician. He was appointed physician to the Army of Ireland in 1647, but did not take up his position until 1649 and he died shortly afterwards. Much of his text is based on information supplied by his brother Arnold Boate, Physician-General to the Army in Leinster who had collected it over a period of eight years. Boate's work was the first regional history in the English language and its coverage is extremely comprehensive.[5] It was the precursor of many surveys carried out over the following two centuries and like them, its purpose was utilitarian.

Boate's section on winds is particularly amusing and instructive: 'With winds it is in this countrie almost as with rain, Ireland not only having its share in them, as other countries, but being very much subject to them, more than most other parts of the world.' He goes on to comment on the infrequent east wind:

> commonly there is no need of a wind to be wafted over into England; where to the contrary, those, who out of England will come over into Ireland, very ordinarily are constrained to wait two or three weeks, and sometimes five or six weeks, yea it hath faln out so more than once, that in two whole months, and longer, there hath not been so much East wind, as to carry ships out of England into Ireland...[6]

The Dublin Philosophical Society was established in 1683. It was comprised of a group of men such as Sir William Petty, its first president, who had come over to Ireland as Physician-General to the parliamentary army; William Molyneux, the founder, and his brother, Thomas; and St George Ashe, provost of Trinity College Dublin. The Society was well placed as many of the members were also members of the Royal Society, London, and were in regular communication with men such as Samuel Hartlib, John Flamsteed, and in the case of William Molyneux, with John Locke.

Petty had carried out the Down Survey of Ireland (1654–56), in which he had tabulated and described the whole country.[7] The survey was not reliable but it was the first attempt to survey the country in a systematic way. As Hoppen has suggested, mapping was undoubtedly an important activity.[8] The interest in surveying that can be noted in the work of both Boate and Petty was continued by William Molyneux in the 1680s when he projected a map of Ireland, with detailed descriptions, which would form the Ireland section of Moses Pitt's *English Atlas*.[9] Molyneux set about the task in a scientific fashion, sending out questionnaires to people throughout the country in order to elicit geographical information. Significantly, Molyneux asked about the nature of the soil, flora, fauna, topography, ports, history, population, seats, towns, trades, antiquities etc., thus anticipating the nineteenth-century Ordnance Survey *Memoirs* by a 150 years. Unfortunately, Molyneux's scheme came to nought: having collected information from a wide variety of sources, Molyneux was forced to abandon the project when Pitt's *Atlas* folded due to the latter's arrest for debt. In the final analysis, only five of the projected eleven volumes of the *Atlas* were published. The Irish section never appeared in print and many of the submissions have not survived.

Remembered by many as the author of *The case of Ireland's being bound by acts of parliament in England, stated*,[10] Molyneux was also the author of a highly influential text, *Dioptrica nova*,[11] which not only became the standard work on seeing and perception, but it so impressed John Locke that he took up Molyneux's ideas in the second edition of his *Essay concerning human understanding*.[12] Essentially, the Dublin Philosophical Society concerned itself with scientific matters and the members published with the Royal Society, or privately. Yet, as Atkinson has suggested, 'In much of Europe, the Royal Society was originally known only as the source of the *Philosophical Transactions of the Royal Society*, which reached a wide international audience in the seventeenth and eighteenth centuries, whether in its original form or its numerous vernacular and Latin translations.'[13] Thus, through their membership of the Royal Society the deliberations of our Irish scientists could extend not only to England but to the continent of Europe. Of the sciences covered, medicine was by far the most frequent topic of discussion. But in line with the Baconian ethos of the Society, and taking into account Molyneux's abortive survey, it should be remembered that the Society also considered antiquarian matters within its scope, and that men such as Thomas Molyneux, Edward Lhuyd and Roderic O'Flaherty laid the foundations for an antiquarian movement that really gained force with the formation of the Royal Irish Academy in 1785.

THE EIGHTEENTH CENTURY

In the early eighteenth century John K'Eogh, a member of an old Irish family, and a minister in Co. Roscommon, published several works, including *Botanalogia universalis hibernica* and *Zoologia medicinalis hibernica*.[14] Again, the aim was utilitarian – K'Eogh was anxious to promote the medical efficacy of using animals for cures. K'Eogh's herbal had been preceded by Caleb Threlkeld's Irish florilegium, *Synopsis stirpium Hibernicarum*, which was published in Dublin in 1727.[15] Threlkeld drew on many manuscripts and previously published sources for his work although Cabot maintains that this text does contain the results of some of Threlkeld's own field work.[16] K'Eogh is interesting for four reasons: firstly, like Threlkeld, and following on from the manuscript tradition, he used the Irish, English and Latin forms of the names of plants and, in K'Eogh's case, of animals also; secondly, the work is still of value to lexicographers because of the inclusion of the Irish versions of plant and animal names (both works are arranged in a dictionary format); thirdly, in the dedication to the *Zoologia,* K'Eogh advocates the promotion of the three branches of the *materia medica*, namely, botany, zoology and mineralogy; fourthly, K'Eogh is another example of one, who, though primarily interested in scientific matters, later wrote a work on the antiquities of Ireland.[17]

The Physico-Historical Society of Ireland (1744–53) was a short-lived, but rather important society. It aimed, rather pompously, to do justice in Ireland and to encourage immigration. It also aimed to set up county committees to collect information on local matters, but this never quite got off the ground. It did employ a botanist to assist Charles Smith, a medical doctor, in the preparation of his surveys of Cork and Waterford.[18] And John Rutty, another doctor, published prolifically on mineral waters. Rutty was also a member of yet another society, the Medico-Philosophical Society (1756–78), which devoted itself to 'the pursuit of truth and the sound method of reasoning first introduced by Lord Bacon'.[19] As

Cabot has pointed out, Rutty's *An Essay towards a natural history of the County of Dublin* (1772) is the first real county natural history in Ireland.[20] It is interesting also for its employment of statistics of population and other statistical sources of information.

The Dublin Society, which later became the Royal Dublin Society, was founded in 1731. The RDS is a household name in Ireland, and is perhaps best loved for the annual Horse Show which attracts horse lovers and show jumpers from far and wide. In fact, the Society was always associated with animal husbandry, the useful arts and manufactures, and originally bore the title the 'Dublin Society for improving Husbandry, Manufactures and other Useful Arts'; shortly afterwards 'and Sciences' was added. Thomas Molyneux and Thomas Prior were two of the founder members. A lawyer and friend of both Swift and Berkeley, Prior was critical of absentee landlords and in 1729 published a *List of absentees of Ireland...with observations on the present trade and conditions of that Kingdom.*[21]

The Society also involved itself in devising practical methods for such things as reclaiming bogs for tillage. Again, we witness the utilitarian tendencies of the societies, which are reflected in their publications. The Dublin Society diverged from the other societies, however, in that it began an active publishing programme. The Society took out advertisements in local papers in order to promote new activities and to let the public know about recent discoveries and other matters. They also paid a printer to publish pamphlets and occasional publications and they later published *Proceedings*. In 1736, the Dublin printer Richard Reilly negotiated with the Society to publish their *Weekly Observations* in his *Dublin Newsletter*, against which the Society undertook to purchase 500 copies of each issue – an interesting example of entrepreneurial activity on both sides! In 1739, Reilly went on to publish a collected edition of selected *Weekly Observations* which was pirated in several other capitals and reprinted in 1763.[22] The collected edition includes articles such as 'General reflections on the present state of Ireland in relation to our trade and manufactures'; 'A method of raising hops in red-bogs'; 'Directions for making roads'; 'Instructions for making cyder', together with several articles on flax. The *Weekly Observations* were meant to be immediate and snappy, and in this they certainly succeeded.

The first volume of the *Transactions of the Royal Dublin Society* was produced in 1800. It included essays on tanning, spirit varnish, scooping out potato eyes for seed, malting, and raising of hops. Importantly, it also included extracts in English of articles from the publications of continental societies, for example the *Transactions of the Agricultural Society of Amsterdam*, and there were queries regarding sheep from 'a respectable farmer near Philadelphia, transmitted to the President of the Board of Agriculture by Gen. Washington'! The Royal Dublin Society continued its work in this vein throughout the nineteenth and well into the twentieth century.

The Royal Irish Academy was founded in 1785 by a group of interested scientists and antiquarians; its aims were to investigate and promote the sciences, polite literature and antiquities in Ireland. The founding president was James Caulfield, the first earl of Charlemont. The Academy had many members in common with the Royal Dublin Society and subsequently with other societies and organisations formed in Ireland, but it differed from these societies in several respects. Firstly, it restricted membership; secondly, it actively involved itself in the three areas of scholarship included in its aims; thirdly, while it laid a certain emphasis on the utility of research, it laid greater emphasis on research per se, and in the case of antiquities, on the preservation and conservation of buildings, artefacts and manuscripts. To quote from the preface to the first volume of the Academy's *Transactions*:

> Let it not be imputed to arrogance when we say that, however former Societies in this kingdom may have failed, the members of this Academy should not be disheartened. From its peculiar nature, and several favourable circumstances attending the time of its institution, it has many prospects of continuance. Uniting in one plan the three compartments of Science, Polite Literature, and Antiquities, it unites whatever is pleasing with whatever is useful, the advancement of speculative knowledge with the history of mankind: it makes provision for the capricious variations of literary pursuit, and embracing all the objects of rational enquiry it secures the cooperation of the learned of every description.[23]

Members were encouraged to share their knowledge and interests with one another, regardless of their own disciplines. Thus we find that the poet William Preston published a paper in the Transactions of the Royal Irish Academy for 1803 on a programme for Ireland's industrial development,[24] and the renowned antiquarian, Charles O'Conor, wrote in the first Transactions that the 'Academists cannot begin better than by display of our natural advantages'.[25]

In 1789, Richard Kirwan, an eminent chemist and author of a work on mineralogy, which was the standard text in that field for most of the nineteenth century, and was widely translated, exhibited a sword from Roscommon at an Academy meeting.[26] And Richard Lovell Edgeworth, father of the author, Maria, published 'An essay on the art of conveying secret and swift intelligence', which was inspired by the activities of the United Irishmen and the need for a swift response.[27] The following are the first lines of a verse he composed on the prospect of telegraphic communication between England and Ireland:

> Hark from basaltic rocks and giant walls,
> To Britain's shores the glad Hibernia calls;
> Her voice no longer waits retarding tides,
> The meeting coasts no more the sea divides.
> Quick, at the voice of fortune or of fame,
> Kindles from shore to shore the patriot flame,
> Hov'ring in air, each kindred genius smiles,
> And binds with closer bands the sister isles.

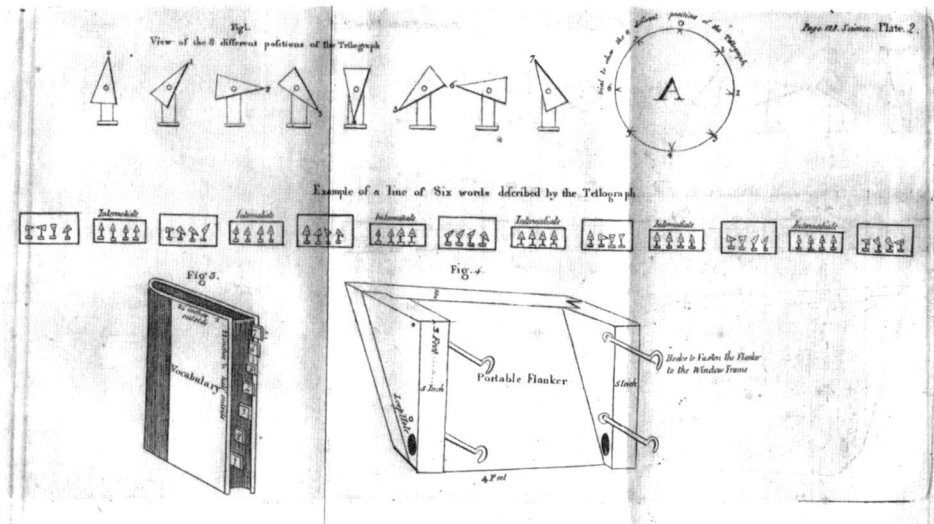

Figure 4.2 Plate illustrating the first line of Edgeworth's verse, 'Hark from basaltic rocks and giant walls.' From Richard Lovell Edgeworth's paper 'An essay on the part of conveying secret and swift intelligence' in *Transactions Of the Royal Irish Academy*, v.6, 1797.

The Academy published *Transactions* from 1787 until 1907. Each volume was divided into three sections and the coverage was as follows:

Science	106 papers
Polite Literature	25 papers
Antiquities	32 papers

The Academy later published *Proceedings* (1836–), the *Cunningham Memoirs* and the *Todd Lecture Series*, facsimiles of the great Irish vellum manuscripts, and Sir William Wilde's museum catalogues, inter alia, and the Society continues to publish in the myriad sciences and the humanities today.

THE NINETEENTH CENTURY

The Geological Society of Dublin (later the Royal Geological Society of Ireland) and the Statistical and Social Inquiry Society were also important in the scientific field in Ireland. The former was founded in 1831 'for the purpose of investigating the mineral structure of the earth, and more particularly of Ireland'.[28] Ireland had been surveyed, as we know, by Petty, Boate and many others in selective ways over the years, but it had not been geologically surveyed. By the late 1880s, however, it had been geologically surveyed more than any other country in the world.[29] The *Journal* of the Society is obviously replete with geological information, but for even the non-geologically minded it contains really first-rate maps. The Society petered out in the 1890s, but by this time the Geological Survey of Ireland was in place.[30]

The Statistical and Social Inquiry Society, founded in 1847 as the Dublin Statistical Society, was utilitarian in its aims, and was influenced by the sciences of political economy and statistics. Rather as Rutty had a hundred years previously, it drew on statistics to bolster social theories. The Society continues to flourish today. Figure 4.3 gives a good example of the type of topic with which this society concerned itself. It is a table showing the amounts of money sent home by emigrants to the United States during the period 1844–53; the information was used by Jonathan Pim, President of the Society in the course of his presidential address in 1854.[31]

Estimate of the number of Emigrants from Ireland to America, and of the amount of remittances in small sums sent by emigrants to their friends in Ireland, in the years **1844** *to* **1853** *inclusive.*

	Number of Emigrants.	Amount of Remittances.
1844	54,834	not known.
1845	75,9114	not known.
1846	106,748	not known.
1847	219,885	not known.
1848	181,316	£460,000
1849	218,842	£540,000
1850	213,649	£957,000
1851	254,537	£990,000
1852	224,997	£1,404,000
1853	199,392	£1,439,000

from Jonathan Pim's address delivered at the opening of the 8th session of the Dublin Statistical Society, 20th November, 1854

Figure 4.3 *Journal of the Dublin Statistical Society*, v.1, 1855.

Other important scholarly societies that were founded in the nineteenth century include the Belfast Naturalists' Field Club, the Dublin Naturalists' Field Club and the Astronomical Society of Ireland. But I would like to conclude my survey with a brief mention of the mapping project of the Ordnance Survey of Ireland which was undertaken between the 1820s and the late 1840s. Briefly, the Ordnance Survey aimed to map Ireland on a scale of six inches to the mile, but the scheme grew to include a *Memoir* exercise reminiscent of Molyneux's which was extremely comprehensive in its coverage. Work on the survey began in Co. Derry. However, the *Memoir* scheme, although comprehensive for the Ulster counties, never extended far south due to the high cost and time factors involved. Nonetheless, the mapping continued, and this in its own way led to problems, primarily with naming and language. A team of Gaelic speakers, led by John O'Donovan, had to go out into the field, literally, to sort out the problem of placenames. This was highly complicated in Ireland and no mean undertaking, considering that practically every field has a name. O'Donovan, never a man to take the easy way out, not only worked on the placenames, but also investigated the antiquities, the lore and topography of each place in which he stayed. His research activities are recorded in the Ordnance Survey *Letters* held by the Royal Irish Academy. The associated Ordnance Survey *Name Books* are in the National Archives. A geological department recorded the geological features and George du Noyer drew them. Du Noyer and others, including George Petrie, the great antiquarian, recorded the antiquities in pencil, pen and ink and in watercolour. It was a glorious, if ill-fated, marriage of science and antiquities. Eventually, the government in London pulled the plug on the *Memoir* venture because of the mounting costs of the project and the fact that the maps, which were the main object of the exercise, were not being produced. However, the Survey had served three useful purposes. Firstly, the whole of Ireland was surveyed on a six-inch scale; the resulting maps are still consulted on a daily basis in the Royal Irish Academy library. Secondly, while the *Memoir* for Templemore and Londonderry[32] was the only one published at the time, the Institute of Irish Studies at the Queen's University of Belfast, in association with the Academy, published the *Memoir* series in forty volumes during the period 1990–98.[33] These volumes serve to provide an exhaustive illustration of life in pre-Famine Ulster. The great pity is that the provinces of Connaught, Leinster and Munster were not covered by the *Memoir* element of the Survey due to the retrenchments that led to the cessation of the collection of statistical and other *Memoir* information. Thirdly, the *Letters* are a tremendous source of local history, topographical information and folklore.[34] In our own time the story of the Ordnance Survey and the lexicographical problems that it incurred inspired the playwright Brian Friel to write his play *Translations*.

CONCLUSION

In some respects scientific development in Ireland from early times to the present was probably not very different from that experienced in other countries, but in other ways it has been fairly distinctive. In the old Gaelic order, medicine and botany played a major role and this trend continued over time. The tradition of surveying was strong, originally in order to make the country attractive to settlers, and to dominate it; later to utilise the land and resources to the optimum. It was not uncommon for scientists to involve themselves in antiquarian, literary, or political activities, as we saw with the two Molyneuxs, John K'Eogh, Richard Kirwan, Sir William Rowan Hamilton and Sir William Wilde. The Irish language played a significant role in various sciences, if only by default.

Scientists, scientific societies and the Royal Irish Academy played a rich part in bringing Ireland to its present state. The sciences were not divorced from everyday life. On the contrary, scientific discourse and publication was very much driven by utilitarian concerns. The scientists were not limited in their outlook, neither were they limited in their research. Many of them had more than a passing interest in antiquities and literature; they even published in these fields. The men and the societies that they founded form an important part of the intricate tapestry that is Ireland, past and present. They played a significant, enabling role in paving the way to make the Ireland of the twentieth century – the Ireland that produced the literary writers with whom our country's heritage has been so widely associated.

Chapter 5
Salome: A Text Unveiled

D. C. Rose

Although almost all of Wilde's texts present points of interest both in their manuscript reworkings and in their publishing history, in this essay I propose to look at some of the questions raised by the history of *Salome*, and in doing so hope to make tremble a veil or two. The accounts of the play's genesis vary; its original French form is owed to more than one writer; the English version presents certain problems; Wilde's concept of the part of Salome herself was subject to change; and the relationship of the play to the opera, which has exceeded it in the number of productions, needs elucidation. We even need to establish whether we pronounce the title with the stress on the first syllable or the second. There is no English orthodoxy here, but perhaps the euphony of the former is preferable, and the fact that in French and generally on the Continent the final 'e' is adorned with an acute accent reinforces this: Richard Ellmann, however, preferred to omit this acute accent, and one may follow his usage.

Generally speaking, the *idées reçues* that *Salome* has attracted are that it was written in French by Wilde for Sarah Bernhardt; that it was contumaciously banned in England by the Lord Chamberlain; that it was produced triumphantly in France; that Richard Strauss[1] took it on as opera and the rest is part of the history of twentieth-century opera. All of these facts are superficially true, and they have also acquired a few accretions of dubious worth, such as that it was banned out of hostility towards Wilde rather than for the official reason that it violated the regulations against the portrayal of biblical characters on stage, that Bernhardt played Salome in France or intended to do so; or that Wilde himself was photographed dressed as Salome.

The last point is best disposed of early on. This photograph, showing a portly lady in 'oriental costume', remained in many editions through which Ellmann's *Wilde*[2] has passed despite efforts to make known the fact that it represents the singer Alice Guszalewicz, playing Salome in Köln in its first flush of productions after the opera's Dresden premiere on 9 December 1905. But this raises a new question: who was Alice Guszalewicz? Given that the role of Salome has been sung by many women who are household names, history has forgotten Alice Guszalewicz, and details of the production in which she sang are similarly elusive.[3] She is mentioned in none of the five most basic reference works in opera.[4]

SALOME AS STAGE PLAY

We then come to the play itself. How good was Wilde's French? It is generally taken for granted, at least among anglophone biographers and critics, that it was excellent.

But where did he learn it? One cannot assume that Portora Royal School, Enniskillen, was a forcing ground for fluency in the language. Generally speaking, one must suppose that he picked it up as a gentlemanly accomplishment, some of it at his mother's knee (although the Merrion Square governess was German), some of it perhaps at school, some of it while travelling, some of it self-taught. Of course he spent a considerable time in Paris in 1883 when he came back from his American tour, and his quick intelligence and lively mind would certainly have ingested a great deal of the spoken language. Frank Harris[5] suggests that this stay transformed Wilde's 'school boy' French into fluency. Leaving aside the reference by Harold Nicolson[6] to Wilde's talking to Paul Verlaine[7] 'in his Chelsea French, of which he was so proud' (for Nicolson never heard Wilde), Joseph Renaud refers to Wilde's *'accent anglais'*, while Will Rothenstein remembered 'a rather Ollendorfian French with a strong English accent'.[8] Wilde praised the French translation of *Macbeth* by Jean Richepin[9] in literal prose, which a recent critic has described as 'woefully inadequate'.[10] Aubrey Beardsley's cartoon of Wilde writing *Salome* with the aid of French dictionaries and phrase books is probably accurate enough – given the exotic words, far from everyday speech, that Wilde introduces. One may note that the Paris writers Wilde most often met with were men like Robert Sherard[11] (who was English), and Stuart Merrill[12] and Francis Vielé-Griffin[13] (who were American): bilingual as these men were, it is perfectly likely that they spoke English with Wilde.

Vyvyan Holland quotes Stuart Merrill: '*Salome* was written in French by Wilde, then revised and corrected by me, Retté and Pierre Louÿs in that order, but solely from the point of view of the language. Marcel Schwob corrected the proofs. Wilde was thus the sole author of *Salome*, any corrections that were made being only for the purpose of drawing attention to the faults in his French.'[14] Holland here was exercising some filial piety by quoting selectively; for Merrill recorded that it was not easy to make Wilde accept all his corrections. The working out of the order and nature of the revision of the text has not been conclusively established: we know that Wilde while engaged in the writing had the company of both Merrill and Adolphe Retté, a poet and editor of the Symbolist reviews *La Vogue*, and *L'Ermitage*.[15] Merrill told Vincent O'Sullivan 'with some amusement that Wilde, resenting some of Merrill's suggestions, put them loftily aside, saying that Merrill was a foreigner and did not know French'.[16] This sounds very Wildean. Robert Sherard claimed that he himself *saw* Wilde write most of *Salome*, which suggests a most unlikely proximity, and further states that he read the draft MS. As he made these claims at the time[17] and Wilde did not deny them, there must be something in them (one is usually reluctant to believe Sherard, whose constant hyperbole and frequent mendacious references make him an unreliable recounter even of events that he may have witnessed).

Francis Vielé-Griffin, another Symbolist, is also said to have looked over the MS. To this Alan Harris, in his introduction to the 1952 edition published by Duckworth, adds that Marcel Schwob is known to have made very few corrections, and even if he did explain later that he had purposely refrained from spoiling the character of Wilde's style, we may be sure that Sarah Bernhardt would not have wished to speak, even in London, lines that sounded linguistically absurd 'to a French ear' (21). This has a convincing ring to it, even if it takes us back to a greater implication of Bernhardt with the play than the record reveals. Schwob, who was one of Wilde's guides to Paris literary life before falling out with him, was much taken with Wilde. Jules Renard, in his terse way, wrote in his journal in 1894, 'Je me rappelle qu'un soir, chez Mme Léon Daudet, où on l'écoutait avec une complaisance charmante, il faillit confondre Wilde avec Shakespeare. On dut l'arrêter.' ['I remember one evening, at Madame Léon Daudet's, where people used to listen to him with a delightful forbearance, he found it necessary to mix up Wilde with Shakespeare. He should be stopped.'][18]

Sherard's version of the part that Schwob played in this was that Schwob read over the MS before it went to the printer 'and told me that the French was perfect throughout'. Sherard also asserts that Wilde was 'as admirable as a French as he is a Greek, a Latin, an English scholar'.[19] Whatever about that, on the whole I think Wilde's French stands up in *Salome*, even though its structure is occasionally more Merrion Square than Montparnasse. Occasionally, his French was shaky. It deserted him: in a letter to Robert Sherard for example, he begins with some sentences in French that he wants Sherard to incorporate into an article Sherard was writing, but switches to English when he reaches what is clearly a more difficult bit.[20] Stuart Merrill wrote in his *Souvenirs sur Symbolisme* that Wilde wrote French as he spoke it, that this gave the flavour of his fantasticated conversation, but that, as far as *Salome* was concerned, it would have given a wretched impression on the stage ('...aurait produit, au théâtre, une déplorable impression').[21]

The text was published in Paris and London on 22 February 1893 by the Librairie de l'Art Indépendent and by John Lane respectively. Lord Alfred Douglas[22] then translated the work into English in a way that displeased Wilde, who did not feel that the translation did justice to the work. This was published by John Lane in 1894 in an edition of 500 copies at fifteen shillings, and 100 copies on large paper at thirty shillings. Since then, no other English translation has been published as far as it has been possible to ascertain except for the commission from Vyvyan Holland and one by R. A. Walker.[23] These versions do not appear ever to have been staged.

Sarah Bernhardt,[24] Wilde's original choice for the title role in the aborted London production of *Salome*, was not the only actress that Wilde saw as Salome; his mind also turned to Eleonora Duse,[25] the leading Italian *tragédienne* of her day. While staying with Bosie Douglas in Naples in October 1897, Wilde wrote to Stanley Makower:[26]

> I am supervising an Italian version of Salome, which is being made here by a young Neapolitan poet. I hope to produce it on the stage here, if I can find an actress of troubling beauty and flute-like voice. Unfortunately most of the tragic actresses of Italy – with the exception of Duse – are stout ladies, and I don't think I could bear a stout Salome.[27]

This suggests that Wilde was still in the high spirits that had characterised him in Dieppe, his first Continental place of refuge, although, as ever, he was inclined to exaggeration. One wonders if it was not the young Neapolitan poet who had the troubling beauty[28] and flute-like voice, for the version that Wilde describes as 'being made', two months later has become only a project intended by the poet.[29] Wilde sent the text to Cesare Rossi, reporting to Robert Ross that the actor-manager was 'astounded with *Salome*, but had no actress who could possibly touch the part. I am going to try Duse, but with not much hope.'[30] Even without much hope, this is a clear indication that Wilde no longer thought of Bernhardt as Salome, but was Salome really a role that Duse would have accepted? According to Anita Roittinger, 'Although Eleonora said she liked the play, she could not imagine herself acting in it, and declined.'[31]

Duse (who had once been a member of Rossi's company) was at this time acting in Venice. She was thirty-nine and at the height of her powers: clearly her age was not any more a bar in Wilde's eyes than Bernhardt's age had been. She had had a number of London seasons, where she so impressed the painter John Singer Sargent[32] that he persuaded her to sit for him,[33] but there is no record as yet of Wilde having seen her on stage there. She came to Naples in December 1897 and according to Ellmann, Wilde and Bosie went to see her 'every night'.[34] If this was so – Ellmann gives no source – it would have been in *Magda* and in *La seconda moglie* at the Teatro Mercadante, the latter being the Italian version of Pinero's *Second Mrs Tanqueray*[35]. Wilde told the publisher Leonard Smithers that Duse was reading *Salome* and that there was a chance of her playing the part: 'she is a fascinating artist though nothing to Bernhardt' is his surprising comment. Our information about Duse and Wilde then dwindles away: Duse's most authoritative biographer makes no reference to either *Salome* or Wilde,[36] and Wilde does not appear to have contacted her when she was in Paris in March 1898.

Salome was banned by the Lord Chamberlain in June 1892 under the antique regulation that biblical characters were not to be presented on the stage. Its subsequent appearance in England can be dealt with quickly.

- Florence Farr[37] produced it for the New Stage Club at the Bijou Theatre for one private performance only on 5th May 1905;
- it appeared twice at the King's Hall, Covent Garden on 10 and 17 June 1906 in a private production staged by the Literary Theatre Society with a third performance at the National Sporting Club on 20 June;
- on 27 and 28 February 1911 at the Court Theatre directed by Harcourt Williams,[38] again in private productions;
- by the Literary Theatre Society once more on 13 June 1916;
- directed by J. T. Grein[39] at the Court Theatre 12 April 1918 (this was the production made famous by the attack on the play by Pemberton Billing[40] and the subsequent libel case taken by Maud Allan).[41]

It emerged from the shadows of these quasi-clandestine productions when Terence Gray[42] produced it for the Cambridge Festival in 1929. For 1931 I have found three productions:

- Peter Godfrey directed it at the Gate Theatre, London, in May 1931;
- Nancy Price[43] directed it for the People's National Theatre at the Duke of York's Theatre in London in October;
- and Terence Gray reprised it at the Cambridge Festival;
- OUDS then produced it at Oxford in March 1942;
- Peter Zadek[44] produced it for the Centaur Theatre Company at the Rudolf Steiner Theatre in London in March 1947;
- Ronald Lane produced it at the New Torch Theatre in London in 1952, and
- Frederick Farley produced it at the Q Theatre in London in June 1954, transferring to the St Martin's Theatre in July.

There were no other London productions until the famous Lindsay Kemp production at the Roundhouse twenty-five years later, and it was another twelve years before the play was, one may say, re-launched by Steven Berkoff at the National in 1989, the most successful of all the play's productions. This had begun at the Gate Theatre in Dublin in April and May 1988, was revived there the following spring and received much acclaim at the Edinburgh Festival in August 1989. Then, Berkoff himself taking over the part of Herod from Alan Stanford, it reached London and a world tour.

The purpose of this litany is to suggest that in comparison to the opera, as I shall discuss, the play's reputation in England was at least until 1977 an indifferent one. The New Torch Theatre, the Q Theatre, the Rudolf Steiner Theatre: these are hardly the venues that Wilde envisaged when he had talked of the Théâtre Français. From all this one can only resurrect Robert Morley[45] and Beatrix Lehmann in Terence Gray's Cambridge production, with its choreography by Ninette de Valois[46] and incidental music by Constant Lambert,[47] and that ever-to-be-honoured day in 1954 when the late Agnes Bernelle[48] omitted her body stocking and became the first woman to strip naked in the legitimate West End theatre.

How much does this tell us of the play, of Wilde's reputation, and of English theatre managements and audiences? This is a subject for further study, this insistence on Wilde as a drawing room comedy dramatist rather than a Symbolist poet. To Ireland falls the distinction of the first mainstream production of *Salome*, when Hilton Edwards[49] directed it at the Peacock Theatre in Dublin (not at the Gate, as one sometimes sees written) in 1928; but it was not produced there again until Berkoff's production. Since then in Dublin there has been one curious production in which it is Herodias who is put to death, by an ad hoc group calling itself the Wilde Child Theatre Company that dissolved with the last veil, and an amateur production by the La Touche Players, both in 1995; and more recently, a revival by Alan Stanford of the Berkoff production, again at the Gate.

All this had been preceded by the very first production, by Aurélien-Marie Lugné-Poë,[50] at the Théâtre de l'Œuvre in Paris in February 1896 while Wilde was in prison. Lina Munte played Salome, Gina Barberi played Herodias, Edouard de Max[51] played Jokanaan and Lugné-Poë himself played Herod. But who was Lina Munte? She played Virginie in the adaptation of *L'Assommoir* at the Ambigu, and also acted at the Gymnase: one contemporary called her the thinnest woman in Paris after Bernhardt.[52] The sources are remarkably silent: *Salome* clearly did not sweep her to fame, and the contemporary critical reaction to the play must be reviewed in this light. I have found one fugitive mention of Munte's name in order to provide a rather forced play on words, in the course of some verses by Henri Beauclaire.[53]

It is upon this production and this production alone that the reputation of *Salome* rests as Symbolist drama: Christopher Innes calls *Salome* 'a major example of Symbolist drama...the earliest and most complete British example'.[54] That said, one must not make too much of it. The play only had two performances, on 10 and 11 February. Maurice Maeterlinck praised the published version which Wilde sent him, and more work on the Paris sources may uncover further responses from the French. It is unfortunate that J. M. Synge left Paris on 3 February and August Strindberg did not arrive until the twenty-first: in establishing the reception of the play the reaction of either would have been useful.

The Théâtre de l'Œuvre also produced seven plays by Henrik Ibsen, as well as plays by Maeterlinck, Strindberg and Gerhardt Hauptmann. It would not appear that Wilde attended *any* of these productions, but given Lugné-Poë's view of Symbolist acting, this is perhaps not surprising.

> A fixed style was adopted: the actors behaved as if drugged, their movements sluggish, their voices hollow and querulous in turn. The whole production was made as unnaturalistic as possible, and Lugné-Poë himself, whether he was playing Rosmer, Solness or Brand, always wore the same long black overcoat and waistcoat buttoning up to the chin, a costume which the young symbolists paid him the compliment of adopting as the unofficial uniform of their movement.[55]

This is a world away – many worlds away – from Beerbohm Tree[56] as Lord Illingworth or George Alexander[57] as Jack Worthing; from scented cigarettes and the Prince of Wales in the Royal Box, from trick bracelets and something sensational to read on the train. For his part, although Lugné-Poë visited Wilde in Dieppe in June 1897, only once again in a long career did he direct a play by him, *A Florentine Tragedy* in 1907.[58] Again, we must paint this into our picture of *Salome*. All this also suggests how it became of interest to the Russians, and it was chiefly as a stage play that it was performed there. A translation of the play had already appeared in Moscow in 1904; two years later Countess Radoshevsky published a new translation in St Petersburg,[59] and in 1907 it was published again in Moscow in translation by a man called Brik. In 1908 there was another Russian version published in Moscow by Mikael Lykiardopoulos,[60] with an introduction by Robert Ross, and one in St Petersburg by the leading Symbolist poet, Konstantin Dmitrievich Balmont.[61] Ida Rubinstein[62] commissioned a production with sets by Leon Bakst, music by Aleksandr Konstantinovich Glazunov[63] and choreography by Mikael Fokine as a vehicle for herself: as the Holy Synod of the Russian Orthodox Church banned the text, the piece was mimed, a silent Wilde. Nikolai Nikolaievich Evreinov[64] produced it for Kommissarzhevskaya's Theatre with a set by Kalmakov, which we are told 'resembled huge female genitalia'.[65] Salome was played by Alisa Koonen, wife of the director Aleksander Tairov.[66] Koonen lived to 1974 and perhaps somewhere there are recorded her experiences of this production.

In August 1917, Ivan Platon produced *Salome* at the Maly Theatre in Moscow, but the most remarkable of Russian productions was that in Moscow in October 1917 at Tairov's Kamerny Theatre, with the Revolution occurring on the streets outside, and freezing, hungry people inside. Tairov wrote of this, and this is worth an extended quotation, because it is as revealing an engagement with the text as I have discovered.

> To become aware of the rhythmic beat of the play, to hear its sound, its harmony, and afterwards as it were to orchestrate it – that is the third task of the director. I have long felt the need for such an approach to the verbal material of a production, but I felt it especially strongly and undeniably in working on the production of Salome. The rhythmic and contrapuntal pattern beats so clearly in its verbal material and appeals so irresistibly for fulfilment, that so far as I am concerned it is absolutely impossible to pass by...
>
> Further on, when the dynamic energy which has been accumulating in measure with the development of the action once more finds an outlet in Salome's sudden cry 'I will dance for you, Tetrarch', the greedy howl of joy which rips from the breast of Herod tears the backdrop asunder and carries it aside with waves of reverberating ether, revealing in the blood-drunk rays of the moon the red curtain of the dance and death.

'Unfortunately,' adds Tairov, 'this idea, beautifully worked out in the model, was not transferred to the stage with complete success for a whole raft of technical reasons.'[67] Some idea of Tairov's conception may be gained from Exter's designs (Fig 5.1).

Together with *The Picture of Dorian Gray*, it was *Salome* that gave Wilde the European reputation that he craved. The bridge to that reputation, however, was not Lugné-Poë but Richard Strauss.

SALOME AS OPERA

The place of *Salome* in operatic history is more secure than its place in the history of the stage. German interest came as early as 1902 when Hedwig Lachmann translated it for a production by Max Reinhardt[68] at Berlin's Kleines Theater, with designs by Lovis Corinth,[69] a painter who himself created two large 'Salome' canvases. This was the version seen by Strauss, who already had his attention drawn to the play by Anton Lindner,[70] and a shortened version of Lachmann's translation, which had been published in 1903[71] and reached five impressions in that year, became the basis of his libretto. Gary Schmidgall has stated that Strauss was 'little interested in the superficial beauties of Wilde's sonorous, bejewelled text... There was a furioso vein in the æsthetic that produced *Salomé* – but Strauss

Figure 5.1 Costume designs by Alexandra Exter for the Tairoff production, 1917.

had to mine for it.'[72] But Strauss's access to the text was, as I have suggested, limited, and although this might indicate a lack of interest, it might also be a misreading (or mis-hearing) by Schmidgall. If there was an imaginative failure – and this is not the usual critical response to the opera – it may have been because there was nothing of the decadent about Strauss. The link between the opera, its original play, and decadence may also need to be sought through set designs, and one recognises that although (again to cite Schmidgall) the conjunction of Wilde and Beardsley made the John Lane edition 'the epitome of English Decadence',[73] stage designers have preferred to go their own way – and here they echo Wilde's unease with Beardsley's illustrations and his remark that one day he would write a play to go with them.[74]

When Strauss told Gustav Mahler, then directing the Vienna Opera House, that he was going to make an opera of *Salome*, Mahler was violently opposed to the idea on both moral and practical grounds, thinking that production might be barred in Catholic countries, and indeed Mahler did not then succeed in getting the censor to pass it for Vienna. Strauss's great admirer, Ernst von Schuch, conductor of the Dresden Royal Opera, premiered it there on 9 December 1905 with Marie Wittich in the title role. Robert Ross, Wilde's literary executor, was in Dresden for the first performance, but, says his biographer, 'Robbie did not enjoy the glittering occasion; his appreciation of the music was clouded by the knowledge that Wilde had always regarded *Salome* as his finest dramatic work, but as an opera it lost most of its mystique'.[75] Of the later, Berlin, production, somewhat tinkered with on the express instructions of the Kaiser Wilhelm II, Mahler wrote to his wife Alma, 'The performance again made an extraordinary impression on me. It is a work of genius, very powerful, and decidedly one of the most important works of our day…Destinn was magnificent!' This was Emmy Destinn[76] who sang Salome. The Kaiser said, 'I am sorry Strauss composed this *Salome*. It will do him a great deal of harm', upon which Strauss remarked that it had enabled him to build his new villa at Garmisch.

Salome was the first opera performed in German in Paris; it was the only German opera ever conducted by Arturo Toscanini.[77] It was hearing Ljuba Welitsch[78] sing Salome that made Leontyne Price[79] determine on an operatic career; it was Grace Bumbry's[80] first soprano role when she decided that she could go no further as a mezzo. The part of Salome has been sung by over sixty sopranos in the last ninety-seven years, which must give it a significant ranking in any list of much performed operas. In 1999 it received its first Dublin production, directed by Joël Laüwers with Karen Notare in the title role. Conductors have included Thomas Beecham,[81] Karl Böhm,[82] Andrew Davis,[83] Christoph von Dohnányi,[84] August Everding,[85] Walter Goehr,[86] Reginald Goodall,[87] Rudolf Kempe,[88] Hans Knappertsbusch,[89] Clemens Krauss,[90] Zubin Mehta,[91] André Messager,[92] Rudolf Moralt,[93] Kent Nagano,[94] Giuseppe Sinopoli,[95] Georg Solti,[96] George Szell,[97] Vilem Tauski,[98] as well as the others already mentioned and of course Strauss himself. It is a roll call of the most distinguished practitioners of the twentieth century, its lustre far outstripping that of the handful of directors of *Salome* as stage play.

One who knew Wilde, and lived to know the opera, was Vincent O'Sullivan, who describes an interesting interplay between text and part before plumping for Strauss as providing the best interpretation (a view countering that of Schmidgall):

> The best performance I recall was by a Russian, Ysovskaya, in Berlin some years after the war. But to appreciate her show you had to make all sorts of concessions on general grounds. Also on the particular ground of Wilde's text. Her Salome was a woman scourged by her passions. Rather a noble character, a victim of fate. Evidently the idea underlying this reading of the part was that Salome never believed the prophet would be killed; she believed a miracle would strike the sword from the headsman's clutch. In the last scene of all it was not insane sensuality that was suggested, but the collapse of a woman who sees that her god can die.
>
> That the reading is far from Wilde's conception all who have his text in mind will agree. Still, that the chief part can be ennobled in such a fashion, that it bears various interpretations, shows that the play is not merely the artificial morbid thing it has often been described. For all that, it seems preferable to see Salome in the opera of Richard Strauss. The music is precisely the right music. It carries the drama through with such a rush that it is impossible to linger on the details.[99]

Other European composers have written music for Wilde in general and *Salome* in particular. I have mentioned Glazunov, but among the Russians there were also Aleksandr Nikolayevich Tchenerpnin,[100] and Aleksandr Abramovich Krein.[101] Strauss's *Salome* was last produced in St Petersburg in April 2002, with the German libretto. The German libretto is not the only one that is sung with Strauss's score, however. A French version, retranslated from the German, was sung in Paris: Strauss consulted Romain Rolland[102] when he ran into difficulties over the musical stressing of the French silent 'e'. In English, it is sung in translations from Hedwig Lachmann's German, either by Maria Massey Pelikan or by Tom Hammond, and there is also a Portuguese translation of Lachmann's libretto by Manuel Rosa. There is clearly scope here for a parallel texts edition.

Strauss's version had the effect of obscuring another version: a score by a naval officer called Antoine Mariotte.[103] This was written without Mariotte realising that the Wilde estate had given Strauss the musical rights; nevertheless a performance was licenced in Lyon on 20 October 1908 and a Paris performance was given in 1910 and again in 1917, but not I think since. The score had been published the previous year by the rather unlikely Imprimerie & Librairie Centrales des Chemins de Fer, and a score for piano and voices was published by Enoch et Cie in 1910.

Florent Schmitt[104] also composed a *Tragédie de Salomé*, which grew out of a scenario by Robert d'Humières,[105] director of the Théâtre de l'Art and an acquaintance of Wilde. D'Humière's version may also have owed something to the interest in writing a score for *Salome* of Schmitt's friend Fritz Delius,[106] who entered into negotiations with the executors of the Wilde estate before abandoning the project. Schmitt's was the version danced by Loïe Fuller at the Théâtre des Arts in 1907 (for which Jules Chéret[107] designed the poster), but it was most famously performed by the Ballets Russes in 1913 with Tamara Karsavina[108] in the title role. Stravinsky called it 'a work of genius'.[109] It was no surprise that Loïe Fuller should have danced Salome, for the part held a particular fascination for solo dancers, Maud Allan and Ida Rubinstein in particular. By then, dancing Salome (or at least the Dance of the Seven Veils) was part of a dancer's repertoire: Sahari-Dejeli (at the Casino de Paris), Odette Valéry, Artémis Colonna, Leonora La Bella – and not least the guest who danced the Dance of the Seven Veils at the London studio party where all those present were dressed as characters in Wilde's plays.[110]

Much of the impact of *Salome* when it was first published must of course be attributed to the illustrations by Aubrey Beardsley. It is surprising that a text that adopts so much of Symbolist synaesthesia, has so many Baudelairean *correspondances*, and exercised so many set designers, has apparently attracted very few illustrators: Marcus Behmer for the earliest Lachmann editions, Frank Martin for the Folio Society, the French artist Alastair for the edition published by Crès in Paris in 1923 and reprinted in 1925, André Derain for an edition published in Paris in 1938, Valenti Angelo for the Heritage Press edition published in New York in 1945.

CONCLUSION

As scholarly attention to Wilde continues to grow and shake itself free from the uninterrogated early biographies, more of the lacunae in the narrative history of *Salome* as hitherto told will become apparent. Jacqueline Groth's research in progress on the Dance of the Seven Veils, Mary Callaghan's work on the Strauss *Salome*, Tine Engelbert's on other musical versions of Wilde, and Jess Sully's work on the femme fatale, all indicate the detailed scrutiny that is now being brought to bear.[111] The present essay is therefore a dipstick into what has been recovered so far, a contribution to the re-ordering of the narrative, and perhaps a guide to what still needs to be done. The history of *Salome* is an interesting one, and had Wilde never written *The Importance of Being Earnest* or *An Ideal Husband*, or *Lady Windermere's Fan* or *A Woman of No Importance* or *The Ballad of Reading Gaol* or *The Picture of Dorian Gray*, he would still be remembered for the text he began to write that autumn evening in 1891 at a little table in the Grand Café on the boulevard des Capucines.

Chapter 6

From the pointed ones to the bones: Beckett's Early Poems

John Pilling

'It is always Irish things and people that vex', wrote W. B. Yeats in a journal entry of early 1909;[1] yet Yeats was by then already a part of the history of the Irish book. Forty years later, long after having left Ireland, Samuel Beckett took an even more jaundiced view: 'I think', he wrote in a letter to his friend Thomas MacGreevy, 'it is impossible to have health in Dublin. Of any kind.'[2] It had never been part of Beckett's plan to find fame and fortune in the country of his birth. The Irish writers he admired he typically analogised with European models of excellence, comparing MacGreevy (somewhat extravagantly surely) with the painter Giorgione, O'Casey (somewhat more reasonably) with Molière, Jack B. Yeats with Ariosto (a comparison of which Beckett was particularly fond), and Denis Devlin (in perhaps the most apt of them all) with Guillaume Apollinaire.[3] Typically, in savaging the Censorship Act of 1929, Beckett spoke intemperately (and in fact outrageously) of the Irish as 'a characteristic agricultural community in this, that they have something better to do than read'.[4] Even with the issue of Beckett's Irishness revived and revised by several important recent publications,[5] it is evident that, in any celebration of 'the Irish book' (above and beyond the books of his friends that had come out of Ireland), Beckett would have considered himself a non-participant, and quite content to be absent from the proceedings.

The story I shall attempt to tell here – of a desperate need to be published, a need which even Dublin could occasionally be permitted to gratify – does little to alter the substance of the situation of stand-off sketched above, but much to change the picture of how and why such a situation evolved and, in due course, took root. It is a story, like the paintings of Tal-Coat in Beckett's Duthuit dialogues, 'complete with missing parts'[6] in the sense that it is impossible to make the surviving specifics wholly coherent and integrated, even with the more or less accurate application of inference and guesswork. It is an attempt to make some sense of a still somewhat neglected body of work – Beckett's poems, and more particularly his early poems – which even as published bristles with difficulty, and which on its way to publication (as here) threatens to become a tangle of threads that may never unravel to everyone's satisfaction. It is not a story of 'neatness', even though it dares to fly in the face of Beckett's dictum to the effect that 'The danger is in the neatness of identifications.'[7] As it happens, it was begun by the issue of the *Irish Studies Review* that epitomised this very 'danger' by reprinting in facsimile the manuscript version of Beckett's one contribution to *The Great Book of Ireland*, the poem 'Da Tagte Es', described on the cover of the journal as

'Beckett's last poem' though rather more accurately characterised in Theo Dargan's article on *The Great Book* as 'the last piece of writing he ever did'.[8] As a poem in holograph this 'piece of writing' literally inscribes Beckett in the pages of *The Great Book*, as if fifty years in Paris were coming to an end with a kind of return home. Yet at the same time the writing shows Beckett in exile even from himself, still living an 'existence by proxy'.[9] In this poignant manuscript version the title, from Middle High German, has gone, and – an old man's memory failing – Beckett has transposed the second and third lines of his poem as first published. And, even more poignantly, there are four false starts, crossed out, the act of a dying man trying, as he had been all his life, to get going, and to keep going.

Beckett's brief but memorable inscription of himself in the story of Irish literature could not, given his frail health, extend beyond poetry into the genres for which he is much better known: prose fiction, and drama. But not until he was over forty years of age, with *Molloy* in 1947, did he achieve something like what he had been seeking with the first, and not until 1952, with *En attendant Godot*, was there a comparable success in the case of the second. At the start of his writing career Beckett seems, indeed, to have had almost no interest in writing plays, though he was certainly very interested in going to watch them. The genres that did then matter to him were poetry and the novel, and whilst he would have been happy to achieve success in either of them, it was undoubtedly poetry, of the two, that mattered most to him. Prose, the prose of *Assumption* (1929) and *Dream of Fair to Middling Women* (1931–32) at any rate, Beckett considered epiphenomenal to poetry, a kind of differently distributed equivalent occupying a larger space but employing very similar techniques. By making the two genres different sides of the same coin Beckett was, in publishing terms, doing himself no favours; editors of every shape and size, even when in charge of magazines encouraging experimental writing, not unnaturally tended to reject submissions that did not at least in part conform to accepted norms. Beckett had no interest in accepted norms when it came to his own writing, though he was something of a classicist in his admiration for the writing of others. In order to get going at all he needed something to kick against, even if that something thereby became the lever or trigger enabling utterance to take place. This being so, Beckett was always rather at a disadvantage in his dealings with editors and publishers, in part because of his own recalcitrant nature, but in part also because circumstance was simply against him. The early years were to prove a struggle with an elusive opponent: the public; whereas the later years were to prove a struggle largely conducted exclusively with reference to the self that had learned to do without a public.

My purpose here is to study one aspect of how Beckett got going by way of a provisional dating of his early poems, and by presenting what is known of his dealings with publishers, Irish or otherwise, in this connection. To this end I consider the available evidence under two broad headings: (a) published and unpublished poems written prior to the appearance of *Echo's Bones and Other Precipitates* in book form (Paris: Europa Press, [November] 1935), but excluded from that collection; (b) the poems that make up the collection as first published, presented in a provisional order of composition.

A. PUBLISHED AND UNPUBLISHED POEMS WRITTEN PRIOR TO THE APPEARANCE OF
ECHO'S BONES AND OTHER PRECIPITATES, AND EXCLUDED FROM THE COLLECTION

1. 'For Future Reference' (published in transition, *19–20 June 1930, 342–3).*

In *Samuel Beckett: Poet and Critic*, Lawrence Harvey describes this poem as
'written when Beckett was at the École Normale' and 'of the same period as his
essay on Joyce' ('Dante...Bruno.Vico..Joyce'); in his private papers (at
Dartmouth College) he dates it 1929.[10] The reference (line 58) to 'Bruno's
identification of contraries' aligns this poem not only with the Joyce essay
(published in the summer of 1929), but also with the squib 'Che Sciagura',
published in *T.C.D.: A College Miscellany,* on 14 November 1929. The memories
of Trinity life on which the poem in part depends in themselves suggest a date
earlier rather than later in Beckett's time at the École (November 1928–September
1930). The poem is presumably one of the 'twice round pointed ones' mentioned
by Beckett in a letter to Thomas MacGreevy[11] as submitted to Jacob Bronowski
(an editor of the Cambridge journal *Experiment* and later editor of the British
section of the 1931 first and only issue of *The European Caravan*) and rejected by
him. Beckett later wrote to MacGreevy: 'I mentioned the poems and he [Charles
Prentice, a commissioning editor at Chatto and Windus] wants to see them. If you
can find For Future Reference in that Transition you might send it along.'[12] This
suggests that at least one of the 'twice round pointed ones' (and perhaps also the
other, assuming 'Return to the Vestry' to be that other) must have been in the
group of poems Beckett hawked round London in the late summer of 1932.

2. 'Return to the Vestry' (published in The New Review: an international
notebook for the arts, *1, no. 3 (1931), 98–9).*

This poem is, with 'For Future Reference', an obvious candidate for the title of
'Beckett's earliest surviving poem', and very possibly the earlier of the two in so
far as it depends in part upon memories of the summer Beckett spent in Tours in
1926, five years before publication. It shares the word 'peace' (line 37) with 'For
Future Reference'; it combines 'grey' and 'silk' (line 43) as does 'Yoke of Liberty'
(described in section A10 below; see lines 1–2); and 'impurity' (line 46) invites
comparison with 'impurée' in the penultimate line of 'Hell Crane to Starling' (see
A5 below). As published – Beckett received his copy of the magazine with his
poem in it in early September 1931 – the poem may be a revision of an earlier
version, since Beckett certainly returned to it again, probably in 1934 (the raw
material by then being eight years old), to produce one of his best unpublished
poems, 'it is high time lover' (see the 'Addendum' to this section pp. 75–6).
'Return to the Vestry' was presumably one of the 'twice round pointed ones'
rejected by Bronowski,[13] which may exclude it from having been the 'something
of mine' that George Reavey intended to publish in the Cambridge magazine
Experiment: 'I was surprised but didn't care much one way or another, perhaps I

would rather they didn't', Beckett told MacGreevy.[14] The editors of *Experiment* were Bronowski and Hugh Sykes Davies, and in any event the short-lived magazine folded in 1931 after its spring issue (no. 7).

3. *'Casket of Pralinen for a Daughter of a Dissipated Mandarin' (published in* The European Caravan, *part one (the only part ever published, on 13 November 1931, with Bronowski as one of the editors), New York: Brewer, Warren, and Putnam, 1931, 476–8).*

Apparently datable on internal evidence to shortly after 'the eleventh's eleventh eleven years after' (line 24; i.e. Armistice Day 1929) and 'the first of the first' (line 9; i.e. New Year's Day 1930), the poem is a reflection of the final rupture between Beckett and Peggy Sinclair in Kassel on New Year's Eve 1929, and is presumably the poem (if poem it was) described by her (as the Smeraldina-Rima) as 'the "thing" you wrot [sic] about my "beauty"' in *Dream of Fair to Middling Women* (Dublin: Black Cat Press, 1992, 61; hereafter *Dream*). 'Casket...' may (in spite of its presentation of the Sinclairs) be the 'pome' sent to 'the Boss' (Peggy's father)[15] and it may also – but see A4 below – be the 'pome' earlier sent back by Æ (George Russell), editor of the magazine *The Irish Statesman*, 'the nice little whimper I wrote specially for him'.[16] 'Già' (line 2) echoes 'Che Sciagura' (summer 1929), and echoes of 'Casket...' appear in the letter to MacGreevy that speaks of 'Armistice Day' and 'a sterile will-less phallus'.[17] It may have been the 'damn thing' (cf. *Dream*, 61) that Beckett would have liked 'to get rid of... anyhow & anywhere (with the notable exception of *transition*)',[18] a pressing need mercifully gratified by the fact that the poem must have been one (with 'Text' and 'Hell Crane to Starling', A4 and A5 below) of the three accepted by Bronowski – as editor of the Cambridge journal *Experiment* – by late August 1930.[19] Not until early 1931 was Beckett, by then back in Dublin, made aware (by George Reavey) that Samuel Putnam had started a review (*The New Review*), and Beckett presumably first met Putnam in the spring of 1931 in Paris. The letter to MacGreevy which dates 'all the early ones – all the Caravan ones' as earlier than 'Whoroscope'[20] can, in the case of 'Casket...', be presumed correct, even if 'all' is probably an overstatement (see A10 below). A few variants occur in the Leventhal material at the Harry Ransom Humanities Research Center (HRHRC), but obviously no significant revision of this poem, arguably one of the least successful of all Beckett's early poems, was attempted.[21]

4. *'Text' (published in* The European Caravan *(see A3), 478–80 and reprinted in* The New Review, *1 no. 4 (1931), 338–9).*

This was written close in time to Beckett's first reading of Proust in mid June of 1930, and perhaps this was all that emerged from 'I am going to write a poem about him'[22] (by the first week of August 1930 Beckett was reading Proust for a second time). 'Text' may be 'the baronial nausea' referred to in a later letter;[23] it was almost certainly one of the three poems accepted by Bronowski by 25 August 1930. The use of material found in the Joyce essay (line 33) and of Musset (line 41) points towards the École Normale and suggests, as the many references to Dante also do, that the bulk of the poem pre-dates 'Whoroscope'. The 'Miserere' of line 1, the first word of the poem, may explain the 'whimper' of the 'pome' sent to George Russell (see A3 above).[24]

5. *'Hell Crane to Starling' (published in* The European Caravan *(see A3), 475).*

Like 'Text', this poem makes recurrent use of the Bible, which suggests that both poems were composed close together in time, probably shortly before 'From the Only Poet to a Shining Whore' (see A7) which also contains biblical references. This is one of the three poems accepted by Bronowski by 25 August 1930, and it is the only one of the three Beckett is known to have extensively revised (probably in 1934), retitling it 'To My Daughter' (HRHRC; 'Hell Crane...' alludes to two daughters in Genesis and two in Ezekiel).

6. *'Whoroscope' (published in softcover binding in an edition of 300 copies by Nancy Cunard at the Hours Press, 15 rue Guénégaud, Paris in late June/early July 1930).*

In late July Beckett sent a copy to Joyce[25] and was told by Nancy Cunard that the pamphlet was selling well, which he found difficult to believe.[26] The much-repeated story of how the poem came to be written (overnight, on the evening of 15 June 1930, Beckett having only just heard of the Hours Press prize, and with the deadline for entries by post having expired) is attractive but almost certainly without foundation; the manuscript version at HRHRC shows that there was time for correction, relineation and general tidying-up. The addition of 'Rahab' to what became line 91 of 'Whoroscope' as published suggests that Beckett may have been working on 'Whoroscope' and 'From the Only Poet to a Shining Whore' at much the same time, perhaps for some weeks.

7. *'From the Only Poet to a Shining Whore, for Henry Crowder to sing' (published by the Hours Press of Nancy Cunard in* Henry-music, *with music by Henry Crowder and poems by Beckett and others, in late 1930).*

Written, according to Harvey,[27] 'in the Dôme Cafe in Montparnasse', probably in summer 1930; Beckett describes it as 'the Rahab tomfoolery' in a letter to MacGreevy.[28] In her biography Deirdre Bair misdates it September 1930.[29] Compare 'Text' and 'Hell Crane to Starling' for biblical references; it is possible that Beckett thought of the three as a kind of trilogy, of which 'From the Only

Poet...' was probably the last to be written. It was later titled 'To Be Sung Loud' but left unrevised (HRHRC). Rahab reappears in *Dream* (53), begun after Easter 1931.

8. *'Tristesse Janale' (unpublished)*

A sixteen-line poem in French, previously titled 'Lamentation Janale' (HRHRC Leventhal collection). Line 1's reference to 'concierges' links it to Jean du Chas and 'Le Concentrisme', and three points of contact with Proust link it to Beckett's attempt to add a section to his *Proust* essay in the autumn of 1930, which in the event he found himself unable to do:[30] 'Janale', cf. 'Janal' (*Proust and Three Dialogues with Georges Duthuit*, London: John Calder, 1965, 35; hereafter *Proust*); 'O flèches de Télèphe', cf. 'the spear of Telephus', *Proust*, 1; 'Abîme et dure sonde', cf. 'gouffre interdit à nos sondes', *Proust*, 31. In a letter to Thomas MacGreevy Beckett writes: 'I read a paper to M.[odern] L.[anguages] S.[ociety] on a non-existent French poet Jean du Chas – and wrote his poetry myself. One that amused me for a couple of days'.[31]

9. *'Ce n'est au Pélican' (unpublished)*

A twelve-line poem, also in French, but in free verse ('Tristesse Janale' is in alexandrines). This is the poem 'given' to Lucien, modelled on Jean Beaufret, in *Dream* (21; with the first two words changed to 'c'n'est'), but retrieved by its author as possibly worth inclusion in a '*POEMS* by Samuel Beckett' volume (HRHRC). The reference in line 5 of the poem to 'Lucie' suggests a possible connection with Lucia Joyce and the events of spring 1930 – Beckett apparently courting her, whilst actually visiting the house mainly to see her father – which led later in the year (probably in July) to a break with Joyce. Beckett refers to Musset (from whose 'Nuit de Mai' the 'Pelican' is taken, by way of Henri Evrard) in a letter to MacGreevy,[32] and also used this poem as a postscript to a letter to George Reavey.[33]

10. *'Yoke of Liberty' (published in* The European Caravan *(see A3), 480).*

Beckett distinguished this poem, explicitly on grounds of quality and implicitly with regard to time of composition, from the three other poems also first published in *The European Caravan* in a long and important letter to MacGreevy, one of his most sustained discussions of poetry, his own and others'.[34] Beckett cites Dante's *De Monarchia* (from which his title is taken) as early as the Joyce essay of 1929, and placed this poem (with its alternative title 'Moly') first in the contents list for the projected '*POEMS* by Samuel Beckett' (HRHRC). But 1931 seems, however, the likeliest date of composition, probably either just before – the more likely option – or very soon after the two 'Alba's (see B1 and B2 below). It was presumably not one of the three poems accepted by Bronowski by 25 August 1930 (since it almost certainly did not exist by that point in time), but it became the fourth of the poems published by him in late 1931. It may possibly have been sent to (and accepted by) George Reavey for publication in the Cambridge magazine *Experiment*, which folded after the spring 1931 issue. As 'The lips of her desire were [sic] grey' it was sent to Seumas O'Sullivan at the *Dublin Magazine*, perhaps on the rebound from his rejection of one of the two 'Alba's,[35] but O'Sullivan was, as in his later dealings with Beckett (at least as Beckett saw them), nervous about material that could be construed as sexual, and the poem was rejected by 9 October 1931. Beckett told MacGreevy, 'I sent it ['Yoke of Liberty'] yesterday to *Everyman*. I can't remember whether I sent it to them before or not',[36] which suggests that it had also been submitted to journals other than the *Dublin Magazine* during August and September 1931. As 'Moly' he sent it, with 'Enueg I', 'Dortmunder' and 'Echo's Bones', to *Poetry* (Chicago) in November 1934 – even though he had agreed terms with George Reavey for a book of poems by June 1934. For *Poetry* Beckett made minor revisions, though there is nothing to suggest that his good opinion of the poem – as expressed in the letter to MacGreevy of 18 October 1932 – had changed for the worse, and every indication otherwise, in spite of its omission from *Echo's Bones*. The alternative title 'Moly' must presumably have been prompted by Beckett's reading of Victor Bérard's translation of Homer's *Odyssey* between August and October 1931; the woman who 'preys wearily' (line 5) is a kind of Circe.[37]

11. 'Spring Song' (unpublished)

A long poem found in the Leventhal material at the HRHRC, which also exists in a variant (Georges Belmont) version, and considered for inclusion in the prospective '*POEMS* by Samuel Beckett'. Given the poem's title and the most probable dates for 'Dortmunder' and 'Sanies II' (see B4 and B5 below), spring 1932 (perhaps April) seems the most likely date of composition. Charles Prentice refers to it in a letter to Beckett,[38] and it was probably one of the poems delivered to Leonard Woolf of the Hogarth Press and to other London publishers (including Derek Verschoyle at *The Spectator*) in the latter half of 1932.[39] Given the date of Prentice's rejection it was probably part of the 'truss of poems' that Beckett sent to Edgell Rickword at Wishart & Co;[40] it is not singled out in Beckett's own letter of [27] August 1932 to Thomas MacGreevy, but its explosive content may have contributed to the dispirited assessment of the early poems which Beckett makes there.

12. 'Home Olga' (published in Contempo *(North Carolina), 3 (1934), 3).*

Written in 1932, in celebration of Joyce, possibly for Bloomsday (June 16), Joyce mentions it in a letter of 22 July 1932, which strengthens the case for Bloomsday (rather than, as has been suggested, his birthday in February). This suggests that it was composed after 'Spring Song' (see A11), as does a letter to MacGreevy that speaks of Beckett having begun 'a poem ['Serena I'], the first since "Home Olga"'.[41] The poem was sent to Stuart Gilbert in the late summer of 1932[42] but it was not acknowledged on receipt and more than two months later Beckett had not heard 'anything further' from Gilbert.[43] Presumably it was not part of the 'truss of poems'[44] being touted around London publishers at the time, Gilbert having expressed an interest in it. Beckett later asked MacGreevy[45] if the poem had appeared – it was published seven months later, about eighteen months after it was written – and Beckett thought sufficiently well of it after publication to consider it for inclusion in '*POEMS* by Samuel Beckett' (HRHRC).

13. 'Gnome' (Published in Dublin Magazine, *9 (July–September 1934), 8).*

Harvey says that it was written '[a]fter Beckett's resignation from Trinity College in January of 1932'.[46] This implies that it was written close in time to 'Dortmunder' (see B4), perhaps, like that poem, in Kassel; but the two poems are so different that a later date for 'Gnome' seems much more likely. The form of the poem is based on Goethe's epigrammatic 'Xenien', and Beckett had certainly read some Goethe as early as 1931,[47] although letters of November and December 1932 show a more sustained interest in German literature. Beckett read Goethe's autobiography in the spring of 1935, and *Faust* more than a year later in the late summer/early autumn of 1936, but must have read more widely in Goethe between 1932 and 1935, as the poem 'The Vulture' indicates. Phrases in German are particularly plentiful in Beckett's correspondence between May and July 1934, and 'Gnome' must surely have been (with 'Da Tagte Es', which also opens with an imperative) one of the 'couple of Quatschrains' mentioned in a letter to A. J. Leventhal of 7 May 1934 (HRHRC). The absence of anything even slightly sexual in 'Gnome' may lie behind Beckett's decision to send it to Seumas O'Sullivan, and O'Sullivan's (perhaps immediate) acceptance of it for the *Dublin Magazine*.

ADDENDUM

The poem 'it is high time lover' which appears with this title in the projected contents of '*POEMS*' (HRHRC) is, as indicated above (see A2), a revision of 'Return to the Vestry', in its later version reduced to twenty-nine lines. The reference to 'hochzeit' in line 2 is consistent with Beckett using German phrases through 1934, and 'spinning-jenny' in line 23 probably derives from the W. B. Yeats poem 'Fragments', which first appeared (stanza one only) in the same (October–December) 1931 issue of the *Dublin Magazine* as 'Alba', and which was added to 'The Tower' section of his *Collected Poems* in 1933. The two unknown poems from the HRHRC contents list – 'Abundance of the Heart' and 'Seats of Honour' – may have been early titles for 'Da Tagte Es' and either

'Gnome' (almost certainly written close in time to 'Da Tagte Es') or (though it does not seem very likely) 'The Vulture'.

B. POEMS INCLUDED IN *ECHO'S BONES AND OTHER PRECIPITATES* (1935), IN A PROVISIONAL ORDER OF COMPOSITION

1. 'Enueg II'

With 'Alba' (Beckett considered 'Enueg II' an 'alba' for at least a year after its composition), this is one of the two earliest poems collected for the 1935 volume, both written in early August 1931. In September 1931, in a letter mentioning 'the green tulips' (cf. line 24 of 'Enueg II'), Beckett told MacGreevy that, three weeks earlier, 'they came together one on top of the other, a double-yoked orgasm'.[48] In a later letter Beckett told his friend of O'Sullivan's rejection of this poem: 'He didn't like "give us a wipe" [line 11] and he didn't like the anthrax [line 25].'[49] Not until a few days later did Beckett tell MacGreevy that O'Sullivan had also rejected 'Yoke of Liberty',[50] which is not an 'alba' but which (like the 'alba's) was almost certainly inspired by the real-life original of the Alba in *Dream*, Ethna MacCarthy. Both the original 'Alba's must have been sent to Charles Prentice at Chatto and Windus in July 1932; Prentice's letter to Beckett of 27 July 1932, rejecting the possibility of publishing a volume of poetry, singles out 'Alba 2' (presumably 'Alba' as published) for special praise. The confusion of 'Alba's' and 'Enueg's' in the '*POEMS*' contents list (HRHRC) leaves the issue of when this poem became 'Enueg II' in obscurity. There seems to be no surviving evidence of Beckett trying to place the poem in the years after the *Dublin Magazine* rejection and before its first publication in *Echo's Bones* – unless it was with the 'stuff of mine'[51] sent to *transition* – which may or may not indicate a lessening regard for it. (The title 'Enueg II' seems to have been first attached to the poem published as 'Serena I' [see B6], sent as 'the little policeman Enueg' – to distinguish it from 'the canal Enueg' [i.e. 'Enueg I' as published] – to George Reavey, with 'Happy Land' [i.e. 'Sanies II' as published] in November 1932.[52] In an undated letter to Reavey (HRHRC; presumably written after Beckett had received a proof copy of *Echo's Bones*), Beckett states: 'there should be a space in *Enueg II* [as published in *Echo's Bones*] between "doch I assure thee" [line 21] and "lying on O'Connell Bridge" [line 22]'. Beckett adjudged this error 'Pas sérieux', however, and it has persisted in most subsequent reprintings, although in *transition* (24, June 1936, 9) a space has been inserted between 'breaking outside congress' (line 20) and 'doch I assure thee' (line 21).

2. 'Alba'

Written in early August 1931; it was accepted – after being examined 'longitudinally, latitudinally and diagonally' for 'fear of an obscene anagram' [ball?][53] – by Seumas O'Sullivan (who rejected the other 'Alba', i.e. 'Enueg II' as published) by late September (Beckett describes it to MacGreevy as 'the "sheet" Alba')[54] and published in the *Dublin Magazine*, vol. VI, no. 4, 4 September–December 1931. Almost certainly the 'Alba 2' of Charles Prentice's letter to Beckett of 27 July 1932, and presumably part of the 'truss' of poems either delivered by hand or sent to London publishers in the summer of 1932. In spite of failing to interest them in a poetry collection, Beckett continued to think well of 'Alba'[55] and later translated it into French with the help of Alfred Péron. The translation appeared in the last pre-war issue of Luc Descaunes's magazine *Soutes: revue de culture révolutionnaire internationale*, 9 (1938), 41.

3. 'Enueg I'

Written in November 1931 after a long walk around the environs of Dublin[56] and sent (with some slight variants from the published version) to Seumas O'Sullivan at the *Dublin Magazine*,[57] who rejected it ('Herewith a pome that Seumas O'Sullivan wouldn't have on account of the *red sputum* [line 2]. I haven't tried to place it elsewhere').[58] One of the 'three or four' poems excluded from Beckett's generally negative estimate of his poems in the letter to MacGreevy of 18 October 1932, which suggests it must have been one of the group of poems shown to London publishers in the summer of 1932, and which also helps to explain Beckett's keenness to place it over the next few years. In a later letter to MacGreevy Beckett describes it as 'the canal Enueg'[59] (presumably to distinguish it from 'the little policeman Enueg' [i.e. 'Serena I' as published]), and he gave a copy of it to the poets Brian Coffey and Denis Devlin,[60] obviously hoping that they might find a publisher for it. Their efforts having failed, Beckett sent it to the *Bookman* who swiftly rejected it.[61] A deal for a book of poems to be published by George Reavey had been struck by June 1934 but a few months later, in November 1934, Beckett sent it (with several variants, and accompanied by the poems 'Moly', 'Dortmunder' and 'Echo's Bones') to *Poetry* (Chicago), who also rejected it. Even though he had agreed terms with George Reavey by June 1934, it was not until early in 1935, after some months of discussion, that Beckett could be quite sure that a volume of poems would appear from the Europa Press ('[Arland Ussher] congratulated me on having secured the co-operation of [George] Reavey'),[62] which helps to explain Beckett's desire for a periodical publication for 'Enueg I'. In her biography Deirdre Bair mistakenly describes 'Enueg I' as 'the poem he wrote when Peggy Sinclair was dying'.[63] In *The Samuel Beckett Manuscripts: A Study*, the late Richard Admussen mistakenly supposes that 'Cascando' (1936) was sent with 'Enueg I' to Seumas O'Sullivan at the *Dublin Magazine* in November 1931, an error deriving from misplacement of material in the TCD MacGreevy collection.[64]

4. 'Dortmunder'

Written 'in Kassel..."under the influence of Dortmunder beer"' early in 1932.[65] Beckett was in Paris by February 1932, which makes January the most likely time of composition of the poem. 'Dortmunder' is too well controlled to have been the extempore effusion that Beckett liked to think it was (he speaks of 'the spontaneous combustion of the spirit' in the letter to MacGreevy in which this poem is singled out from others 'of little worth').[66] It was sent to *Poetry* (Chicago) in November 1934 (with 'Moly', 'Enueg I' and 'Echo's Bones'), and must have been one of the poems submitted to London publishers in the summer of 1932. Presumably the sexual content of the poem precluded Beckett sending it to Seumas O'Sullivan at the *Dublin Magazine,* where it would probably not have found favour.

5. 'Sanies II'

In her biography Deirdre Bair writes: 'One of the earliest poems dating from 1929 is "Sanies II".' [67] This dating is almost certainly too early by some three years, and derives from the copy of *Echo's Bones* annotated by Beckett (HRHRC). But in writing 'École Normale Paris 1929' beside 'Sanies II' in this copy Beckett is, I think, remembering his *first* experience of Paris from the perspective of his *second* lengthy stay (February to July 1932), having suffered a nostalgia for the city almost from the moment of his returning to Dublin.[68] It is referred to by Charles Prentice in his rejection letter to Beckett as 'There was a happy land', and by Beckett in a letter to MacGreevy (saying that it has been sent, with 'the little policeman Enueg' [i.e. 'Serena I' as published], to George Reavey) by the same title.[69] It was given the title 'Happy Land' in the *'POEMS'* contents list (HRHRC). Written in Paris between February 1932 and 12 July 1932, when Beckett left for a holiday in Toulon and Le Lavandou, but making use of books read, and of Dublin experiences, in late 1931.[70] 'Sanies II' was almost certainly included in the poems submitted to London publishers in the late summer of 1932.

6 'Serena I'

This is the poem referred to as 'begun…yesterday' in a letter to Thomas MacGreevy, which speaks of 'ardour and fervour absent or faked' in phrasing similar to the variant opening of the untitled poem sent with a later letter to MacGreevy.[71] In the latter Beckett describes it as 'the only bit of writing that has happened to me since Paris [which confirms the Parisian origin of 'Sanies II'] and that does me no particular credit as far as I can judge'. Beckett's excitement of 30 August 1932 ('Desire to write coming. Feel it coming') was obviously tempered by the outcome, as is also clear from a letter to George Reavey of 8 October 1932, to whom Beckett sent this poem (with the title 'Enueg II') and 'Sanies II' (as 'Happy Land') a few days later. 'Serena I' uses material from Beckett's first long stay in London (mid July to late August 1932), but most if not all of the poem was written after his return to Dublin, too late to be part of the 'truss' sent to Edgell Rickword at Wishart & Co on 30 August 1932. In the *'POEMS'* contents list

(HRHRC) it appears as 'I put pen to this' (the first line of the version sent to MacGreevy on 8 October 1932), a title scored through and replaced by 'Cri de coeur I' (cf. B7 and B9 below).

7. 'Serena II'

With the title (from the first line) 'this seps of a world', this is included in the letter to MacGreevy of 4 November 1932; the same title (crossed out and replaced by 'Cri de coeur 2') occurs in the *'POEMS'* contents list. Beckett refers to it as 'the bitch and bones' in a letter to MacGreevy, and it may perhaps be the 'filthy commodity' of an earlier letter (although a curriculum vitae for a possible job may have been more in Beckett's mind).[72] Beckett later adjudged this poem 'a complete failure' as Lawrence Harvey's notes on their conversations indicate, and his poor opinion of it may have set in within a short while of writing it. In the copy of *Echo's Bones* annotated by Beckett (HRHRC), his note to this poem reads 'Glencullen – Prince William's Seat Enniskerry', a walk south of Foxrock of which Beckett was particularly fond.[73]

8. 'Sanies I'

This was written after a cycle ride around Portrane and other North Dublin locations on Easter Sunday (16 April) 1933; described in a letter to MacGreevy of April 1933 but filed at TCD with a later letter, where it bears the title 'Weg Du Einzige!'[74] This remains the title (minus the exclamation mark) in the *'POEMS'* contents list. In an earlier letter to MacGreevy recording a cycle ride to Donabate and back on 26 December 1932 Beckett speaks of 'The first flicker in the mash-tub since the bitch and bones [i.e. 'Serena II']', but may be referring to ideas for a short story ('Fingal'?) rather than to this poem.[75] It must presumably have been one of the poems, together with any or all of the 'truss' put together in late August 1932 (see B6, above), given to Colin Summerford of Methuen, to whom Beckett had also given *Dream*.[76]

9. 'Serena III'

This poem, with the first line 'gape at this pothook of beauty on this palate', is filed with the letter to MacGreevy of 9 October 1933 at TCD. It is inspired by Beckett's affection for Nuala Costello, whom he met in September 1933, having by this time (as he told Lawrence Harvey, who recorded the fact in his Dartmouth College notes) given up all hope of Ethna MacCarthy's favours. Unless an early version of the much-reworked 'Malacoda' pre-dates it, this may have been the first poem Beckett wrote after the death of his father on 26 June 1933, although the published version of 'Malacoda' shares material with the short story 'Draff', despatched with nine other stories to Charles Prentice at Chatto and Windus early in September 1933.

10. 'Malacoda'

This poem may have been begun in the immediate aftermath of Beckett's father's death (26 June 1933), but is much more likely to have assumed something like its final shape some months later, and it was certainly a poem that Beckett worked on more intensively than most because of its subject. It did not assume its final printed form until as late as October 1935, a month before the publication of *Echo's Bones* (see B11). A letter of 4 March 1934 to Maurice Sinclair (personal communication) uses the motif 'Muss es sein' as found in 'Malacoda', and it may have been the specific difficulties Beckett was having with this poem which prompted him to tell A. J. Leventhal, 'My poems are worthless.'[77] The '*POEMS*' contents list gives it the title 'Thrice he came', which is crossed out and replaced by 'The Undertaker's Man'. Beckett was still calling it 'The Undertaker's Man' with the publication of *Echo's Bones* only some three months away,[78] by which time he was expecting 'proofs which have not come', but had in any case reached the depressing conclusion that it 'never was a poem'. When proofs finally arrived in October Beckett worked on them and described the poem as 'well changed'.[79]

11. 'Echo's Bones'

This poem was written after Charles Prentice had rejected the story ('Echo's Bones') which he had asked Beckett to add to the ten already received for the collection to be published in May 1934 as *More Pricks Than Kicks* (Beckett's working title for which was *Draff*).[80] Beckett quotes the poem in a letter to MacGreevy,[81] and sent a version of it (with a few variants, and with 'Enueg I', 'Moly' and 'Dortmunder') in November 1934 to *Poetry* (Chicago), who rejected it. The date of '1935' added to this poem in some reprints – it is not found in *Echo's Bones and other precipitates* – is spurious.

12. 'Da Tagte Es'

Almost certainly one of the two 'Quatschrains' (with 'Gnome' the other; see A13) mentioned in Beckett's letter of 7 May 1934 to A. J. Leventhal. A letter to Leventhal written more than a year later[82] quotes the poem, adding that the poem was with Seumas O'Sullivan at the *Dublin Magazine* ('He has a quatrain of mine, due in the last awful issue'). Beckett's comments on the situation make it clear that he was expecting O'Sullivan to detect sexual images in a poem which, for Beckett, was much more a belated response to his father's death, an attempt to 'redeem the surrogate goodbyes', and one that was very probably written in the wake of difficulties with 'Malacoda'. It is also evident that O'Sullivan had not unreservedly committed himself to publishing the poem, a faint-heartedness which obviously irked Beckett, who was remembering the suspicions that had bedevilled their relationship four years earlier, when O'Sullivan had accepted 'Alba' but had turned down 'Enueg II' and 'Yoke of Liberty'. In a letter to MacGreevy Beckett wrote: 'The *Dublin Magazine* is out, but my poem not in.'[83] O' Sullivan must have rejected it sometime in the spring of 1935.

13. 'The Vulture'

The first poem in *Echo's Bones*, but almost certainly the last to be written, probably early in 1935. An April 1935 letter to MacGreevy shows Beckett visiting cemeteries near Dublin; there are points of contact between the poem and a later letter to MacGreevy,[84] but Beckett was by then expecting the proofs of *Echo's Bones* to arrive (they arrived in October) and in late August 1935 he had begun writing what would become *Murphy*, which suggests that 'working over the poems' later in the year[85] was more a matter of revision than new creation.

In tracing how Beckett moved – uncertainly, and often in considerable distress of spirit – from haphazard magazine opportunities to a book half the size of the projected '*POEMS* by Samuel Beckett', the absence of precise indicators comparable, say, with the manuscript of *Molloy* – where you can pinpoint the actual day on which the 'sucking stone' episode was written – is very much to be regretted. Yet even from such patchy evidence as we possess, it is clear that Beckett was desperate to place his poems with publishers whenever and wherever they might be interested. It was after Dublin, London and Paris had, as he thought, failed him that Beckett was trying *Poetry* (Chicago), even when Reavey was being encouraging: the idea of a volume had surfaced in May 1934 and terms had been agreed in June 1934. At much the same time, and perhaps as a direct consequence of Reavey's acceptance, Beckett was obviously privately wondering whether his poems were 'worthless', as most subsequent commentators have done. In this connection it is not necessary to claim that Beckett (either at this early stage or later) was a major poet, and if W. B. Yeats is to be taken as the major poet of Beckett's young manhood – as he surely is – no such claim could survive for very long. Beckett could probably have admitted well before he felt obliged to do so during his interviews with Lawrence Harvey that the desire to be a poet tended, in his case, to get bound up with what he had in fact achieved, making it difficult to evaluate what he had actually accomplished that was distinctive and specific, however idiosyncratic it might at first sight seem. Before 1934 (when finally a solution of sorts seemed to offer itself in the shape of George Reavey), Beckett had obviously realised that different editors found different aspects of his work unsympathetic, which made the issue of where to send the poems a delicate one. The clearest example of this is Seumas O'Sullivan at the *Dublin Magazine*, whose taste was (from Beckett's point of view) very fastidious with regard to material likely to fall within the terms of the Censorship Act of 1929. After *Echo's Bones*

O'Sullivan accepted Beckett's poem 'Cascando', but infuriated him by cutting the first three lines to leave it 'circumcised' – albeit with sufficient space around it for Beckett once more to regret the 'circumcision'.[86] Given the climate, it is perhaps not surprising that when O'Sullivan offered Beckett the editorship of the *Dublin Magazine*, he declined.[87] It probably did not help that Beckett, who had not expected to find much of a welcome on home ground (and in this, at least, had not been disappointed), had for the most part chosen over the previous four or five years to bypass the routes whereby he might have found an audience in Ireland, even though few other avenues were opening up for him. It clearly did not take until his appearance as 'The Atheist from Paris' in a court case of late 1937 for Beckett to seem something of a stranger, and indeed something of a *persona non grata*, on home soil.

After Dublin, London would not prove much more hospitable once the always encouraging, but shrewd and discriminating, Charles Prentice had decided that Chatto could not countenance a book of poems.[88] Paris was just about all Beckett had left; but in Paris the émigré magazines that had flourished in the 1920s were succumbing to the rigours of the 1930s. Here, too, Beckett could hardly have failed to notice the ill fortune whereby he always seemed to be having work appearing in the last issue of particular magazines (*This Quarter*, *The Bookman*, then later in *Soutes* and again in pre-war *transition* ['Ooftish' and 'Denis Devlin']); this was more a sign of the times than any rejection slip might have been, though it must have seemed a kind of rejection by proxy. (Beckett also managed to match this baleful record later when he appeared in the last post-war *transition* with his translation of Apollinaire's 'Zone'.) It must have been painfully clear, as W. H. Auden began to turn heads in England and as the Surrealists' capacity to disintegrate into factions continued in France, that the times were changing in a way inimical to Beckett's own future as a writer, or such little future as he seemed prepared to allow himself in the way he cavalierly alienated now this group, and now that. The mixed feelings he had registered about pre-war *transition* – where only five of Beckett's poems appeared, one in June 1930 (*transition* 19/20), one in April–May 1938 (*transition* 27), and three reprinted from *Echo's Bones* in July 1936 (*transition* 24) – were perhaps not only attributable to the difficulty of emerging out of the shadow of Joyce, with Beckett often doubtful of his ability to do so; part of the problem was being obliged to belong to a recognised 'set'. (A letter to MacGreevy reads, 'I had no notice of *transition* and no doubt no wonder', which probably reflects how he felt at seeing his name co-opted (without consultation) for Eugene Jolas's Verticalist manifesto, although it is probably also an index of Beckett's lingering disappointment that, of the 'stuff' he had submitted to Eugene Jolas,[89] no poems had been selected, and the piece chosen – 'Sedendo et Quiescendo' (the '?' / 'my thing' of letters of August 1931) – sported a glaring linguistic error in the title on its appearance in *transition* in March 1932.) Without George Reavey – committed to experimentation as he had previously been to the short-lived Cambridge journal *Experiment*, and unusually open to influences from across Europe as a whole – it seems unlikely that there would ever have been an *Echo's Bones*, which no one in Dublin or

London had taken much note of, if only because Beckett had known in advance –
his experience with his novel *Dream of Fair to Middling Women* painfully fresh in
his mind – that nobody would. Even as it was to be, and had to be, Beckett's Paris
friend published only a few (327) privately printed copies, and when eventually
Echo's Bones arrived at Foxrock it was greeted with so little interest by his family
– Beckett had given his mother three copies – that he could not really be sure it
had even been noticed.[90] At this point, as he told MacGreevy, he could console
himself by remembering that it had taken them some time to acknowledge the
More Pricks Than Kicks stories published eighteen months earlier – 'perhaps
before midsummer the *Bones* will be similarly disinterred'; but he gave vent to his
real feelings a few days later when he told MacGreevy that he was 'only interested
in those I like having copies' and that he had been disappointed by the muted
reaction of 'Ruddy' (T. B. Rudmose-Brown), Ethna MacCarthy and A. J. ('Con')
Leventhal.[91] And, as the months passed, they brought only an anonymous brief
review in the *Dublin Magazine* – described by Beckett as 'five lines of faint damn'
– and a mention by 'M.C.' of the three *Echo's Bones* poems reprinted in *transition*
24 in *The Irish Times*.[92] With copies for the most part restricted to 'those I like', it
was becoming painfully clear that there were not many who reciprocated by liking
the poems. As is now much clearer, and as hopefully justifies what I have
attempted here, 'liking' the poems is ultimately less important than valuing them,
some ('Alba', 'Yoke of Liberty', 'Enueg I' and others not actually given special
status by Beckett, 'Serena II' for example, which in Lawrence Harvey's notes is
dismissed by Beckett as 'a complete failure') for their own sake, as poems in their
own right, and all of them for what they tell us of how Beckett thought he might
still achieve something of note, some literary respect, in spite of having had to
jettison *Dream*, and in the teeth of the profoundly embarrassing failure to engage
with the taste of the time with *More Pricks Than Kicks*, of which fewer than 400
copies were ever actually sold.

Chapter 7
Irish Censorship: Some Uncomfortable Revisions

W. J. McCormack

Perhaps I should begin by explaining whence this present essay arose, and how it relates to a rather larger project on which I had been working for the previous four years. This was *Fool of the Family*, a biography of J. M. Synge, in the course of which the *Playboy* riots of January 1907 naturally take up some pages. I don't have much to add to the history of these disturbances, except to say that there were supporters of Synge who, despite their personal loyalty, felt that the play was not wholly satisfactory from either an aesthetic or psychological point of view. Among these, two of the most perceptive were Ellen (or Eileen) Duncan, an art curator, and a person signing him or herself La Linge. At the public debate in the Abbey Theatre organised by Yeats, Duncan was prevented from speaking by the chairman, who claimed he was protecting her from the insults of Synge's detractors. These latter ranged from militant Catholic nationalists to the pacifist Frank Sheehy-Skeffington.[1] Here, in essence, are some of the notable features of the long and familiar argument about censorship which began almost as soon as the Free State was founded and which continued up to (and perhaps beyond) Brian Lenihan's liberalisation of the Censorship of Publications Act in 1967.

The dispute about Synge's play brought into conflict ideological groupings that had not previously locked horns. The Parnell scandal of 1891 had certainly mixed politics and sexuality, but it had no literary or 'high cultural' dimension at the time. Conflict between Church and State in nineteenth-century Ireland had not been in short supply, but the element of personal transgression or (in a different register) personal martyrdom was absent. It may be significant that, where one looks for heroes in pre-Syngean public controversies, the central figures are often Catholic priests – George Tyrrell and Walter Macdonald in the theological arena and (to switch to literary reflections of other figures), the embattled priests in Sean O'Faolain's 'A Broken World' (1937), and Tom Kilroy's *The Big Chapel* (1971). There may be some allegorical significance in the Abbey Theatre's view that Synge's two-act play, *The Tinker's Wedding*, was 'too dangerous for Dublin'; in it a priest is assaulted for attempting to exploit his authority.

The principal opposition to *The Playboy* had come, not from the Church but from the future State in ideological embryo. It was Arthur Griffith's Sinn Féin which articulated all that was unacceptable in Synge's play, abetted by Patrick Pearse.[2] After the riots had died down, a judge named John Ross told Lady Gregory: 'You have earned the gratitude of the whole community. You are the only people who had the pluck to stand up against this organised intimidation in Dublin.'[3] Indicating that battle lines were being drawn between new forces of obscurantism and the upholders of individual freedom, Ross's comment not only anticipates the trouble that would arise over Sean O'Casey's *The Plough and the Stars* in 1926, but implies a state of semi-permanent conflict that would later erupt on other issues – abortion, birth-control, censorship, divorce, homosexuality – with a tiny liberal, aristocratic or upper-middle-class minority holding the last ditch against organised intolerance. The *Playboy* riots inaugurated a tradition of controversy which persisted well into the 1970s, and perhaps even to the X case of 1992.[4]

Inside this long history of disputation, book censorship has served a symbolic role. The act of reading is deemed such a private, personal and reflective thing that interference with it stands as the representative of all violations of personal liberty. Moreover, reading potentially covers every theme or detail of human activity – from metaphysics to mud-wrestling – and does so within a range of discourses that set fiction alongside inquiry, history beside exhortation. Consequently, when the new state began to show an interest in controlling the circulation of books, its opponents on this issue regarded the conflict as far more wide-ranging than a government interference in personal liberty.[5]

Ezra Pound saw the Irish Government's willingness to introduce a comprehensive censorship as craven imitation of recent American law. Of Desmond Fitzgerald, then an Irish government minister he inquired privately, 'Are you a nation or a dung hill?' Fitzgerald explained later in 1928 that the proposed arrangements might 'make it a little less easy for people to read about every rape and incest performed in England'.[6] Pound, who emerges briefly here as a man of sense, advised keeping 'condoms and classics' in separate parts of the legal code. But the popular and political mood of the 1920s did not approve of fine distinctions.

In this perspective, the opposition to censorship is raised essentially by a literary elite, notably W. B. Yeats as an individual but also *The Irish Statesman* as a magazine of general interest. Its editor was the poet/painter/co-operativist, George W. Russell ('Æ'). But, in fact, Æ's magazine was broadly approving of the Censorship of Publications Act as eventually passed in 1929. It was only when the authorities began to announce the names of those appointed to the Censorship Board that disillusion set in. Ironically, *The Irish Statesman* ceased publication due to financial difficulties just as the lines of battle were being drawn. The liberal opposition then turned to the daily *Irish Times* as its mouthpiece.

Three points are worth considering at this juncture. Firstly, it is the 'nonentity' characteristic of the Board members which distress George Russell, not the principle of censorship as such. Secondly, the distinction between book circulation and magazine or newspaper circulation opens up a more complex analysis of censorship in Ireland. Thirdly, Yeats was not an unqualified opponent of censorship either. He too believed that 'if you think it necessary to exclude certain books and pictures, leave it to men learned in art and letters, if they will serve you, and, if they will not, to average educated men'.[7]

At this point the new State was less than ten years old. The practice of censorship had been introduced by the Provisional Government during the Civil War, principally to exclude certain British newspapers, but it was not enthusiastically supported even by the redoubtable Michael Collins. In relation to artistic works, especially where they employed new technology, there was some greater desire for control. Michael Adams recorded the crucial moment wittily, when he wrote, 'In 1923, under cover of night, a Censorship of Films Act was passed by the Oireachtas (the Irish Parliament).'[8] The emotive name of the Committee on Evil Literature (which reported in 1926) gives a clear indication of the prevailing moral, even theological, influence. The Committee consulted statutes and such like in force in at least a dozen foreign countries or colonies. An important focus for their inquiries is summarised in the solitary piece of non-anglophone legislation cited: a French law of 1920 prohibiting the advocacy of abortion or contraception.

France played a major part in the background to the establishment of book censorship by a native Irish government. In Paris in January 1922, an Irish Race Conference was held, to demonstrate to Europe and the world that native rule was indeed in safe hands. (The occasion was marred by high tension between factions who quickly descended into civil war when they got back home.) During the Race Conference, Ezra Pound renewed his acquaintance with Desmond Fitzgerald, who had been a minor Imagist poet and was soon to become a leading figure in Irish government. In the course of the decade Pound would soundly berate Fitzgerald for the pettiness of the censorship proposals, though in larger political matters they increasingly saw eye to eye.

Yeats, when casting himself in the unlikely role of Thomist or scholastic philosopher, was in fact applying to local Irish problems the authoritarian politics of Charles Maurras, founder of *Action française*, and in the 1920s a leading light for T. S. Eliot's *Criterion* magazine. Whereas it has been customary to regard Yeats's views on censorship as a subset of some larger Anglo-Irish liberal tradition, in fact his points of reference are immediately contemporary, international, and increasingly pro-fascist. Writing in the London-based *Spectator* in September 1928, Yeats deplored the activities of ignorant Catholic ecclesiastics and young armed men who stopped trains to search for English newspapers. Against these he evoked 'our men and women of intellect, long separated in politics' who have 'in the last month found a common enemy and drawn together'. He also evoked the *Playboy* riots, and proceeded directly to observe that 'the well-to-do classes practise "birth-control" in Ireland and the knowledge is spreading downward'.[9]

Ten years later, writing in the privileged circumstances of self-publication, Yeats announced that 'the English mind, excited by its newspaper proprietors and its schoolmasters, has turned into a bed-hot harlot'.[10] Yeats died in January 1939 and so did not live to see the outcome of those forces whom he discreetly but persistently approved. The Second World War – it is usually argued – accentuated the isolationism and provinciality of Irish cultural life, and Sean O Faolain's heroic founding and sustaining of the *Bell* is cited as evidence of an otherwise featureless era. Censorship undoubtedly persisted, and the controversy surrounding the banning of Eric Cross's *The Tailor and Ansty* in October 1942 marked a particular mid-war low point. James Joyce's *Stephen Hero* suffered the same fate in November 1944. Mention of Joyce, however, requires an acknowledgement that *Ulysses* was never banned in Ireland.

During the war, a far more regular and vigilant version of censorship was imposed on Irish cinemas, magazines and newspapers. Pathé newsreel was censored in individual cinemas, with managers obliged to remove all material that might suggest or exhort approval either of the Allied or the Axis forces. This left little of interest for picture-house enthusiasts. The story is told that General Tom Barry insisted on a private viewing of an uncensored newsreel in February 1942 at a cinema in Cork city. The manager, reluctant to offend the victor of Kilmichael and (more recently) Chief of Staff of the IRA, sat with the great man to see film of the British surrender at Singapore. Shyly asking why Barry had wanted to see just that one episode of the war uncensored, he was informed that an officer who had taken a prominent role in the humiliating ritual had surrendered to Barry himself in 1920 – 'the bashtard is still at it!'[11]

Newspaper censorship was far more repressive and active in Ireland than in other neutral states such as Sweden and Switzerland. But, in a recent detailed study of the primary materials, Donal Ó Drisceoil has effectively shown that, at the highest level, the ultimate objective of State censorship during the war was to assist the Allies by neutralising the pro-German tendencies of republican and right-wing factions. This additionally involved the censorship of books, for example, in April 1941 bulk consignments of *The Persecution of the Catholic Church in German Occupied Poland* were seized by customs officials and returned to the publisher in London. Nevertheless, Irish Government attitudes were very different from the callousness apparent in this act of censorship. In relation to the Allies, 'co-operation was extensive', Ó Drisceoil writes. 'The British were supplied with "a constant stream of intelligence information".'[12]

The extreme difficulty which de Valera's government found itself in with reference to partition, IRA collusion with Berlin, and the appeal of Italian fascism in certain corners of Irish Catholicism (even certain corners of the Abbey Theatre), is little appreciated by those who invoke a liberal tradition of the kind anticipated in 1909 by Judge Ross. In the 1920s and after, Yeats did not subscribe to any such tradition, and in his condemnation of 'mob censorship' in 1928 we should pay more attention to the first term of that contemptuous phrase as indicating the real object of his animus. Furthermore, the experience of 1939–1945 – while it is punctuated by incidents of crassness and victimisation – also powerfully suggests that the world is not so pure or simple as a self-styled liberal tradition likes to believe (on occasion).

Yeats, who tends to get a rough time from me whenever his politics is discussed, should be credited with one particularly acute observation on the concept of censorship. Writing in 1937 on the issue of his own timidity, in which he feared there might lurk 'a dread of using ill-chosen words', he speculated that there might be at work within his mind 'some censorship like that of the psycho-analysts – yes, there must be a censorship'. The grammatical ambiguity of this – does Yeats announce the certainty, desirability or necessity, of what he terms censorship? – should not disguise Yeats's recognition of the difficulties involved in any notion of an uncensored utterance. He proceeds, 'Now that I have all my critical prose before me, much seems an evasion, a deliberate turning away. Can I do better now that I am almost beyond caring?' The endorsement of German race legislation in 1938 may represent Yeats 'beyond caring'.

The long established consensus has insisted that censorship in Ireland originated in the 1920s and resulted from cultural insecurities exposed by the achievement of limited independence. In this analysis, censorship is of course a reprehensible device, the enemy of enlightenment. Reconsideration of the *Playboy* riots strongly suggests a longer history and a more complex figuration of hostilities and alliances. The much mocked *Register of Prohibited Publications* (Government Stationery Office 1931–85) may serve as a guide to modern literature in that it lists the work of Samuel Beckett, William Faulkner, Aldous Huxley, Kate O'Brien, Sean O'Faolain, George Orwell, Jean-Paul Sartre and other victims of the censors. But to contemplate this historical document without reference to Irish press laws today, contemporary Irish legislation on libel, persistent questions of class, new corporate monopolies and a problematised sexuality is to miss the point. For example, effective censorship of the trial of Mary Cadden in the mid 1950s led to the closing down of the *Dublin Evening Mail*. More recently, timorous compliance with libel laws which protect the wrong-doer contributed to an aura of splendour surrounding Charles J. Haughey and his cronies. Haughey as the patron of contemporary culture was also Haughey the beneficiary of institutionalised repression. For him, the necessity of censorship recognised by Yeats was the corollary of power.

It is ironic that this essay should move towards publication as the sewage system of Haughey's regime is gradually exposed at tribunals whose power freely to inquire into financial records is repeatedly challenged in the courts. On the day that the former Taoiseach last gave public evidence to the tribunal, the strange and wonderful body known as *Aosdána* was meeting in another set of Dublin Castle apartments. During his Camelot heyday, embarrassed members did little more than murmur of 'a climate of fear' at the round table.[13] Now *The Irish Times*, most assiduous chronicler of these autopsies of corruption is in financial crisis. Meanwhile in the Abbey audiences are not treated to the latest tribute to Synge's influence, the symptomatically awful *Lieutenant of Inishmore*. Dublin theatre bosses shun the play, not for aesthetic reasons nor out of any lingering respect for the republican violence Martin McDonagh's play exposes; box office, which equals bums in tourist coaches, connives in censorship.

Chapter 8

Blacklists and Redemptions: The Publishing History of Francis Stuart

Anne McCartney

Working in the area of Irish book history where primary sources are often difficult to come by, the researcher becomes accustomed to finding information in unexpected places. Having completed a study of the works of Francis Stuart who died in February 2000, and whose writing career spanned more than seventy-five years, it struck me that his publishing history provides a unique insight into the overall development of publishing in Ireland in the twentieth century.

Stuart was born in Townsville, Australia in 1902, both parents having emigrated from the north of Ireland to set up a sheep station. When his father committed suicide some six months after Francis's birth, his mother brought him back to Ireland where he lived with various relatives until going to school in England when he was ten. After a rather unhappy and unsettled schooling he returned to Dublin in 1918, at the age of sixteen, to be tutored for the Trinity College entrance examination by a relative, H. O. White, who later became Professor of English at Trinity. Within months Stuart met Iseult Gonne, the daughter of Maud Gonne, at one of George Russell's poetry evenings, and after eloping to London, they returned to Dublin at Maud Gonne's insistence and were married just before Stuart's eighteenth birthday. In this way Stuart found himself at the heart of Dublin's literary circle.

His first published work appeared in *Aengus: An All Poetry Journal* which ran for four issues between midsummer 1919 and July 1920. This was hardly surprising as, apart from the first issue, which was edited by H. O. White, Stuart was editor of this publication, a late example of the so-called 'little magazines' such as *Beltaine* which were spawned by the Literary Revival and tended to centre on the Irish Literary Theatre and the same core of literary talent – Yeats, George Moore, Lady Gregory, Æ, Lord Dunsany and Alice Milligan. *Aengus* adopted the Revival typographic style and physical format but, true to its title, contained no editorial, no advertising, nothing but a frontispiece and a series of poems in a large, clear type. Along with Stuart, contributors included F. R. Higgins, who later was director of the Abbey Theatre, and fellow Northern poets, E. R. Dodds (who went on to be Chair of Greek at Oxford and literary executor of Louis MacNeice), Richard Rowley (who later published Sam Hanna Bell and others) and R. N. D. Wilson who grew up close to Stuart. Moving away from the all-poetry format, the final issue, which is marked 'New Series', contains several pieces by 'H. Stuart' including two short prose works. 'In Church' captures many of the themes that were to mark his entire œuvre – the outsider, the madman, religion and sex – and

'A letter to a young lady, more sincere than most letters, yet not entirely so' gives the first hint of his belief that art 'cannot remain abstract' but must be marked by personal experience. The listed 'Five Poems – H. Stuart' are in fact only three, 'War', 'Criminals' and 'Forgiveness', which are dated either January or February 1920.[1] The final piece in the publication is 'A Drama' by Maurice Gonne, a pseudonym used by Iseult Gonne.

Like *Samhain* and *Dana* and many of the little magazines, *Aengus* was short-lived. The troubled nature of the Stuart's marriage may have had something to do with the demise of the publication as July 1920 was also the date of a violent row between the couple when Iseult smashed a heron plaster cast Stuart had made at school and, in retaliation, he poured paraffin over her clothes and set them alight. Stuart wrote of this incident in *Things to Live For* (1934) and *Black List, Section H* (1971), making the smashed heron a symbol of the state of his marriage. Following this incident the couple were estranged for a few months and Yeats was asked to negotiate reconciliation. Despite this, the next few years were difficult emotionally and marked with many arguments and separations. Stuart's next publication is a privately printed poem entitled *To Our Daughter*, in which he tries to justify to Iseult his absence from the christening of their first child, who unfortunately died a few months later, again in his absence.

The turmoil of his early marriage and his involvement in the Civil War meant that it was April 1923 before Stuart managed to get more poems published, this time in *Poetry: A Magazine of Verse*, a Chicago journal. He later received the Young Poet's Prize awarded by Mrs Rockefeller McCormick for these, though by this time he was interned in Maryborough Military Prison and Tintown Prison Camp for some months. While he was imprisoned Iseult arranged for Fred Higgins to have a collection of Stuart's poems, including those written in prison, published privately. *We Have Kept the Faith* by H. Stuart appeared in January 1924, a few weeks after Stuart's release. Bound in cardboard with a cloth spine, the printed label on the cover giving it an 'Arts and Crafts' look, the book is the only publication of the Oak Leaf Press of 13 Fleet Street, Dublin. This was the address of the General Advertiser and Wood Printing Company, the printers of the first three issues of *Aengus* and Stuart's next short-lived publishing venture, the magazine *To-morrow*.

When he was preparing *We Have Kept the Faith* for publication Higgins was also involved with Con Leventhal, who at that time was running a book shop in Dawson Street but who succeeded Beckett as lecturer at Trinity College Dublin in 1932. Together they published the one and only issue of *The Klaxon, An Irish International Quarterly* which appeared Winter 1923/24. This was a fiercely Modernist magazine which paid homage to Dada and Picasso and was against not just the forces of Church and State but also the new literary establishment.[2] Leventhal's reason for producing this magazine was to publish his long review of *Ulysses*, which he did under the pseudonym of Lawrence K. Emery. The *Dublin Magazine* under pressure from their printers had refused the article. *The Klaxon* also included a translation of Merriman's *The Midnight Court* by Percy Arland Ussher, a poem from Higgins and a personal essay by Thomas MacGreevy.

Provocative and promising, *Klaxon* was to provide some of the impetus for *To-morrow*.

Stuart's involvement with *To-morrow* came about through his neighbour at Glencree, Co. Wicklow, Cecil ffrench Salkeld. Salkeld was the son of Blanaid Salkeld who was a writer and an actress at the Abbey Theatre. He had studied art in Germany where he had been part of the New Objectivity group and had exhibited with Picasso. Salkeld's daughter Beatrice was later to marry Brendan Behan. Stuart and Salkeld shared an attraction for the bohemian way of life and together with Higgins and Leventhal decided to produce a monthly literary magazine devoted to their unconventional views on art. As well as using the new magazine as an outlet for their own work, they solicited contributions from Liam O'Flaherty, his wife Margaret Barrington, Joseph Campbell and Lennox Robinson. Yeats was also approached and enthusiastically gave them a new poem 'Leda and the Swan' and an anonymous editorial. In *The Cat and the Moon and Certain Poems* (1924) Yeats recalls that he wrote 'Leda and the Swan' because Æ asked him for a political poem for *The Irish Statesman* but as he wrote 'bird and lady took such possession of the scene that all politics went out of it, and my friend tells me that his conservative readers would misunderstand the poem'.[3] Writing later in *The Yeats We Knew* (1977) Stuart praises Yeats's generosity and was obviously unaware that the poem had previously been rejected by Æ.

> The idea attracted Yeats and to our surprise and delight he offered to give us a new and unpublished poem of his to print in the first number. The poem was 'Leda and the Swan' and when I read it I realized that because of this poem our paper would be of importance. But Yeats's interest in the project went even further. He wrote an editorial for us, not, of course, to appear above his signature. In it he deplored the lack of any cultural standards in the new Irish State and in the Church in Ireland. I don't think we realized what a bombshell we were exploding when we printed this article, to say nothing of the poem with its strange, perverse eroticism. I know I didn't.[4]

The magazine ran into trouble even before it was printed, not because of Yeats's contribution, but because of Lennox Robinson's story of a young girl named Mary, who, having been seduced by a tramp, dreams that she will give birth to the Christ Child in his second coming, only to give birth to a girl and die in childbirth. When the proof was set up by the printers in Fleet Street, Dublin, they refused to print it unless this story was changed as they thought it was blasphemous. Writing to Olivia Shakespear, on 21 June 1924, Yeats describes the drama surrounding the publication.

> Last night I received a deputation from a group of Dublin poets, a man called Higgins and the Stuarts and another, whose name I do not know, who were about to publish a review but it was suppressed by the printers for blasphemy. I got out a bottle of Sparkling Moselle, which I hope youthful ignorance mistook for champagne, and we swore

alliance. I saw a proof sheet marked by the printer 'with no mention meant to be made of the Blessed Virgin' – the good lady as we all know being confined to church. My dream is a wild paper of the young, which will make enemies everywhere and suffer suppression. I hope a number of times.[5]

The magazine was eventually printed in Manchester but only ran for two issues, August and September before the controversy it aroused forced its young editors to discontinue. In a letter to Lady Gregory, Sean O'Casey wrote: 'There is a very bitter article in this month's *Catholic Bulletin* about the recent happenings around the publication of *To-morrow*. It is so vulgar in tone that I am reluctant to send it on to you.' In the article, the editor of the *Catholic Bulletin*, after a long tirade condemned 'the filthy Swan Song of W. B. Yeats and the ribald obscenities and brutal blasphemies of the prose story signed Lennox Robinson'.[6] The controversy led to the dismissal of Robinson as Secretary of the Carnegie Library Committee. The fate of Robinson and of *To-morrow* shows something of the way censorship actually worked in Ireland at this time, in that it was not only a prohibitive measure but also a reactive one. This first venture into publishing confirmed for Stuart his assertion in the second editorial that his was 'a voice in the wilderness' and it was to bring to a close his attempts to produce a radical journal, although a late novel, *Faillandia* (1985), has as its central plot the publication of such a journal.[7]

Stuart's dream of creating a new kind of literature is closely bound up with his political beliefs at the time. Earlier in 1924 a lecture on 'Nationality and Culture', which he seems to have delivered some time before, was published by Sinn Féin Árd-Comhairle. In this he writes of his hope that modern Irish writers and poets would counter cheap English fiction and stand 'side by side' with all that is best in foreign literature:

Our bookshops are crammed with cheap English novels and magazines. These books are there because of the demand for them; it is going to be a difficult thing to do away with this demand . . . We want to see Fintan Lalor's Essays, the Essays of Davis, Mitchel's Jail Journal and other books, Pearse's Essays and stories, Connolly's Labour in Irish History, Mangan's poems, and of course, our modern Irish poets and writers in our bookshops side by side with what is best in foreign literature. But we won't see that until there is a demand for it, until the English novels and magazines are left unsold upon the hand of the booksellers.[8]

As if to confirm the difficulties facing the Irish writer at the time, the period from 1924 to 1931 was a barren time as far as Stuart's publications go with only a few poems and a pamphlet published. Two poems – 'Introduction to a Spiritual Poem' and 'Night Arrival' – appeared in the October 1924 edition of the *Transatlantic Review* edited by Ford Maddox Ford in Paris, while five others appeared in the October 1926 edition of *Poetry: A Magazine of Verse*. The pamphlet *Mystics and Mysticism* (1929) was published by the Catholic Truth Society of Ireland which was set up in 1899 to 'create a taste for a pure and wholesome literature'. In the first ten years of this Society's existence the four hundred and twenty-four pamphlets issued had a circulation of over five million copies. While religious pamphlets obviously had a healthy market, the same could not be said for literary publications where the demand was surprisingly low, a situation which Seumas O'Sullivan noted in the *Dublin Magazine*.

> There is little or no demand for books in Ireland, and consequently, Irish publishing languishes and Irish authors cease to write or are published in England. Even in Dublin books are borrowed rather than bought – there are thousands of people in Dublin who can afford to buy books, but only when all hope of borrowing has gone will they purchase, and then, perhaps only at second-hand. In the face of this it is difficult to see what the Dublin Industrial Development Association can do in the matter. Its favourite remedy, a prohibitive tariff, would not only be useless but pernicious, and even if the clause in the American Copyright Act, which compels printing in the United States, were adopted here, it would only prevent the importation of books by those who need them. Only by increasing the demand for books of all kinds in Ireland can the Association hope to effect any improvement upon the conditions now prevailing. When the people of Ireland are reading books by Irish authors in large numbers will there be Irish publishers to publish and to print them in Ireland.[9]

Despite the difficulty in finding a local audience Stuart had not completely given up the dream of being a writer and in 1929, following a summer working as a stretcher-bearer in Lourdes, he was encouraged by Iseult and Liam O'Flaherty to write a novel about his experience. The friendship between O'Flaherty and Stuart brings us to one of those links that makes it impossible to write a history of Irish publishing which does not include consideration of Irish books published outside Ireland. From quite early in his career O'Flaherty had been guided and encouraged in his writing by Edward Garnett,[10] who was a reader for Jonathan Cape from 1921 until his death in 1937. Garnett played an extremely important role in encouraging Irish writers, including Yeats and Hyde in the 1890s, and famously also turned down Samuel Beckett's *Dream of Fair to Middling Women,* saying that 'he wouldn't touch it with a barge pole. Beckett is probably a clever fellow, but here he has elaborated a slavish and rather incoherent imitation of Joyce, most eccentric in language and full of disgustingly affected passages – also indecent.'[11] Garnett had the habit of closely tutoring his authors and O'Flaherty's correspondence with him shows that he had a tremendous influence on his thinking and writing and indeed reading.[12] O'Flaherty recommended Stuart to Garnett and, despite the fact that the novel struck neither Garnett nor Jonathan Cape, they agreed to publish it with revisions. *Women and God* was published in 1931 at the same time as O'Flaherty's *The Puritan.* The Cape archives in Reading show that the print run was only 1,500 and of these 600 were wasted.[13] Like most Irish writers of the time Stuart had turned to England to find a publisher. This is hardly surprising since Irish publishing houses such as M. H. Gill, Browne & Nolan or Talbot Press found it more profitable to produce educational or religious books. Indeed it is interesting to note that in 1931 none of these houses produced a novel. James Devane writing in *Ireland Today* around this period questions whether an Irish-published novel is even possible.

> I have heard it costs three hundred pounds to publish a novel. Four thousand copies must be sold to pay costs, and of these four thousand, four hundred at most may be sold in Ireland. From this fact it is obvious that an Irish novel is not possible today. An English publisher decides the fate of the Irish novel. English critical standards measure its worth.[14]

O'Flaherty certainly had no love of Irish publishers, telling Garnett when he recommended Peader O'Donnell to him in 1927 that 'The Talbot Press wanted to print *Islanders* but they are outrageously vulgar people and they must not get a work of art'. He went on to promise Garnett that Cape would 'undoubtedly have a big sale in Ireland, at least two thousand in Ireland alone' which puts into perspective the low sale of *Women and God*.[15]

The extent of O'Flaherty's involvement in Stuart's publishing is not clear but the following year, when O'Flaherty was in dispute with Cape over the film rights of *The Informer*, both of them turned to Victor Gollancz. Gollancz had set up his own imprint at 14 Henrietta Street, London in 1928 following a period working with Ernest Benn. Gollancz got his authors by paying large advances, guaranteeing them publicity and sales and by commanding personal loyalty. He spent lavishly on advertising rather than multicoloured jackets, opting instead for a gaudy yellow cover, a fact which gave O'Flaherty some misgivings.[16] The combination of religion and popular appeal in Stuart's work was bound to appeal to Gollancz who is described in *Mumby's Publishing and Bookselling in the Twentieth Century* as

> ... a latter-day St. Joan with all the conviction and single-mindedness of Shaw's saint. He didn't work scientifically but emotionally, explosively even, always one-hundred per cent committed to whatever involved him. He did not know the meaning of half-heartedness. He was a large man, in every way, and often a tiresome one, but his socialism was based on humanitarianism. For V.G. publishing was always a crusade as well as a business.[17]

Certainly Stuart's next four novels, *Pigeon Irish* and *The Coloured Dome* in 1932, and *Try the Sky* and *Glory* in 1933 were published by Gollancz in London and simultaneously by Macmillan in New York. In keeping with Gollancz's promises on publicity they were widely reviewed in London, Dublin and New York. Opinions on Stuart varied. The *New York Times* proclaimed him a genius, and Father Talbot, editor of *America* and the President of the Catholic Book Club, declared *The Coloured Dome* 'the most interesting Irish literary work of recent years'.[18] Others seriously questioned his ability to write at all.

It is all quite unconvincing. It is all in the wrong plane. And no more can
be said. Yet Mr. Stuart can write, if only he can let himself. But then he
will be modern and clever, and yet not clever enough to avoid a convention
that is cheap and brassy and thin, especially thin. The words at the end of
the book gathering to themselves no glory, no wonder from what has gone
before.[19]

Even O'Flaherty, when approached by Gollancz for a foreword for *Glory*, wrote
back, 'I don't know what to say about *Glory*. Really, it's a bit too mad to tell the truth.
Please say if you like 'what magnificent extravagance! But I think it's just insanity.'[20]

Whatever the artistic merits of the works there is a telling recollection in *Black
List, Section H* (1971) where Stuart worries that, despite Gollancz's instinct for
picking winners, he might let him down and it is made clear that his early novels
were not economically successful.

Victor Gollancz doesn't know what to think [of one of Stuart's novels] so
he says something nice about it. He has an idea that if he's patient, and
meanwhile doesn't actually lose money on me, I'll once write something
that could add to the prestige of the firm.[21]

But if Stuart was not earning much from writing he was certainly gaining publicity
and was deemed sufficiently well established for Jonathan Cape to commission his
memoirs, which were published in 1934 under the title *Things to Live For: Notes
for an Autobiography*. Again the print run was 1500 but this time the records show
that this collection of autobiographical and fictional pieces eventually sold out, no
doubt helped by the facts noted by one reader: 'Mr. Cape has lavished all his fine
artistry in format on *Things to Live For*, and yet it costs only seven and
sixpence.'[22]

Aware of O'Flaherty's success in selling the film rights to his novels, Stuart
attempted to write a film script of Synge's *Riders to the Sea* for Brian Hurst but,
even though shooting is recorded as having started in June 1935, the film was
never completed.[23] Instead, breaking his own rule of never writing for money,
Stuart quickly completed a comic attack on the insincerity of the film industry, *In
Search of Love*, which was published by Collins in September 1935. Collins was
Compton Mackenzie's publisher and, since he had championed Stuart's novels in
his reviews for the *Daily Mail* right from *Women and God*, it is likely that he
recommended Stuart to them.

In contrast to the light-hearted comedy of *In Search of Love*, the novel
published just a few months later, *The Angel of Pity*, is a profound philosophical
treatise on warfare and compassion. With this work Stuart again seems to have
followed O'Flaherty in his choice of publisher, since *Shame the Devil* was also
published in 1935 by Rupert Grayson, whose firm Grayson & Grayson published
a series of popular fiction that year under the imprint of Grayson Books. Other
writers featured were Sean O'Faolain and Graham Greene. O'Flaherty had been
introduced to Grayson by a close friend, Patrick Kirwan, a German translator, with
whom he had shared rooms in the 1920s. Neither book brought success for its
author. O'Flaherty wrote to Stuart a few months after publication:

I'm afraid your *Angel of Pity* got about the same treatment as my Hollywood shocker, except from a different point of view. They attacked me most foully and said about your book, to use Rupert's words, that it was rather odd.[24]

Since the market outside Ireland had, for the most part, failed to respond to Stuart's work, he turned his attention to home, responding to a letter in the *Irish Press* with his thoughts on creating a market for Irish writers in Ireland:

Sir – I had hoped that Mr. Diarmuid O Dalaigh's letter of a few days ago would have elicited some views from other Irish writers on the question of the home market. As it has not done so I would like to say that I at least agree with almost everything he said. Countries as small as ours support their own writers, if not in luxury, at least decently. Why does Ireland not?

For two reasons, I think. The Irish reading public has two other great sources of supply: England and America, especially the former. And as a corollary, the Irish writer has the same two alternative markets for which he can afford to neglect the home one. There are two ways of altering this state of affairs: a sufficiently large reading public to support Gaelic writers, or a prohibitive tariff on all English and American authors in Ireland.

The first remedy seems to me difficult to attain in any case not for some generations, if at all. The second is possible but there are such things as reprisal tariffs and I wonder how many Irish writers would be willing to become victims of a tariff war?

Is there a less drastic remedy? How about a quota system such as is applied in England for English films? Could something of the sort be applied to publication of work by Irish writers in Ireland?

Maybe someone has a suggestion to –

Yours faithfully, FRANCIS STUART[25]

Stuart did have an Irish publication at this time, a small paperback book, *Racing for Pleasure and Profit*, published by Talbot Press in 1937, but for his next four novels he turned again to Collins. *The White Hare* (1936), *Julie* (1938) (one of the first novels to be produced by Collins in its especially commissioned Fontana typeface), *The Bridge* (1938), and *The Great Squire* (1939) brought to an end this first phase of Stuart's publishing career. He had written eleven novels in eight years and all of them had been published outside Ireland. From the numerous reviews collected by Iseult in her scrapbook it is clear that he had achieved a considerable public success as a writer.[26] Sean O'Faolain, for example, writes in his review of *The Great Squire*:

It is always exciting to follow the imaginative adventures of Mr. Stuart's mind. One is, indeed, kept on tiptoe: as when an acrobat takes to the tightrope. His progress makes it an uncomfortable performance to attend. Here, I think, Mr. Stuart has got safely across, though with some painful, heart-shaking stumbles. *The Great Squire* should increase his already large public.[27]

Whatever success he had achieved was brought to an abrupt end by his decision, in April 1939, to take up an offer made by Helmut Clissman, Head of the German Academic Exchange Service that he should undertake to lecture in Berlin.

The reasons that lay behind this decision were the source of controversy for the rest of Stuart's life, some critics asserting that he went to Berlin because he was sympathetic to the Nazi cause. Most recently it has been suggested by Brendan Barrington in his introduction to *The Wartime Broadcasts of Francis Stuart* (2000) that despite Stuart's declared lack of interest in party politics, his decision was motivated by an 'allegiance to the Third Reich in the Second World War'.[28] He also states, quite provocatively, that readers 'knowing of Stuart's collaboration with the Third Reich'[29] would be disappointed when they look at his depiction of Jews in his pre-war novels, even those written just prior to his departure for Germany, *In Search of Love, Julie* and *The Great Squire*.[30] However, Barrington argues that in *The Great Squire* 'Stuart is guilty at the very least of a sort of abdication of the fiction-writer's duty to create fully human characters, and at worst of perpetuating a stereotype that, in 1939, the year of the novel's publication, was being used to frightful ends in Europe'.[31] He continues:

> ...there is no evidence that anti-Semitism was a motivating force in Francis Stuart's decision to live, teach and broadcast in Nazi Germany. At the same time, it is difficult to avoid the conclusion that some strain of anti-Semitism was a necessary enabling factor in that decision.[32]

As proof of Stuart's pro-Nazi propensity at this time Barrington offers a letter published in *The Irish Times* on 13 December 1938 in which Stuart argues that the Irish plans to aid refugees from Europe was a hypocritical gesture to 'prove the humanitarianism of the democracies' given the way in which the poor of Ireland were treated:

> ...until democracy has proved its humanitarianism more thoroughly in the spirit of the Gospel it scarcely enhances its appeal by these gestures on behalf of suffering foreigners.[33]

Barrington also cites Stuart's article 'Ireland A Democracy? The Real State of Affairs', published in *The Young Observer* of 1 December 1939, as further confirmation of his fascist leanings. In this article Stuart warns that the freedom of the Press so cherished by democracies is an illusion.

> It is merely a good trick to enable the people to let off a little of their freedom-fervour harmlessly! For the views of these papers can never be any but those which are reconcilable with the financial activities of their proprietors and large shareholders, and therefore they can never achieve any important reforms either sociologically or even nationally.[34]

The basis of Barrington's argument appears to be that criticism of one political system necessitates the endorsement of another.

> Here Stuart's political beliefs trumped all other considerations. He had whipped himself into believing that hypocrisy (which, needless to say, was

present in Éire's derisory refugee programme) and what General Porteous calls 'organised benevolence' were greater evils than state-organized racial persecutions.[35]

Writing in his diary after the war Stuart clearly states his position: 'I came under suspicion not because I was a Nazi, which God knows I never was, but because I was not on any side. Because I did not believe in one propaganda or the other.'[36] His novels corroborate this position, particularly since in these Stuart was always at pains to show the danger of assuming the moral high ground. In *Julie*, for example, a rather rancid description of the Jewish hero seems to fulfil all the anti-Semitic charges levelled at Stuart:

> A toadstool that had sprouted in one of the cracks that were beginning to split the concrete. An underground fungus. His small blue eyes were almost hidden between the heavy lids above them and the fleshy pouches underneath. They appeared to blink across the court as though dazzled by sunlight, by the rays of sunlight filtering in, by the light of justice. He looked indeed like one of those puff-balls, full of a dry, frothy substance. Something that one cannot resist kicking with the toe of one's boot to see it burst.

But the final sentence, 'Or that is how he was presented by the press', shows that Stuart was intent on revealing the anti-Semitism that was rife in the British press at the time.[37] By calling into question the right of the Éire government to present itself as humanitarian, or the British press to call itself free, Stuart is making the point that the official bodies of democracies need to own up to and address their own failings before they can stand in judgement of others. This is a message that had permeated all his novels to date, so his views in the letter and article should not be read as a coded espousal of fascism on Stuart's part.

Whatever the reason for his decision to remain in Berlin, and Barrington admits that marriage and financial difficulties were motivating factors,[38] the effect was a nine-year gap in Stuart's publishing, with only two pieces published in 1940, an essay on de Valera in *Irische Freiheitskämpfer* ('Irish Freedom Fighters') and *Der Fall Casement: Das Liben Sir Roger Casement und der Verleumdungsfeltzug des Secret Service*, a translation of William J. Mahoney's *The Forged Diaries of Casement*. So during the war the only outlet for Stuart's creative energies, apart from the broadcasts he made to Ireland for Irland-Redaktion from 1942 to 1944, were his diaries. In these he continued to plan his writing career while recognising that publication would be a problem.

> August 20. This morning a letter from Scherl saying the Propaganda Ministry had refused permission for *Winter's Song*'s publication in German. The Propaganda Ministry has neither interest in nor knowledge of the truth. This book could not now be published in England or America either, though it is in no way political. At least that is something – to know I have written what would please none of the Propaganda Ministries. Later I may publish it at home.[39]

Stuart could only envisage one way around the problem – to set up his own publishing company in Ireland after the war.

> I would like to have a small publishing concern in Dublin where I could publish my books – *Winter Song* first, my poems and then the one I am writing. Then I would be independent of America and England where in any case it is doubtful if they would be taken.[40]

This was not to be, as his return to Ireland after the war was delayed, firstly by his imprisonment by the French occupying forces and then by his efforts to bring back his lover, Gertrud Meissner. In fact Stuart did not return to Ireland until 1958, by which time Iseult had died and he had married Gertrud, or Madeleine as she was known. The second phase of his publishing career was drawing to an end.

At first the difficulties envisaged in finding a publisher for his work seemed to be realised when his manuscript for *The Pillar of Fire* (later revised and published as *Victors and Vanquished* (1959)) which Stuart sent to Victor Gollancz from Freiburg in January 1947, did not receive an immediate acceptance but was sent out to a second reader. At this time he was still depending on food parcels from Iseult and in his diary he prepared for the inevitable blow of refusal:

> My novel is too different to the other novels to be quickly or easily accepted. It should not surprise me that Gollancz hesitates so long to find a decision on it. It should not even surprise me if he finally rejects it. But what is difficult is not to worry over its fate.[41]

When the rejection finally came Gollancz wrote that he had received widely differing reports about the work; because of the post-war slump in publishing, the book could only have a minute sale and while this would normally not have worried him, he was already committed to other titles. But any worries that Stuart had that he would never be published again were dispersed in March 1948 when Gollancz wrote that he was accepting *The Pillar of Cloud* without reservation, stating, 'from the report I judge it to be a novel of very great beauty and significance'.[42] The relationship with Gollancz was to last through the publication of Stuart's next six novels, *Redemption* (1949), *The Flowering Cross* (1950), *Good Friday's Daughter* (1952), *The Chariot* (1953), *Victors and Vanquished* (1959) and *Angels of Providence* (1959). The American market was more resistant, with Macmillan turning down *The Pillar of Cloud* and *Redemption* despite Gollancz's appeal to Harold Latham, the Vice-President that '*Redemption*, in particular is too wonderful a novel to be handled by any publisher as "just another book"'.[43] In fact of all Stuart's post-war novels, only two were published in America, *Redemption* by Devin-Adair, New York in 1950, and *Black List, Section H* which was published by the Southern Illinois University Press in 1971 as a result of an intervention by a student, Jerry Natterstad, who was undertaking a doctoral thesis on Stuart. The reluctance on the part of American publishers is the only evidence of any form of blacklisting of Stuart's work, though Gollancz reported 'a great deal of advance "sales resistance" to *Redemption*, in view of its subject'.[44]

The letters from Gollancz held in the Francis Stuart collection at the University of Ulster show a very warm personal relationship between the two men with Gollancz willing to publish the work despite poor sales.

> I want to let you know that I read *The Chariot* over the weekend with the deepest appreciation. I thought it movingly good and beautiful. As it is clear, from what you say in the book itself, that you have faced all this, I must tell you that (while I shall do everything I possibly can for it) you must not expect sales. The English are being almost as bad as the Americans in their failure to understand your basic attitude to life, which is the only one that corresponds to reality.[45]

The relationship only ended in 1960 when Gollancz could not bring himself to publish 'A Trip Down the River', which remains unpublished. The letter he wrote to Stuart at that time reveals his personal commitment to the writer.

> Having published you so long, and in good times and bad, so to speak, I feel horrible about turning down a novel by you. The fact that book after book of yours has not been in any way 'a commercial proposition' has never worried me: I have published them because I have enormously liked them, and I haven't worried a bit about the financial results. But here is a book that I cannot bring myself to like; and that does change things.[46]

Although the days when publishing houses could respond to the philanthropic urges of their owners were disappearing with the onset of the multinational chains, Victor Gollancz was one of the few that remained in family hands, his daughter Livia taking over as chairman and director with John Bush after Victor's death in 1967.[47]

In 1961 Stuart began work on a new novel the working title of which was *We The Condemned*. Work went very slowly and the manuscript was not completed until 1967. Over the next five years it was sent to numerous publishers and agents all of whom rejected it.[48] No one it seemed wanted to take a chance on the work, some worrying about the threat of libel in a work so recognisably autobiographical while others rejected it on its literary merits. As previously noted the novel was published under the title of *Black List, Section H* by the Southern Illinois University Press, in January 1971. Stuart's next work, *Memorial* (1973) was quickly accepted by Timothy O'Keeffe,[49] who had then just become a partner in Martin, Brian & O'Keeffe, and who also wished to publish *Black List, Section H*, even though he had turned it down when he was with McGibbon & Kee. He also published *A Hole in the Head* (1977) and *The High Consistory* (1981) and when Tim Binding at Penguin reissued *Black List, Section H* in the King Penguin series in 1982, the sales of which were 6,064 in the first year, Stuart was at last enjoying commercial success. A three-year grant from the Arts Council added limited financial security as did his appointment in 1983 to the newly formed *Aosdána*, a body of creative artists to whom the Irish state paid an annual income. The conditions that Stuart was arguing for in his letter to *The Irish Times* in 1938 had finally come to be.

Arts Council funding for writers and for literary publication, as well as the innovations in desktop publishing, brought about a burgeoning of the publishing industry in Ireland in the 1980s. Dozens of small Irish houses began publishing works to the highest standards of design and marketing. Typical of these was Raven Arts Press, which was set up by Dermot Bolger in 1977 to fill what he saw as 'a big vacuum in relation to Irish writing'.[50] Bolger primarily published new Irish writing but he also reissued Stuart's *We Have Kept the Faith* in time for his eightieth birthday celebrations in 1982. He also took over from O'Keeffe as Stuart's publisher after they had co-produced *States of Mind* in 1984. Raven Arts published *Faillandia* in 1985 and, following the death of Madeleine in 1986, Stuart wrote a small philosophical treatise on his work, *The Abandoned Snail Shell* (1987), which was published along with a short collection of his poetry, *Night Pilot* (1988). His final full-length novel, *A Compendium of Lovers*, was produced in 1990 when he was eighty-eight years of age. *We Have Kept the Faith* was reissued in 1992. Raven Arts Press metamorphosed into New Island Press and reissued *The Pillar of Cloud* and *Redemption* in 1994. Stuart's final works, a small collection of poems, *Arrows of Anguish*, and a short novel, *King David Dances*, appeared under the New Island imprint in 1996 and 1998 respectively. In the last twenty years of his life then, Stuart was able to have his work published in Ireland, each new publication bringing with it equal measures of praise and condemnation. His works, whether published in England, America, Europe or Ireland, have never sold in large numbers and most are long out of print; as a result they are quite valuable on the second-hand market.

Looking back over the range of Stuart's publishing history it is possible to discern patterns that reflect the development of the Irish publishing industry in the twentieth century – the importance of the Little Magazines in the Literary Revival; the self-published Arts and Crafts editions; the limited Irish market for novels and the need for British and American publishers; the dearth of publications during the war; censorship; the slow post-war recovery and the revival of small presses in the latter part of the century. Given its longevity, Stuart's publishing career provides an interesting microcosm for historians of the twentieth-century book.

Chapter 9
Thomas Kinsella and the Peppercanister Press

Derval Tubridy

In conversation with John Haffenden in the early 1980s Thomas Kinsella describes his poetry as a process that is never closed, containing within itself the potential for development. He said: 'I hope the echoes of one poem or sequence go on and get caught up by the next.'[1] Kinsella's poetry is written out of a sense of progression and recapitulation. It reaches out to explore both the public and the private through an examination of events such as the assassination of John F. Kennedy or the death of his father, and does so by situating these events within the context of a larger frame of understanding, whether this is a Platonic ideal of leadership and politics, or the sociopolitical situation in Dublin at the turn of the century. When Kinsella talks about his poetry in terms of a sequence, he is referring to his work as a whole, from the early Irish translations, through to such significant collections as *Downstream* and *Nightwalker*. However, I would like to suggest that it is really in the Peppercanister Poems that we can most fully see the structure that is developing throughout the poet's mature writing; it is there that we see how, as Kinsella himself puts it, 'the whole thing works'.[2]

The Peppercanister Poems are a series of slim volumes issued under Kinsella's own imprint, The Peppercanister Press. The Press takes its name from St Stephen's Church on Upper Mount Street, Dublin, known locally as 'the peppercanister'. It is visible from Percy Place, where Kinsella lived at the time. The device of the Press is based on a sketch of the church by Liam Miller, founder of the Dolmen Press, and it is through Miller's influence and support that Peppercanister came into being. The idea for the Peppercanister Press arose initially from Kinsella's long association with the Dolmen Press. Dolmen was set up in 1951 by Miller in response to the dearth of publishing opportunities in Ireland with the demise of journals such as *Envoy* and the *Bell*. Miller's aim was to publish Irish writers in well-crafted editions, and within a few years of its foundation Dolmen was publishing writers such as Frank O'Connor, Padraic Colum and Austin Clarke. Kinsella's early translations were published by Dolmen, including *Longes Mac Nusnig: Being the Exile and Death of the Sons of Usnech* (1954), *Thirty-three Triads, Translated from the XII Century Irish* (1955) and *The Breastplate of St Patrick* (1954). The young poet's collections of poetry were also published by Dolmen, beginning with *The Starlit Eye* (1951) and including *Poems* (1956), *Another September* (1958), *Moralities* (1960), *Downstream* (1962), *Wormwood* (1966) and *Nightwalker and Other Poems* (1968). As a result of a co-publication agreement between Dolmen and Oxford University Press, Kinsella's latter collections came out in Oxford as well as Dublin.

In 1964 the Dolmen Press was incorporated and Kinsella became one of its founding directors. This placed the poet in a difficult position since as a director he could not justify Dolmen publishing all of his work.[3] He needed to find another outlet for his poetry and, rather than moving to another publishing house, Kinsella decided to found his own imprint, the Peppercanister Press. One of the reasons that Kinsella has given for publishing his poetry initially with the Peppercanister Press before it is published by the larger English or American presses such as Oxford and Knopf, is that it gives him the opportunity for the kind of interim publication usually provided by magazines and journals through which the poet can assess the progress of his work. As Kinsella explains: 'Peppercanister became an alternative to the publication of poetry in literary journals. I had always found this unsatisfactory, with the poems placed between stories and articles and disappearing with a particular issue.'[4] However, Kinsella did not abandon serial publication altogether. For example, certain poems in *Song of the Night and Other Poems,* published by Peppercanister in 1978, were first published in journals such as *Tracks,* Philadelphia; *The Chowder Review,* Madison, Wisconsin; and *The Sewanee Review.* And indeed this practice continues. Kinsella's recent journal publications include poems in *Agenda, Poetry* and *Ploughshares.*

In his preface to the Dolmen/Oxford edition of his poems *Fifteen Dead* (1979), Kinsella explains how the idea of the Peppercanister Press was originally to publish 'fine books in the forms and material most suitable to the longer poems and sequences' that he had started writing around the late 1960s.[5] These limited edition volumes would, Kinsella felt, satisfy the market for his work, but they would, 'when appropriate' as he puts it, be collected later in ordinary trade editions. Kinsella's intention that Peppercanister focus on limited edition collector's volumes emulates Miller's focus on fine materials at Dolmen. Indeed, Kinsella's *Three Legendary Sonnets* (1952) was, as Robin Skelton describes, 'published in an edition of 100 copies, hand-set by the poet himself. Five of these copies were printed upon hand-made paper and signed. From this time onward the majority of Dolmen editions included a small number of specially bound and signed copies.'[6]

Though the remit of the Peppercanister Press was initially the production of fine limited editions, history intervened to change that remit. Instead, on 26 April 1972 the first Peppercanister was issued as a slim, cheaply produced pamphlet which aimed to reach the widest audience. This was *Butcher's Dozen,* a poem written in haste and in anger in response to the findings of the Widgery Tribunal concerning the shooting of thirteen civilians during a civil rights march in Derry that year:

> [Peppercanister] originated with Butcher's Dozen, written in April 1972 in response to the Widgery Report on the 'Bloody Sunday' shootings in Derry. The poem was finished quickly and issued as a simple pamphlet at ten pence a copy; cheapness and coarseness were part of the effect, as with a ballad sheet.[7]

The poem reached an inordinately wide audience but also incurred an extraordinary amount of vitriolic criticism in which Kinsella was even accused of cashing in on the tragedy of others. However for other readers, the poem cauterised the wound of a deeply felt injustice and served to remind that poetry is not the preserve of the drawing room or the lecture theatre, but has a place also on the streets. The trade edition, priced at ten pence, had a tan wrapper displaying a coffin device with the number thirteen. This device was modelled on the badge issued for the civil rights protest march in Newry on 6 February 1972. Though distributed by Dolmen Press *Butcher's Dozen* was printed at the Elo Press simply because it needed to come out in a larger edition and at a greater speed than Dolmen could accommodate.[8] The trade edition had two print runs and was followed by a limited edition bound in quarter morocco over red cloth, retaining the coffin device blind stamped on the cover and a library edition bound in red cloth with the coffin image embossed in black and the number thirteen in red. Twenty years after Bloody Sunday, on 19 April 1992, Kinsella reissued *Butcher's Dozen* in a somewhat similar format to the original trade edition, though moving from 5 x 8 format to 6 × 9¼. This was priced at a very reasonable £4.95 and distributed by Dedalus Press, Dublin in an edition of 500 copies.

The Peppercanister editions that followed also dealt with public events. Two elegies for the deceased Irish composer Seán Ó Riada, and one for the American President John F. Kennedy form what can be considered the first series of Peppercanister Poems. 'It seemed', Kinsella notes, 'that Peppercanister was developing as a means of dealing with occasional public items.'[9] The first of these, *A Selected Life,* was written just under a year after Ó Riada's death in October 1971 at the age of forty. The composer's death had a significant impact on people from all walks of Irish life, and the importance of his contribution to Ireland's culture was celebrated by his contemporaries. In the same year that Kinsella's *A Selected Life* appeared, John Montague dedicated 'Patriotic Suite', the eighth part of his poem *The Rough Field,* 'for Sean O Riada'.[10] A few years later, Seamus Heaney's poem 'In Memoriam Sean O'Riada' appeared in the 1979 collection *Field Work.*[11] Aidan Matthews emphasises the public importance of Ó Riada when he writes:

> Most of our more senior poets have made encomia to the memory of Sean O'Riada: for Kinsella, he is 'the vertical man'; for Montague, he represents a mythic coalescence of O'Carolan's music, renaissance recklessness and the usages of the great Gaelic houses in the seventeenth century. Heaney's notation is less aristocratic, but it encapsulates a similar ambition – that of establishing a cultural epitome and, in consequence, an affective norm in one's art.[12]

A Selected Life, described by Kinsella as 'a funeral poem', appeared in August 1972.[13] Possible alternative titles for the poem were 'Sound and Echo' and 'Moments Musicaux'.[14] It was issued in both a limited and a trade edition and the proceeds from both went to a foundation, *Fundúireacht an Riadaigh,* established to help the composer's family. The limited edition was issued in quarter leather binding over blue cloth with the author's name and the title of the book embossed in gold on the spine, and the trade edition was in green wrappers with black and brown print. The covers of both feature an image of Ó Riada which was derived from a medallion by the sculptor Seamus Murphy based on the death mask of the composer. It is a haunting image which captures Ó Riada's profile in chiaroscuro, eyes closed as if in meditation rather than death.

A Selected Life was followed by *Vertical Man* in August 1973. The title comes from Ó Riada's Claddagh Records recording, *Vertical Man*. Here, Ó Riada's 'Hercules dux Ferrariae Nomos no. 1', played by the London Philharmonic Orchestra and conducted by Carlo Franci, is joined by a number of poems by Holderlin, Thomas Kinsella, John Montague, and Seamus Heaney set to music by the composer and sung by Bernadette Greevy. The title also refers to W. H. Auden's dedicatory verse from his 1930 collection, *Poems*; Aiden was a poet whose work exerted a strong influence on Kinsella's early writing:

> To Christopher Isherwood
>
> Let us honour if we can
> The vertical Man
> Though we value none
> But the horizontal one

Vertical Man, titled 'a sequel to *A Selected Life*', was published in both limited (100 copies) and trade editions, the former bound in quarter calf over light brown cloth, the latter in light brown wrappers, both editions using Baskerville type with Perpetua initials. Like the previous Peppercanisters these were printed at the Dolmen Press, a practice that would continue until the ninth Peppercanister, *Songs of the Psyche*.

On 22 November 1973, exactly ten years after John Fitzgerald Kennedy's assassination, *The Good Fight* was issued by Peppercanister Press in tandem with *Vertical Man*. The poem was begun, as Kinsella explains, soon after the Dallas assassination but was not completed until the tenth anniversary:

> With this fifteenth death many things died, foolish expectations and assumptions, as it now seems. I began the poem soon after Kennedy's assassination – with how many other poems written for a while, as people roamed the nights to relieve themselves of obscure pressures. But the poem jammed and allowed time for the foolishness to digest.[15]

The Good Fight mourns the deaths of both John F. Kennedy and of a certain kind of optimism and confidence which he had come to embody. Through the figures of Kennedy and his assassin, Lee Harvey Oswald, the poem sets up a series of oppositions between the public and the private, the popular and the isolated, the politician and the poet, rhetoric and philosophy, only to undermine the clarity of those oppositions through a complex intertextuality that draws on Plato's writing, near-contemporary accounts of the Kennedy administration, and journalism on the inauguration and assassination. Kinsella is clear-sighted in his analysis of democracy and alert to the risks inherent in a system that lays greater store on mass hysteria than on reasoned argument. The poem is illustrated by images drawn from Greek portrait statues of Plato taken from *The Portrait of the Greeks* by Gisela Richter.[16] Kinsella arranges the images in descending order, starting with a complete full frontal image of Plato's head, and progressing through stages of physical attrition by which the details of the face are progressively effaced until the last image looks little more than a skull. The limited edition of 125 copies was printed on Glastonbury antique laid paper, quarter bound in calf over olive boards with a front image of Plato on the cover. The trade edition of 1,500 copies differed from previous ones, bound now in white wrappers, stapled, with red and black print. It sold for fifty pence. In both editions, Times Roman font was used.

Between 1974 and 1978 Kinsella returned to writing the more private poetry for which he had received recognition and acclaim in the 1960s. Once again he turned inward in an exploration of how the self deals with the experiences from which it is formed. Using imaginative frameworks such as the stories of the ancient peoples of Ireland, or the eighteenth-century French Enlightenment project of Denis Diderot's encyclopaedia, Kinsella developed a type of poetic sequence that is characterised by free verse and an open form. The fifth Peppercanister, *One,* returns to Kinsella's concerns with Celtic mythology and Jungian psychology. The title announces a beginning that has already been pre-empted by the zero of 'Notes from the Land of the Dead':[17]

> what shall we not begin
> to have, on the
> count of
> 0

One is part of the numerological system Kinsella has described as 'an enabling idea' that allows him to explore the 'profound personal and family matters' which concern his poetry.[18] Influenced by Jung, Kinsella developed a system that draws together the isolation of the individual, its connection with the other, and the foundation of community, in a sequence from nought to five:

> One begins as zero, one develops as one, one meets another and becomes two, with luck, three emerges . . . Something like a psychic zero is in an act of preparation, and something like a personal unit in its finding its way into existence. The scheme I have found most useful can count up to five; that is as far as it gets.[19]

One is beautifully illustrated by W. B. Yeats's daughter, Anne Yeats (1919–2001), whose delicate line drawings emphasise Kinsella's Jungian explorations. The sequence was published in September 1974 in three forms: de luxe, limited and trade. The de luxe edition consisted of twenty-six lettered copies printed on handmade paper and fully bound in calf. As Stephen Enniss notes, '15 copies of the de luxe edition sold for £65'.[20] They were all signed by Kinsella and Anne Yeats, and each included a verse in the poet's hand. The limited edition consisted of 124 copies on handmade paper, quarter bound in brown calf over dark green, and also signed by poet and artist. These sold for £12. The trade edition consisted of 750 copies, bound in stitched, stiff paper wrapper with a light brown dustwrapper glued at the spine.[21] These sold for £2. With *One*, Peppercanister returned to Pilgrim type first used in *A Selected Life*. It would be the type of choice until Peppercanister's production moved to the Dedalus Press with *One Fond Embrace* in 1988, though with variations between twelve-point in those editions printed by Dolmen and eleven-point in those printed by Reprint in Dublin.

The most complex and beautiful of the Peppercanister editions is *A Technical Supplement*. Published in May 1976 it contains six illustrations taken from the engravings of Denis Diderot's *Recueil de planches sur les sciences, les arts libéraux, et les arts méchaniques, avec leur explication*, published between 1762 and 1772. These volumes were produced to accompany and illuminate the seventeen volumes of text prepared over the period 1751 to 1772 which together form the '*encyclopédie, ou dictionnaire raisonné des sciences, des arts et des métiers*. Kinsella has chosen two details from plates illustrating the Art of Writing, one from Drawing, one from Anatomy and two from Surgery. He has placed these images throughout the twenty-four numbered sections of the poem in such a way as to form a symmetry of location, through which the sense of one group of images overlaps on to another, informing the work as a whole. For example, in *A Technical Supplement* Kinsella juxtaposes an engraving of the ideal proportions of the statue of Laocoon with the subsequent sections dealing with the 'Vital spatterings'(vii) of life, the 'hot confusion'(vi) of the slaughterhouse. The discrepancy between appearance and reality which forms the main theme of Virgil's tale of the destruction of Laocoon and his sons serves to reinforce Kinsella's own exploration of the dissonance between the substance and the surface of reality.[22] Twenty-five copies of the de luxe edition, printed on handmade paper and bound in Basil, were offered for sale at £75. Though the colophon of the library edition states that 550 copies were printed, Stephen Enniss tells us that this is a misprint: 'Only 50 copies of the library edition were printed, as reported in a Peppercanister prospectus and confirmed by note in the Thomas Kinsella Papers at Emory.'[23] The library edition was bound in dark green buckram and sold for £9. The trade edition was bound in grey wraps with dark blue lettering, including an image of a penknife on the front. It came out in an edition of 550 copies and sold for £2.85.

In the two years between *A Technical Supplement* and *Song of the Night and Other Poems* Kinsella moves from visceral and numeric concerns toward an evaluation of love and the nature of understanding, once again taking direction from Jung. 'Gentle quietism' well describes the change in tone from the vigorous interrogative of *A Technical Supplement* to the considered meditation of *Song of the Night and Other Poems*.[24] Published in June 1978 in the now familiar three-part format of de luxe, library and trade editions, the cover of *Song of the Night* is illustrated by an image of a heron by the poet, based on a drawing by Hokusai.[25] The de luxe edition is bound in black leather (50 copies at £80), the library in black cloth (50 copies at £15), and the trade in simple white paper wrapper (300 copies at £5). As the colophon notes, certain poems from the collection appeared in serial publications sometime earlier: 'C. G. Jung's First Years' in *Tracks*,

'Anniversaries' in *The Chowder Review,* and 'Tao and Unfitness' in *The Sewanee Review,* thus providing an additional form of interim publication before being collected by trade publishers such as Oxford University Press and Wake Forest Press.

Song of the Night and Other Poems was published simultaneously with the eighth Peppercanister, *The Messenger.* This is an elegy for the poet's father, John Paul Kinsella, who died in May 1976. Unlike Kinsella's other elegies, the subjects of which are connected with the poet through politics, culture or friendship, *The Messenger* looks to the connections of blood and family from which the poet, and his father, have come. Designed by Jarlath Hayes (1924–2001), the master typographer and designer, the cover of *The Messenger* is a visual tour de force. On a blood-red background the artist has redrawn the emblems and motifs of the devotional magazine *The Irish Messenger of the Sacred Heart; organ of the apostleship of prayer.* In place of Christ there is an image of the winged god Mercury/Hermes carrying a caduceus, the staff entwined by two snakes and bearing two wings on top which is symbolic of the herald. It is used to symbolise the physician, and is also associated with the alchemical symbol for *coniunctio*, which means the marrying of opposites. The figure of Mercury on the refashioned cover of *The Messenger* does not so much banish Christ as incorporate him, since Mercury, or in alchemical texts, Mercurius, is the analogue of Christ.[26] Twin snakes encircle Mercury, drawn in the interlaced style of old Irish illuminations, illustrating the circularity of the uroboros dragon with which Mercury is associated, and alluding once again to the Christ figure (and connecting also with Anne Yeats's drawing of the uroboros in *One*):

> As the uroboros dragon, he impregnates, begets, bears, devours, and slays himself, and 'himself lifts himself on high,'...so paraphrasing the mystery of God's sacrificial death.[27]

To the left of the figure, the image of the papal crown featured on the *Messenger of the Sacred Heart* is replaced by a label for Guinness Extra Stout. To the right, the image of an Irish harp featured on the devotional magazine is replaced by an emblem of the Irish labour movement, the plough and the stars. Religion gives way to business, and patriotic idealism to social realism. Of all the Peppercanister trade editions (525 copies at £5), *The Messenger* is surely the most striking and visually inventive, and is complemented by a de luxe edition bound in full vellum with red ribbon stitching (50 copies at £100), and a library edition bound in black buckram (75 copies at £15).

Publishing through the Peppercanister Press allowed Kinsella the freedom, and the control, to broaden the scope of the poetic work by introducing visual imagery into the text of his poems, thereby deepening the significance of the poems themselves. The influence of Liam Miller must not be underestimated in this regard, since it was the high standard of craftsmanship and the astute eye for presentation notable in the Dolmen editions which provided Peppercanister with an example. In his preface to Stephen Enniss's *Peppercanister 1972–1997,*

Twenty-five Years of Poetry: A Bibliography the poet describes how he 'had admired Liam Miller's commitment to quality in materials and design, and for a while this was confused with the Peppercanister idea'.[28] This influence was most evident in the special and limited editions printed on handmade paper, with full leather bindings, that Peppercanister produced between 1972 and 1987. These were, initially, printed by the Dolmen Press for Peppercanister with what may be considered the second series of Peppercanister editions: *One* (1974), *A Technical Supplement* (1976), *Song of the Night* (1978), and *The Messenger* (1978).

Though the trade edition of *The Messenger* contains a note in the inside flap announcing that edition as the beginning of a new series, Peppercanister instead entered a period of silence, a silence that was broken seven years later in 1985 with the publication of *Songs of the Psyche*. Interestingly though, the Kinsella papers at Emory University show how the fragmentary writing Kinsella did during this period is incorporated into later volumes right up to the early 1990s. For example, drafts of poems included in the folders for *Songs of the Psyche* are included in the much later volume *Madonna and Other Poems*, published in 1991. During this period Kinsella was also occupied with two editorial and translation projects. The first, with Seán Ó Tuama, is an anthology of Irish poems in the original and in translation called *An Duanaire, 1600–1900: Poems of the Dispossessed*. Published by the Dolmen Press in 1981, in conjunction with Bord na Gaeilge, it makes available to a wide audience the Irish-language poetry of the period. The second was *The New Oxford Book of Irish Verse*, published in 1986, which includes poetry from the Irish and the English, and seeks to 'present an idea of these two bodies of poetry and of the relationships between them'.[29]

There were also, however, two projects that might have become Peppercanister editions. The first was a collaboration with the Irish artist Cecil King published in a limited edition by Monika Beck of Saar, Germany.[30] Kinsella was in correspondence with Beck around August 1981. The project was titled *King and Kinsella* and contains a series of Kinsella's poems illustrated with four screenprints by King. Among the poems for the edition were 'Percy Lane: A Gloss', 'Wyncote, PA: A Gloss' (a version of which had already been published in *New Poems 1973*). The Peppercanister edition of these poems was to be titled 'From My Desk, May 1981'.[31] Two of these poems echo the form of the glosses written by the mediaeval scribes on the margins of their transcriptions, glosses which Kinsella was translating for *The New Oxford Book of Irish Verse*. The idea of the additional poem or comment on a prior text is evident in earlier works such as *A Technical Supplement* which is a supplement both to Diderot's *Encyclopédie* and to Kinsella's own œuvre. The second possible Peppercanister 9 was a collaboration, on the theme of love, with the artist Pauline Bewick called 'Men and Women'. Kinsella notes plans for the book: 'possible P/C with Pauline Bewick (from NOBIV)'.[32] On 29 May 1978, just before *Song of the Night and Other Poems* and *The Messenger* came out, Bewick sent Kinsella an invitation to a private showing of her works at the Cork Arts Society Gallery, enclosing a note: 'I haven't forgotten Cúchulainn's dream, have you written it yet? if so I'd love to see it to see if I could illustrate it – Pauline.'[33] The poems for this Peppercanister were a selection of thirty from Kinsella's *New Oxford Book of Irish Verse*.[34] Neither of these projects came to fruition.

Out of this period of silence from 1978 to 1985 comes *Songs of the Psyche*, a complex sequence of poems that explore the development of an individual and communal psyche through the interrelationship between personal biography and social history as glimpsed through a Jungian lens. Though it was published in tandem with *Songs of the Psyche* in 1985, *Her Vertical Smile* moves away from a consideration of the inner processes of the psyche and toward an examination of how the actions of the individual and of society combine to write a history in which all are implicated. It also explores art and politics as systems through which we make sense of experience.

Rather than being printed by Dolmen as previously, the 1985 editions, *Songs of the Psyche* and *Her Vertical Smile,* were set by Nuala and Raymond Gunn (still in Pilgrim type but now eleven-point rather than Dolmen's twelve) and printed by them at Reprint of Dublin. Since Dolmen was no longer involved in the printing and design of the Peppercanister books, Kinsella looked to Liam Miller one last time to provide direction and expertise regarding technical matters. With his customary generosity, Liam Miller responded to Kinsella's query on 9 March 1984, with the following letter:

Liam Miller   The Lodge/Mountrath/Portlaoise/Ireland

9 March 1984

NOTES TOWARDS A GENERAL SPECIFICATION FOR PEPPERCANISTER BOOKS

Format: US Royal octavo. Trimmed page size 235 x155mm (6 1/8 x9¼") This is based on using Artlaid Natural paper or similar as available ex Dublin stock from O'Sullivan'S.

Type: Photoset Pilgrim Roman with Italic. Type size will be determined by the text to be set. i.e. Poetry, set 13/14 point to 26 ems. All lines should be set so that the page seems optically centred on the type area. Setting should be close and evenly spaced.

Type page of text : 39x26 ems. This will accomodate 33 lines set on 14 point body.

Folio: Set in text size, one line under text page. Can be centred or set left and right, as desired.

Make up: double spreads. Margins on page are,
          Inner: 4 ems from fold
          Head: 5½ ems from trimmed head of page.

Display matter: title pages, special initials etc, and the positioning of illustrations should all be planned on layout sheets before making up book for press.

As the books are short, it might be best to impose pages to print in 8-page sheets for sewing.

All books should be threadsewn in sections and bound as individual binding specifications.

An outline double-page layout is enclosed which can be photocopied for planning titles.

Liam

Figure 9.1 Letter from Liam Miller to Thomas Kinsella, 9 March 1984.

The practice of producing both limited, library and trade editions continued with the Peppercanister volumes 9 to 12 published between 1985 and 1987: *Songs of the Psyche, Her Vertical Smile, Out of Ireland* and *St Catherine's Clock*. The de luxe edition of *Songs of the Psyche* (25 copies at £180) was full bound in calf, the library edition (50 copies at £25) in full black buckram, and the trade edition (350 copies at £12) in grey wrappers over stiff card. All carried on the cover an image of an ornament comprising 'a flat circular disk, half-inch thick, the body of dark blue glass, with a wavy pattern of white enamel, like an open flower, on the surface' taken from P. W. Joyce's *A Smaller Social History of Ancient Ireland*.[35] *Her Vertical Smile* also drew its cover image from Joyce's history. The image depicts two spheres, one in orbit around the other. Kinsella notes in the colophon of the volume that:

> the design on the title page, taken from P.W. Joyce's *Smaller Social History of Ancient Ireland*, is a diagram in an astronomical tract of about 1400 AD in the Royal Irish Academy. The lower circle is the Sun (*sol*); the middle circle is the Earth (*terra*), throwing its shadow among the stars.

The de luxe edition (25 copies at £140) was bound in full green calf, the library edition (50 copies at £20) in green cloth, and the trade edition (350 copies at £10) in green paper wrappers.

The year 1987 saw the publication of *Out of Ireland* and *St Catherine's Clock*. The title of *Out of Ireland* continues the themes developed in *Her Vertical Smile* expanding them to include an examination of notions of national identity in the context of history and culture. *St Catherine's Clock* focuses on the writing of history itself. By questioning the possibility of writing one single history out of the multiple narratives that arise from an event, Kinsella once again emphasises the importance of place for an understanding of society, and cautions us on the uncertainties of historical positioning. Yeats's poem 'Remorse for Intemperate Speech', in which he writes, 'Out of Ireland have we come. / Great hatred, little room, / Maimed us at the start.'[36] Issues of origin and influence are explored in both Yeats's and Kinsella's poems, but it is *Out of Ireland* which juxtaposes contemporary identity with cultural history as it asks some unsettling questions. What does it mean to come out of Ireland? How do we constitute the place, or space, called Ireland? Where does one go, once one is out of Ireland? The phrase 'Out of Ireland' suggests a movement or passage that is defined by its origin. But this origin can only be understood from the distance of departure. Key to *Out of Ireland* is the ninth-century Irish scholar John Scotus Eriugena. His image, again drawn from P. W. Joyce's *Social History of Ancient Ireland*, graces the cover of the volume. The de luxe edition (26 copies at £150) was bound in full calf, the library edition (100 copies at £35) in blue cloth, and the trade edition (350 copies at £10) in cream wrappers.

Kinsella's twelfth Peppercanister, *St Catherine's Clock*, explores the relationship between public and private histories and questions the choices involved in writing about each. Kinsella juxtaposes images from Irish history with images from his family history and, through an analysis of both, the poet destabilises the certainties upon which they stand. It was published also in the three usual formats, the de luxe edition

(26 copies at £130) bound in full black calf, the library edition (100 copies at £25) in full grey cloth, and the trade edition (350 copies at £8.50) in grey wrappers.

In 1980, during that period in which there was little activity from the Peppercanister Press, Kinsella entered into correspondence with Peter Fallon of Gallery Press about publishing with Gallery.[37] One year later Gallery Press (then of Dublin) published a first version of the poem *One Fond Embrace* in association with the Deerfield Press of Massachusetts. It was beautifully illustrated with two woodcuts by Timothy Engelland. This was, of course, a Gallery Press edition rather than a Peppercanister one. Gallery did not assume the relationship with Peppercanister that Dolmen had in the past, preferring only to print those editions that would be published under Gallery's imprint.[38] *One Fond Embrace* provides an interesting example of how successive publication influences Kinsella's writing. The Gallery edition of the poem can be seen as a draft of what would become the 1988 Peppercanister edition which contained additions and changes to the poem. When the poem was republished in Kinsella's *Collected Poems* by Oxford in 1996, it had once again been extensively revised, this time by excision rather than addition.

In 1988 Peppercanister ceased publication of the special editions of poetry and concentrated on issuing only trade and library editions giving no priority to either. This change coincided with Peppercanister's move to John F. Deane's Dedalus Press from where the Peppercanister Press would now be printed and distributed. *One Fond Embrace* was the first volume to come from Peppercanister's association with Dedalus, and was followed by *Personal Places* and *Poems from Centre City* in 1990, and *Madonna and Other Poems*, and *Open Court* in 1991. After a break of five years during which he published an essay on poetry and politics in Ireland called *The Dual Tradition* – issued by Carcanet Press in Manchester as Peppercanister 18 – Kinsella returned with a volume of poetry called *The Pen Shop* which was published by Peppercanister in 1997. Then came *The Familiar* and *The Godhead* in 1999, and *Citizen of the World* and *Littlebody* in 2000. Kinsella was careful to distinguish Peppercanister from Dedalus, refusing to be included in Deane's anthology of Dedalus poets and taking exception to the *Times Literary Supplement* review of *Personal Places* and *Poems from Centre City* which attributed the volumes to the Dedalus Press.[39] This misunderstanding can be attributed to the fact that neither volume contains the usual colophon giving publication details, and indeed the previous volume, *One Fond Embrace,* states in its colophon that 'Peppercanister 13, One Fond Embrace, has been printed by the Carlow Nationalist and published by The Dedalus Press'.

These new Peppercanisters came out in library and trade editions, the former hardbound and the latter softbound in wrappers. *One Fond Embrace* had an edition of 100 hardbound (£10) and 500 paperback (£6). *Personal Places* and *Poems from Centre City* came out in 150 hardbound (£10) and 450 paperback copies (£5.95). *Madonna and Other Poems* lists a library edition of 200 copies (£10) and a trade edition of 400 (£5.95), as does *Open Court*. Peppercanisters 13, 14 and 15 omit details of the font used, but *Madonna and Other Poems* and *Open Court* were set in eleven-point Galliard type. *The Pen Shop* (1996) is set in eleven-point Palatino, but *The Familiar* and *Godhead* in twelve-point Times New Roman, as are *Citizen of the World* and *Littlebody.*

The Peppercanister editions printed by Dedalus are somewhat less adventurous in terms of style and design than those printed by Dolmen. However, they do retain Peppercanister's interest in the visual, at least in terms of cover imagery. *One Fond Embrace* displays an intriguing cover. Albrecht Dürer's etching of the Last Supper was redrawn by Brendan Foreman, in collaboration with Kinsella, omitting the figures of Jesus and John. In a letter to John F. Deane of Dedalus Press, Kinsella explains the image:

> The idea I had was of taking out Jesus entire, with John, from the picture, then filling in the lines of the table, the dark background, radiation, etc., so that it looked like an empty place at the table.[40]

Kinsella also thought of using an image of the crucified Christ from another of Dürer's etchings, with the head replaced by the number thirteen. *One Fond Embrace* is the thirteenth Peppercanister, and thirteen is the number of figures depicted on the cover. Thirteen is also the number of the dead remembered in the device used to illustrate the cover of *Butcher's Dozen,* and in his notes Kinsella makes an explicit link between both poems.[41]

The covers of *Personal Places* and *Poems from Centre City* are less complex, the former displaying a line drawing by Kinsella of a pair of lips in an enigmatic smile, the latter a profile of Dante Alighieri whose 'elderly down-tasting profile' features in the poem 'The Back Lane'.[42] Both editions sport an uneasy pattern of parallel lines, the former light brown, the latter light blue, that disrupt the integrity of the cover and minimise the impact of the line-drawn motifs. The covers of *Madonna and Other Poems* and *Open Court* are more successful, returning to the more reserved style associated with Dolmen-influenced Peppercanister. Picking up on the sky blue associated with the Madonna, Peppercanister 16 returns to Dürer for an image of a 'Woman with the Zodiac'.[43] She stands, supported by the trajectories of the planets, her arms reaching to enclose the heavenly spheres which are named by the signs of the zodiac. Her curling tresses are echoed by the flourish of the conifer branches and cones that guard each corner of the image, evoking both fecundity and endurance. In a similar style, and drawing also on Dürer's woodcuts, the cover of *Open Court* features an image of a man's head that was used in Dürer's time 'for the purpose of the study of phrenology'.[44] This image illustrates the now discredited science of phrenology which argued 'that the mental powers of the individual consist of separate faculties, each of which has its organ and location in a definite region of the surface of the brain' (OED). We might argue that in *Open Court* Kinsella gives us a phrenological examination of the state of poetry in Ireland in which the surface evidence does not always correlate with what is at work in the centre. Taking the cover of *Open Court* in tandem with the image on the cover of *Madonna,* we might remember the connection Ralph Waldo Emerson makes between astrology and phrenology: 'Astronomy to the selfish becomes astrology;...and anatomy and physiology become phrenology and palmistry.'[45]

The visual style of *The Pen Shop* is quite different. Here Kinsella chooses to focus on a photograph of the statue of Cúchulainn that stands in the General Post

Office of Dublin thereby situating an aspect of the Irish mythology that is fundamental to his poetry in a specifically political context and, through subject and situation, questioning the use of mythology for political purposes. Peppercanister 20, *The Familiar,* samples an image from Courtney Davis's *Celtic Ornament: Art of the Scribe* that is described there as one of 'various ornaments from the book of Kells' and also includes within the text a 'Portrait of Christ, centrepiece of a three panel triptych "Spirit of the Gael"'.[46] The cover image is placed against a plain pale grey background. Returning to his Jungian concerns in *Godhead* Kinsella chooses an image of a Celtic mandala by Klaus Holitzka. The sequence 'Godhead' comprises four poems – 'Trinity', 'Father', 'Son', and 'Spirit' – in which Kinsella situates the power of the poet within the larger force of the triune god. The cover of *Godhead,* placed on a deep buff background, combines the bearded face of the paternal god with an image of a snake which signals the carnality of the son.[47] Taking its cue from Oliver Goldsmith's *The Citizen of the World,* Kinsella's twenty-second Peppercanister of similar title displays an inverted image of Goldsmith on the cover, against a pale blue background. The image is taken from an engraving on the frontispiece of William P. Nimmo's edition of *The Works of Oliver Goldsmith.*[48] *Littlebody,* or *luchorpán* in Irish, is represented by what Kinsella describes as the image of a piper taken as a rubbing from a fifteenth- or sixteenth-century stone carving from Woodstock Castle[49] and is placed against a pale green background.

It is interesting that since 1978, with just two exceptions, Kinsella's Peppercanisters are issued in pairs. When asked whether this was as a result of the practicalities of publication or part of a working practice, Kinsella explained that he usually works on two volumes in tandem, letting one stand for a while, as he works on the other. And indeed when we compare these pairs of Peppercanisters we find that they often contain a contrasting approach, the one public, the other private, as in, for example, *Songs of the Psyche* which deals with the development of the self, and *Her Vertical Smile* which explores the responsibility of community. However, the Peppercanister editions are not simply a form of interim publishing. When we consider how Kinsella's writing constantly reincorporates fragments from earlier work and builds a structure that is open ended, allowing each Peppercanister book to comment upon the others, we must understand Kinsella's work coming from the Peppercanister Press as a form of the modern poetic sequence – a grouping of poems that contain lyric, narrative and dramatic elements – poems which are often self-analytical but that seek to understand the larger historical and social context. Most importantly we must understand the editions of the Peppercanister Press as an organic whole. In conversation with Denis O'Driscoll, Kinsella describes his writing as a totality that is never fixed. He compares the Peppercanister poems with his early writing, noting that:

> One of the things that has disappeared, by comparison with the early work,
> is the notion of a 'complete' poem, the idea that a poem can have a
> beginning, middle and end and be a satisfactory work of art thereby. The
> unity is a much bigger one than that. And it isn't a sequence, or a set of

connected long poems. It's a totality that is happening, with the individual poem a contribution to something accumulating.[50]

Kinsella's Peppercanister editions explore the issues and questions that have occupied Ireland for the most part of the twentieth century. He has looked to politics, to tradition, to history and perhaps most importantly, to the very personal, in order to write a poetry that never goes for the easy answer, or the easy rhythm. He pushes the reader as hard as he pushes himself. He brings the reader on journeys in which the processes of exploration and discovery are more important than the destination. And the very process of publication has been vital to Kinsella's project.

Chapter 10

A Poet's Journey Home: The Making of Michael Longley's *No Continuing City* (1969)

Ruth Ling

Published at the very outset of his career, *No Continuing City* establishes Michael Longley as a writer of volumes. While the graceful, often decorative forms of its poems have been appreciated, the overall design of this, Longley's first volume, has been overlooked. Yet it is such architectural care that anticipates much of his subsequent work. The thoroughly organic means by which Longley produced and then most definitively rearranged the material of *No Continuing City* (1969) for its inclusion in *Poems, 1963–1983*, looks forward, for instance, to the especially cohesive and self-referential quilt of each volume produced from *Gorse Fires* onwards.[1] Most convincingly too, it inaugurates a lifelong devotion to aesthetics through which Longley increasingly brings an almost physical, artefact-type feel to both poem and book. Such attention to a volume's making and subsequent remoulding holds promise too of the faith Longley is to invest ultimately in his 'papery house' – in the permanence of carefully-constructed artifice.

In comparison with his fellow poets from Ulster, Longley seems to have been slow to find his voice. Unusually for a young poet, however, he was quick to identify what would become one of the constant themes of his work – marital love. At the narrative level, *No Continuing City* follows a lover's progress from temporary lodgings to a lasting home. Yet as Edna Longley – the volume's dedicatee and first reviewer – realised, because marriage should 'augur the beginning rather than the end of self-discovery for a young man', this arrival can only ever be provisional.[2] As St Paul warns in the letter to the Hebrews that provided Longley with his title, an earthly 'continuing city' does not exist. 'The point about a title', Longley stated at the publication of his second volume, *An Exploded View*, 'is that it should reveal its relevance after a complete reading of a collection', and the deepest resonances of his first title are indeed felt when the poems are encountered in the order in which they finally stand in *Poems*.[3] By examining this version of the volume, this essay will demonstrate how ordering can highlight an already evident meaning. Both the difficulty of gaining the marital 'city' and its failure to prove 'continuing', is made much more explicit, I want to argue, through the revised arrangement. Ironically, such mimesis involved turning from an order that he thought respected his themes 'back to their original sequence of composition' as he reported in a poetry reading.[4] His exception to this rule – his withholding from this chronology what might be termed the 'arrival' poems from 1963–64, the first year of his marriage – further facilitates this plan. Laid out at regular intervals across the first half of the volume, 'Epithalamion',

'Odyssey', 'No Continuing City' and 'The Hebrides' now more obviously function as intermediary goals and harbours on the way home. Conversely, each 'nostalgic scheme' of these domestic arrivals is undermined by the struggle and conflict of the intervening 'journey'. This journey is undertaken in part, by several of the 'good uncompromising knobbly little poems' that comprise *Secret Marriages*, the formative pamphlet Longley published in 1968.[5] Sacrificing the particularly homogenised unit achieved by the chapbook's pairings of these poems, their scattering through the pages of *No Continuing City* brokers instead the volume's more necessary 'gradual' marriage.

Marriage, however, is only the means by which the volume comes home in its true sense. *No Continuing City* self-consciously charts the voyage of a young poet towards his first creative domain. The ardent complaint this volume's title makes against there being *No Continuing City*, originates not merely in the mouth of a prematurely grieving husband, but in that of an artist who is by definition, continuously adrift amidst the waters of creativity. An early occurrence of the phrase 'No continuing city' beside the draft line 'And my sandals of spindrift and flotsam' would seem to verify this.[6] Again, looking forward to the growth of an entire œuvre, this first creative, essentially Odyssean, voyage anticipates the way *Gorse Fires* decorates the path back to speech after long silence.

Longley's work always reflects on the nature of its own enterprise. Yet, what particularly distinguishes *No Continuing City* is that the very trajectory of what are already highly self-referential poems, should discuss its own making and validity. First, placing the poems mainly in the order in which they were written provides a literal portrait of the aspiring poet. Then, just as the mainland shore offers respite from the lover's intrepid island-adventuring, each of the major 'arrival' poems becomes a steady harbour around which new tentative material can flow. Each a stage in the 'marriage' between life and art, 'Epithalamion', 'Odyssey', 'No Continuing City' and 'The Hebrides' serve as an anchor or depth charge in the volume's quest to poetically deserve each personal 'berth'. The means by which the first half of *No Continuing City* explores the poetic vocation aligns itself therefore along the contours of Auden's Romantic version of the sea's iconography. Just as it dramatises 'a necessary evil, a crossing of that which separates or estranges', *No Continuing City* is simultaneously 'visited by desperate longings for home and company'.[7] The ebb and flow between the four particularly expansive 'arrival' poems and the shorter 'journey' ones in between – magnifying their sway of alternating long and short lines – enacts the poet's traumatic odyssey. Considering just *how* tortuous this odyssey, the report one of the *Secret Marriages* poems makes on its own progress – 'We drew together by easy stages' – becomes then highly ironic. Indeed, representing for Longley 'something of a caretaker form' with their 'temporary address between more permanent lodgings', these poems' rhyming couplets continue the struggle of the volume to come poetically home.[8] In both its structural reticence and thoroughness, the volume might even be seen to do so in a particularly Northern Protestant way.

As opposed to presenting the autobiographical material of love blossoming into marriage in any predictable manner, the volume's new patterning provides a myriad of perspectives through which, as Edna Longley comments, the poet more than ever 'never repeats himself'.[9] *No Continuing City* not only appreciates then the importance, as Longley termed it, of 'looking after the words' so that such 'themes look after themselves'; its meticulous construction immediately makes good his apprehension that it is by attending to these themes that 'you become a writer'.[10] Eel-like in the immense distances it travels in order to reach its mate, the convoluted course of this volume's 'wide Sargasso' considerably deepens what might otherwise have proved a rather predictable story. What Rainer Maria Rilke recommends as a mining of 'inner' as opposed to merely 'outer' experience, is especially reflected in the new design of the volume.[11] The psychological and poetic growth enshrined in this trajectory constitutes a particularly rigorous response to what Stephen Regan characterises as the Movement's 'shallow denial of human potential for change and development'.[12] Rather than merely proceed 'on words *from* experience', this first work of a young man to whom little had yet happened as Longley admits, succeeds, through its well-plotted progress, in travelling 'on words to experience'.[13] Structure and ordering can release, as much as obey subject matter.

The themes of love and marriage are merely the blocks with which *No Continuing City* rebuilds the crumbling mortal city as the potentially more durable house of poetry. Longley's juvenilia sequence of 'Domestic Sonnets' lays down one floor of this edifice.[14] Already detecting the struggle ahead, this sequence parallels the aspirations of emotional development by undergoing formal destabilisation; each poem is continually interrupted by the next. Most notably, one sonnet's aspiring conclusion on the word 'home' – enacting the 'actual stopping place' suggested by *stanza* – is itself truncated. Through its analogous dispensing with each anterior poem – the 'bed and breakfast' of the title poem stays – the first half of *No Continuing City* becomes engaged, like John Clare in 'Journey out of Essex', in continuously 'unpicking' its own 'whereabouts' (*Poems*, 56). To come home poetically incurs just as much loss as emotionally coming of age. Yet it is due precisely to this perpetual state of wandering, that the volume so thoroughly earns its first potentially lasting 'arrival' as represented by 'The Hebrides', which, in the new arrangement, changes places with the title poem, 'No Continuing City'. Because the experience of being 'lost' leads in an especially Protestant way to being 'found', losing its 'way at last, / So far from home' becomes cause for celebration here rather than for lament. Having completed both the personal and the artistic journey, *No Continuing City* can then go on to undertake the more literal ones of 'Leaving Inishmore', 'Homage to Dr Johnson' and 'Journey out of Essex'. Such expeditions are more easily accommodated by the more formally stable and more explicitly elegiac second half of the volume.

Setting out to emulate Sextus Propertius, who 'expresses himself with love poetry' rather than merely to write 'about love' like Catullus, Longley certainly aimed to make autobiography as impersonal as possible.[15] Through his extensive reworkings of his earliest poems – mere 'raw material' for his own long-term 'vision'[16] – Longley manages, however, to retain his big themes without making them simultaneously 'shout from the page' as he found other domestic poetry of the fifties to do. 'As a reaction to the rationality of the 50s many poets are now writing from the psychiatrist's couch, as it were', Longley observed of his own generation. 'Theirs', he believed 'is a poetry of confession in which one wears one's neuroses on one's sleeve confident that everyone will be interested.'[17] Crude in comparison with how the 'Domestic Sonnets' were transformed into barometers of poetic growth, 'Old House', for instance, has Peter Redgrove – one target of Longley's criticism – suffering rather mawkishly 'in an agony of imagination as the wind / Limped up the stairs and puffed on the landings'. Longley rejects such 'exaggerated autobiography', which he further identifies in the work of Lowell, Sexton, Plath and Scannell, as literal 'deceit or just disguises'. His contrasting efforts to make art 'close to' rather than 'true to' life, heeds Yeats's advice that poets should become 'good liars'.[18] 'These Devious Shores' – Longley's title for a mock-up pamphlet of 'Poems and Translations' – reminds us how the surreptitious ebb and flow that exists between each poem and its vehicle in *No Continuing City* contributes to successful art.[19]

Longley's juvenilia divined much more, however, than the importance of compositional canniness. It established the constant need for industry. Making rich use of the cliché of rebuilding a marriage – of putting 'a roof over our heads', as one draft line puts it – 'At Home', for instance, pledges to spend a lifetime reconstructing 'the floors and ceilings' and 'friendly walls' should the married pair find themselves 'untenanted and homeless'.[20] This early promise to keep building recognises that the 'councils of continuity are unceasing' (as Gaston Bachelard formulates in a philosophical study that especially fits the overarching project of Longley's œuvre). Without this plan, Bachelard continues, 'man would be a dispersed being. It maintains him through the storms of the heavens and through those of life.'[21] The vow of 'At Home' to recognise in marital 'collapse / Material enough to use again', anticipates the arduous programme of revisions, incisions, and drafts Longley required to set his first volume's 'house in order'. His 'bed and board in ruins', he carefully attends, however, to 'emblems / Of survival, regalia of decay' by producing lyrics such as 'Gathering Mushrooms'.[22] Such patterns of loss and retrieval make *No Continuing City* especially Orphic in impetus, for like the lyricist of Longley's early unpublished version of this story, the volume 'Wanders where memory charms / The bones of the past in an endless tide, / To recover...'[23]

Long before his poetics go on to quilt the 'world's sunny side' in *The Weather in Japan*, this 'endless tide' of Longley's first volume is stitched together from old material. The metaphor with which he negotiates his father's death in the elegy 'In Memoriam' derives from this very poem for instance, where Euridice, the 'recreated bride', can 'materialise / On the verge of light and happy legend'. Again, because the title poem opens with the line that concludes 'At Home' – one of the 'Domestic sonnets' – Longley not only reinforces the sense of *in medias res* that fuels its creative impulse, but verifies the volume's deliberate, if intrepid tactics of delay: 'My hands here, gentle, where your breasts begin'. With such a staggered presentation of parsimoniously recycled 'material', the volume more literally constructs, moreover, not merely a poetic house but an entire 'avenue of houses'. Certainly, as the volume's coda verifies, the 'ghosts' of poems still gathering around the volume's 'hearth' are just as crucial to this avenue as its permanent buildings. They too, as 'Birthmarks' declares, can be 'Icon / And lares of the poet's soul'. This poem's renaming – from 'To Derek Mahon' – and repositioning as the final poem, privileges the weaning of the poet as the volume's ultimate theme. As his own archivist, Longley insists that there are utterly no 'barren increments' in the mining of an œuvre – there is no 'false dawn' of a poem. Just as Longley will go on to encounter his own dead relatives and poetic forebears, the volume makes good this claim by continually arranging and re-encountering anterior poetic 'incorrigibles' along its avenue.

However temporary and makeshift, the architectural discoveries of the 'Domestic Sonnets' provide much of the figurative and metaphorical scaffolding of No Continuing City. The most palpable signs of 'remnant yet part raiment still' of the juvenilia recur in the defensive construction of the 'corridors', 'walls', 'vicinity', and 'vestibule' of 'Epithalamion' – the marriage song that opens the volume (Poems, 7–19). Because it will go on to provide the cornerstone of an entire œuvre, the origins of the 'marriage bed and coffin' exchange initiated with this poem are also particularly important. For Longley 'most poems' are 'love poems', but because as he reasons, no occasion is complete until it is written about, they also become 'elegies as well'.[24] Reminiscent of how the young Yeats ironically opened his œuvre by lamenting the passing of time through myth – that of Oisin, a version of which Longley also worked on incidentally in the 1960s[25] – Longley's own first collected poem is also darkened by a specific source – the 'Cornelia' elegy of Propertius. In fact, Longley originally intended to include a shortened version – 'The House-wife's Testament' – of this final Propertius elegy in No Continuing City.[26] Much more organically however, rather as the pieces of Cornelia's furniture are 'infinite [in] their appetite for hurt', the entire poetic household of the volume's first half becomes 'littered' instead with Propertian hints of mortality. Descendants of the moths that were 'glutted' on Cornelia's 'tapestries' nibble away most noticeably for instance at the opening poem's diction. Vocabulary was the facet of poetry Propertius immediately taught Longley to privilege, and while the adjectives and verbs depicting the new lovers' world are 'all dark the element', they are simultaneously bathed in a visionary light.[27] This dichotomy resounds most clearly from the poem's rhymes – 'fatal appetite'/'window catches light'; 'frantic stars'/'folded flower', and 'stars ignite'/'dwindling by a night'. Then, the transformative potential Longley discovered in the language of Propertius's elegies, whereby the words are 'not merely doing, but [are] becoming something', is achieved in 'Epithalamion' through an extensive use of binaries: 'silently/silent...all/All...because/because...dark/dark... fills/full.'[28] The final few stanzas' identical rhymes – 'dissolved/ revolved/involved' – and the slight but notable phonological shift from 'remnant' to 'raiment' at the last moment, manages both to delay and at the same time, secure such change.

Assessing some of the early work Longley was sending him in Canada, Derek Mahon warned of the drawbacks of recollecting dramatic conflict from a secure perspective, and Longley's own admission of an initial tendency to write 'in a blind sort of way' finds its way into 'This Room' of the 'Domestic Sonnets'.[29] The speaker admits that the personal 'arrival' each sonnet celebrates may not yet have been poetically merited:

> ...I regret that I have journeyed through
>
> No distance sufficient nor alarms
> To match my rich arrival in your arms.[30]

And yet even as he laments,

> with such an intimate address
> I now deplore how happily from you
> I lay apart and you from me...

the speaker stumbles upon the discord needed for the shaping of poetry. The dichotomy between proximity and distance here already affects an unprecedented separation of sestet into quatrain and couplet. The analogous 'delays', 'distances' and 'impediments' similarly incurring a 'Lack of speed' in the brief opening suspension of 'The Journey' – another of the 'Domestic Sonnets' – further shape Longley's forms. This summative, yet at the same time, temporary 'unarranged / And infinite arrest' the young husband meets in marriage finds its most full technical expression in 'Epithalamion'. Just as Longley had hoped that 'a kind of poisonous, enervating, love-killing uncertainty' would find relief through marriage, for one moment, the heavy mortal 'pandemonium, its freight' of the poem's long ongoing syntactical 'train' of stanzas appears to find resolution.[31] A complete coincidence between period and stanza manages to place love at the very centre of the poem:

> I hold you close because
> We have decided dark will be
> For ever like this and because,
>   My love, already
> The dark is growing elderly.

Such stillness momentarily mirrors the endstopped stanzas of Louis MacNeice's 'Trilogy for X' where individual identity is successfully preserved behind his 'door for ever / Closed on the world, its own world closed within it'.[32] Longley will similarly need to close an 'open door' in *Man Lying on a Wall* when external pressures threaten creativity – a state dictating the deliberately more disordered structure of the volume. Yet here the acute awareness of mortality that marriage has immediately, and almost involuntarily, induced, forces disintegration back into the frame. *Thalamos* (bridal chamber) must make room for *thanatos* (death). The double tow of caesura and enjambment, and the 'attractive arrangement of varying line lengths' Longley inherited from George Herbert, brings the lovers together, and at the same time, crucially, keeps them apart.[33] The fragile state 'where we, the only two, it seems, / Inhabit so delightfully / A room' is barely held in place. The instruction for the strain enacted through such tortuous syntactical inversion – an early hallmark of Longley's work – came from the poetic rhythm of Yeats, who, along with Herbert, Longley considered to be the greatest 'stanzaic and metrical artist in English'. Regretting 'the decline of the subordinate clause', Longley deliberately set about reversing the tendency of contemporary verse to depend 'on an artificially tight-lipped utterance, on terseness rather than tension. Sentences are not encouraged to travel very far.'[34] Representing his sudden realisation that love ineluctably brings knowledge of 'Pure Death' – as Robert Graves entitles a poem subsequently important to Longley – calls for stanzaic shapes and rhythms where conversely, the 'grammatical unit, the sentence, and the metrical unit' are put into conflict. Just as trimeter pulls against tetrameter within the poem's stanzaic tides, the concentrated marriage room of each intricately rhymed stanza fights therefore to maintain itself within the larger surrounding expanse of the poem. Such unresolved tension between syntax and stanza, and between stanza and long sentence, extends ultimately to the safe positioning of homecoming poems within the twisting and turning trajectory of the volume at large. And as a broadening of the 'contrived' look Longley conceded of this, his first collected poem, *No Continuing City* in its entirety far outstrips the blandness he associated with Movement poets.[35]

Notwithstanding the intimacy of its direct address, 'Epithalamion' seems to have yielded to something Longley disapproved of in contemporary verse – a slight 'dissociation of sensibility' from his original passion.[36] While far from invoking the 'neutral tone' Longley so disliked in Movement poets, such detachment is largely due to the diction of predominantly masculine rhymes which, if not quite 'irrelevant' as one unidentified publisher deemed them, tend towards the flat and unmusical.[37] Some dramatic urgency – 'A proper change of heart' – is immediately introduced into the volume, however, with its next poem, 'A Questionnaire for Walter Mitty' (*Poems*, 20). Besides the 'vocabulary and mythology' and the 'sincerity' as reflected, for instance, in the quiet and fearful grace of that still central stanza of 'Epithalamion', Longley had singled out 'drama' as one of the qualities that drew him to Propertius.[38] The striking change of pace and tone secured by 'A Questionnaire' does several things. Firstly, it immediately exhibits the Audenesque 'curiosity, resourcefulness and protean involvement with life' Longley found to be especially rare in contemporary poetry.[39] Then, because Longley's immediate search for 'new' more continuing 'properties' interrupts the insular, almost sacred, mood of 'Epithalamion', it enacts the threat undergone by the marital home. Yet, such new adventures are required to earn the next poetic homecoming, and particularly one that is entitled 'Odyssey'. Certainly, these adventures, which, in a first equation between the feminine archetype and the muse, are figured as discarded 'bodies' comprising the long way home, are required by the volume's quest to merge life and art.

The volume's progress towards its 'devious shores' is measured through the 'deceit or just disguise' of this series of poems that boldly uses fantastical, offbeat artists. As a metaphor, it is apt that disguise should be so ubiquitous in a volume so intent on concealing its own artifice. Indeed, it is due to so thorough and wide an application of its metaphors that the volume manages to be so 'imaginatively' rather than merely personally profound.[40] Transcending what Longley considered the all-too-frequent and uneconomical use Movement poets made of similes, Longley first makes his metaphors travel the entire length of the poem. For instance, his thorough treatment of the practice of taxidermy in 'The Ornithological Section', manages to blur any distinctions between the elegist, his elegy and its subject. Yet it is more appreciably because he makes his metaphors stretch over the entire length of his volume that *No Continuing City* more definitively establishes 'a wide imaginative state'. For all its light-heartedness and 'change of colour', the form of 'A Questionnaire for Walter Mitty' – the *terza rima* Dante famously used to chart *his* 'voyages to legend' amidst the shades – suggests that it is still epiphany, artistic if not now personal, that the volume seeks.

The relationship between an artist's life and work considered here – 'At which side of the glass does Mitty stand' – is examined further in 'Graffiti' (*Poems*, 21). This next poem's placing of the artist outside the very dwellings his work creates, makes one of the personal capsizes necessary to the volume's artistic homecoming. Grieving that the artist cannot share in his own creative 'metamorphosis', 'Graffiti' anticipates therefore, Longley's later, more direct lamenting of the fruit of his own productive 'fifties' – the 'bouquet' of elegiac 'flowers without leaves' he depicts in 'The Blackthorn', a lyric from *The Weather in Japan*. Predicting the extent of his subsequent ability to create out of loss, the poet already registers the lifelong burden of the artist for whom when 'such passion [is] thwarted', only then is 'such artistry released!' Nonetheless, in what will become a linguistic paradox central to Longley's work, 'Graffiti' wraps its subject in 'paper palaces' in order to mitigate decay. Again, despite its deceptively light-hearted approach, the poem's references to *The Tempest* and to fairy tale imagery reminiscent of *The Winter's Tale*, stress that Longley already aims for nothing less than the reversal of tragedy and death. The volume's new ordering charts the progress of an art that might do so. In addition to renovating the final image of the flags that linger at half mast at the close of 'Epithalamion', the disappearing 'queen' has now been transformed into a fairy tale 'princess' who takes up more permanent residence in Longley's first papery 'city'. Yet despite the onward force of Longley's syntax spinning around a meticulously positioned 'she', the simultaneous 'wintering' of this princess comes close to reproducing the freeze-frames and embalming stasis induced by Thomas Kinsella, for instance, in his parallel attempts to preserve love in *Wormwood*. The decorative arrangement of the poems of *No Continuing City* recognises, conversely, however, that movement and change, are needed to 'imply a sort of spring' for love.

The self-reflexive lessons of 'A Questionnaire' and 'Graffiti' would appear to have paid off since the volume is now ready to enter its first real dwelling by means of the papery house of 'Emily Dickinson' (*Poems*, 22). Certainly, the positioning of this little 'gradual' of a poem with its antiphonal structure of two binding, yet dividing stanzas, signals the first significant, if 'gradual', step bringing the poet into his proper dwelling. Yet despite being much more empty and airy than the dense stanzas of the intervening poems, the lexical exchanges of the two sestets sense that, despite their distillation from the three of the 1969 version, there may still have been inadequate 'perfect progress through / Such cluttered rooms to eloquence, delight'. The unequivocal 'rich arrival' of that early 'domestic sonnet' has not yet perhaps been poetically matched. Certainly, a newly-concentrated diction, characterised by verbal paradox, exhibits the strain an as-yet unbridged gap between life and art still exerts on the poet. Dickinson's counterfeit 'dressing with care for the act of poetry' might be artistically productive, yet, in the absence of any equivalent 'act of love', it begins to look hollow. Again, the creative 'light' rhymes expressing the 'delight' of 'writing' vie hopelessly with the heavily consonantal 'house in Amherst Massachusetts' full of 'dust' and 'rust'. In addition to the poem falling two lines short of the sonnet form that had previously encapsulated unity, its binary strategy continues to keep art and home apart. Its culmination in a pair of self-reflexive similes makes poetry 'gradual as flowers', but life still, 'gradual as rust'.

The ongoing strain of the quest for a more balanced world is again registered in the stylistics of 'Camouflage', the poem that follows in the new ordering (*Poems*, 23). Here, the perfect paradigm between home and artistic sleight of hand, the parenthesis '(Amid the sanctuary of camouflage)' suggests, is merely provisional. Initially, the mirroring artifice of repetition – 'itself reflected, its streams reflecting these' – *appears* to accrue real mimesis: Longley's continued search for 'the proper cloth' *appears* to have 'so deftly' transformed 'habit . . . to habitat'. Yet the suspensions and syntactical tricks executed over the last two stanzas considerably destabilise any such exchange until ultimately, such syntactical delay connotes an art that is still a long way from fully negotiating its 'change of colour, a risk taken'. Stalling him further is the discovery made by 'The Ornithological Section' that now follows – that the preservative quality of art is nothing other than artifice. It is only some desperate 'great need of ours' that produces such 'unnatural treasury'. Indeed this poem's still ornate and highly artificial stanzaic scheme seems to suggest that the envisaged exchange of an ornithologist's art of naming for an elegising 'taxidermist', might itself be a little too glib. Certainly, the poem's diction draws attention to how artificial its qualities of transcendence are. The cumulative effect of unswerving near rhymes ('feats/feasts), doublings (without/without; have/have; so/so; toward/toward), and endstopped stanzas enclosing the birds in their glass houses, seems aware of its own inadequate artistic 'momentum'. Yet for all that it is conscious of failing to deliver, this poem does manage to envisage a lyric art somewhere further down the line – one produced by instinct rather than by intellect, 'where science ends and love begins'. 'Camouflage', as a subsequent 'journey' poem is called, must prove a great deal less formulaic than an art that uses mere 'white for weddings, black for funerals'.

In addition to returning to the force that instigated the poetic homecoming in the first place, the 'love' lingering at the very close of 'An Ornithological Section' also highlights the Orphic means by which poetry is continually brought 'into land' in this volume. It is completely fitting that elegy, as the product of such self-reflexive and summative of artistic processes, should become Longley's most prevalent form and mode.

Longley suspects, however, that while elegy sums up our histories, it might also replicate 'our long delays' as we 'hesitate' through life. That poetry both 'preserves *and* perpetuates' is reflected in the volume's structuring frisson between stasis and movement.[41] The bird capable of migrating 'to his best intent' above 'our broken homes' in an early draft poem, 'St Francis to the Birds', prefigures this structural sway between centripetal and centrifugal direction. Because they can both maintain nests and migrate, birds become particularly fitting exemplars of the lyric poet whose work must resist, being solely 'placed on a rock' and 'closed' like 'the chestnut in its purse' (as the new layout of *No Continuing City* so successfully does). Descending from one such 'inextinguishable bird', 'The Osprey' – the next poem in both versions of the volume – becomes a particularly 'suitable emblem for the poet' (*Poems*, 26). Two lexical shifts – 'he *lives*...his unamphibious two *lives*', and '*waters water*log' (my emphasis) – constitute Longley's next step towards regaining the double shore of love and art 'without compromise'. As he subtly distinguishes elsewhere, a 'minor' talent remains all 'at sea', while a major one has 'to fight continually against becoming waterlogged'. The very phonology of 'The Osprey' seems to depict this struggle when the comparative music of its assonantal middle stanza is complicated by the syntactical and consonantally effortful third to make sure 'No lake's waters waterlog' the poet. Fulfilling the prediction that any grief withstood in the wedding chamber would end up 'fracturing syntax and undoing rhyme', two crucial relaxations to this tension manage however, to tilt the volume towards the air-bound habitat of lyric.[42] While the volume's habitually entwined syntax settles into a more lyrical ellipsis and statement, its more typical true rhyme resolutely turns towards half rhyme – 'removes/lives...whom/him'. Heralding such arrival, the poem's opening suspension repudiates too, the self-consciousness that characterises previous poems: the art of poetry should leave few traces of its 'talents'. Any wielding of the 'Webbed feet' of metre, or of the various 'oils' of linguistic devices should, the poem's self-reflexive codes suggest, be invisible. As the manifesto of 'A personal statement' declares immediately afterwards – albeit somewhat ironically given its formal weightiness – the poem's vehicle should 'sail body cargoless towards surprise'.

Gaston Bachelard suggests that ultimately the house should constitute no less than 'body and soul'.[43] Certainly, the 'chamber' and 'narrow neighbourhood' of each stanza of 'A Personal Statement' erects a site wherein experience might itself be interiorised and therefore somehow transformed (*Poems*, 27). It does so through its linguistic strategies of elaborate punning, metaphysical paradox and witty collocations. The extreme difficulty of trying to earn its own 'way back' / To fire, air, water, earth' though, is mirrored by an appropriately slower Latinate syntax than the volume has previously used. Yet crucially, the volume appreciates how the young poet must progress in his own time, no matter how slow and 'uncorrected by the sun even', as 'Circe' teaches him. The extreme artificiality of the means through which this highly metaphysical poem strives towards lyric waters enacts this delay. Unfortunately, however, such delay may not be entirely deliberate. In contrast to Longley's lyrics where ideas emerge 'naturally out of the poetry', 'A Dialogue' tends, as R. S. Thomas says of the George Herbert templates upon which it is modelled, to make form 'subordinate to an idea'.[44] Compared with 'Narcissus', say, where the application of myth fully disguises, deepens and animates a draft lyric about the artist – in this case, J. S. Bach – such direct discussion as 'A Dialogue' makes of the poet's tactics proves almost too unwieldy for its vehicle.

Such failure is reflected in a throwaway remark of 'Odyssey', the next poem in the new arrangement (*Poems*, 30–1). *No Continuing City* has indeed '(been out of touch)' with experience, the use of parenthesis again emphasising how still unnatural and forced the artifice. Yet the new 'easy-going...through going steady' rhythm of 'Odyssey' where more frequent breathing spaces punctuate a still comparatively tortured, inversion-rich syntax, suggests that the 'adulterous' experimentation upon the waters of creativity *has* been formative. Accordingly, the pace of the volume now begins to quicken. Indeed, the original published title of 'Odyssey', 'En Route', underlines how the still restless trajectory of the volume is equally engaged in seeking beginning as much as resolution. While it acknowledges the value of an art of the quotidian that has kept it 'going, despite delays' – echoing Blake for whom 'practice is art. If you leave off you are lost' – the volume's structure implies that there will always be a 'long way home' to go.[45]

'Circe' then marks further progress towards the paradoxically liberating conditions of a 'widowing calm' (*Poems*, 32). Unsurprisingly, this allegory of the poetic craft grew from a portrait of the artist. Indeed, Longley's titles for some of the first versions of these Odyssean poems – 'The Beachcomber', and 'All my own work' – belie subsequent efforts to disguise their self-reflexive origins. 'The Flying Fish, – the formative working poem for 'Circe' – reaches a realm between sea and air – a lyric halfway house where the known and the unknown might meet. As a young poet, Longley quickly seems to have profited from the long journey MacNeice underwent in his 'middle stretch'. Through his own 'Hankering roaming un-homing up-anchoring' from security, Longley is prepared much earlier than his master to have neither 'floor nor ceiling'. Much more quickly than MacNeice, he reaches the place where 'Sea met sky.'[46] While it has not yet become the more spiritual shelter of *Gorse Fires*, 'The Flying Fish' establishes a shoreline cove between the physical and the metaphysical as Longley's new place of writing. Again, the poem's linear decoration matches the duality of this papery realm:

> The flying fish whose total world this is
>   – The sea shore, the depths, their decoration –
> Has slipped the tides' pull and for all its size
>   Disowned the shallows, such comfortable margins.[47]

One very tangible way in which Longley links the everyday and the extraordinary in the final poems, is through placing modified clichés in the mouths of their mythological characters. Above all other contemporary books of poetry, Longley cherished *The Less Deceived,* and while its author Philip Larkin would presumably not have approved the use *No Continuing City* makes of the 'properties or personae from older poems', he would certainly have applauded its ironic use of everyday idioms.[48] As Douglas Dunn recognises, '[t]he poems of *No Continuing City* are beautifully poised in a language just on the colloquial side of vernacular'.[49] Learning too from MacNeice's later poetry which, Longley apprehends, 'not only relishes idioms and clichés but probes their hidden codes', the ambitious young poet now begins to mine each proverbial phrase for lessons of a creative sort.[50] Circe's words – 'I stand uncorrected...bad and good weather...spring and neap tides of their life' – become watchwords of the poet's growth. So for all that they might seem overburdened here by a plethora of adjectives, and by a less than expertly-controlled syntax, such fresh new poetics as 'Circe' initiates continue to keep the artist and his book 'afloat'.

The apparent construction of 'Nausicaa' – the volume's next poem – from disparate draft lines and statements confirms Longley's art as being one of accumulation rather than of mere revision (*Poems*, 33). While the title of one of its drafts, 'Sea-Changes', continues, like 'Circe' to 'extend the sea, its idioms', the poem again suggests how gradual has been any overcoming of linguistic hurdles: 'Her *partial* sea-change *partly* changes him' (my italics). As a vehicle that might suggest as much, the couplets manage to enclose the hero and crucially, continue to keep him free. Enacting 'love at first sight', which Longley identifies in a reading as the literal subject of 'Nausicaa', again the frequent endstops within such a short airy poem achieve security within the wider conditions of freedom. Such duality continues to vacillate between safety and adventure: the tension in each pair of distichs, deriving from what Propertius, he tells us, calls the 'strange light falling between two individuals', combines cohesion and containment on the one hand, and emptiness and disjointedness on the other.[51] Love and the muse at last indistinguishable, the poem's last couplet describes a lyric that is both accomplished and yet still full of potential for further development: 'All evidence of dry land he relearns. / The ocean gathers where your shoulder turns.'

Longley goes on from his reading of Propertius to formulate how in 'high poetry the words love each other', and however tentatively, arrival at his title poem, 'No Continuing City', indicates how Longley's creative hands are now ready to quite literally 'love' their subject (*Poems*, 34–5).[52] Like many of his most haunting phrases, its almost tactile opening, 'My hands here, gentle, where your breasts begin', had, as we have seen, long been preoccupying his mind. Longley has remarked that the 'last two lines' of MacNeice's 'Mayfly', from which his metaphor grows, 'say it all' on the evanescence of earthly life which 'the emotional intensity of falling in love' instils, and certainly, the elegiac tone underlying these lines – 'But when this summer is over let us die together, / I want always to be near your breasts' – infects all of Longley's subsequent love poetry.[53] Apart from the intervening objectivity of the volume's

Homeric masks, this explicitly self-conscious metaphor of creativity owes a debt to several other sources. Several lines from two formative draft poems contribute, for instance, to this marking of the formative steps love and poetry have now taken toward each other. Firstly, a short lyric that takes 'shape beneath his hand like a breast' brings Bach's masterpieces back to light from the 'dusty windows' of domesticity.[54] Then, deciding that 'Some of the best poems are like women…when they stand or walk, fold their arms / To cover up their breasts which are tiny', 'Comparison' initiates his lifelong equation of poetry with prayerful protection – a protection particularly characterising the poet's own care of his actual building materials.[55]

Longley's crucial attempt in 'No Continuing City' to record the past that continues to 'linger still in Photostat' in poetry, holds echoes of Larkin's memories in 'Lines on a Young Lady's Photograph Album' from *The Less Deceived*. Yet however much he too seeks mimesis, Longley is equally wary of the deadening potential of Larkin's ability to make his lover 'lie / Unvariably lovely there.'[56] Again, Longley's language of renovation – 'Ripping the billboard of my mind' – originates in his compositional processes, in this case in the perennial spring cleaning of his juvenilia. It is because the volume has been formed from draft material that it is able to declare with another of Larkin's poems, 'Such attics cleared of me! Such absences!' As a result of this continual process, the poetic 'sea' of *No Continuing City* is kept 'tirelessly at play'.[57] Acknowledging the heavy losses incurred in the making of a poet, 'absences', the final nihilist word of this Larkin poem of the same name, is echoed in Longley's apprehension that a subject will continually eat a poet 'out of house and home'. Yet because the volume has gradually explored how much an artist must resist, as much as aim, for home, it seems ready to pay the price. 'Odysseus to the Sirens' – an unpublished poem closer both in form and content to Tennyson's 'Ulysses' than 'Odyssey' itself – had already detected distinct menace in the music of home:

> No more distressing scene can you devise
> Than Ithaca, the land for which I lust
> Against which here and now I grip the spear.[58]

Already merging love and art through metaphor, the lover's dread of kissing his love only to find 'her mouth closed', harbours the dread of poetic silence. Again the poet has to resist 'wifely hands that shut' his creative 'eyes'. This overriding suspicion that domestic homecoming might be as disabling for the imagination as it might be for the perennial wanderer, makes Longley opt for a particularly fluctuating arrangement in the volume – one that might continually militate against arrival. Yet deploying a growing metaphysical wit to make the 'last girl' of the drafts both guest and host for the final version of 'No Continuing City', the aspiring poet now sees how the 'last rooms' of poetry circumnavigated through 'Circe' might actually 'last'.

Maintaining the volume's particularly MacNeicean intimations of mortality, another crucial phrase from 'Mayfly' – 'But when this summer is over' – which finds its way into 'No Continuing City', further dictates the plans for the volume's building programme. As a wintry system of enclosures, poetry will counteract to some extent, this 'summer country' – the phrase that gave one draft of the poem its title.[59] Quoting Paul Eluard, Bachelard concurs, 'doesn't winter add to the poetry of a house',[60] and like the narrator of one of Longley's radio broadcasts who revels in the cold months when 'a bird will ruffle its feathers to keep itself warm and the squirrel turns to homemaking', Longley's early work fully realises the creative potential of winter.[61] Moreover, as a draft line of 'Leaving Inishmore' makes clear, this wintry landscape firmly originates in our 'frozen country' – the Northern climes in which the poet lives. Yet Longley also discerns that attempts to stay mortality through dormant natural imagery can in turn immobilise the muse. This is apparent from the direct address the volume now makes to 'Persephone', the erstwhile underground goddess who had, in an early draft, appeared to have signed the 'death warrant' of poetry:

> Not many months ago,
> In winter time,
> Our footsteps burrowed silence from the snow,
> My poetry run underground,
> Rhythm and rhyme
> For good, it seemed, ice-bound
> ...Writing for all I was worth
> As antidote.[62]

Such periodically-voiced concerns about the unsettling, even contractive effect mourning might have on his love will eventually reach a crisis point by *The Ghost Orchid*. Here, any sort of 'Form' whatsoever, the poem of that name suggests, deeply disturbs both life and art: 'Trying to tell it all to you and cover everything...Mislays the hare and the warmth it leaves behind.' Yet by expanding the 'big indoors' landscape of *No Continuing City* through contrastingly fluid and enlightening paradoxes, 'Persephone' manages, on the other hand, to successfully reverse the longed-for 'freeze-up' and its merely 'catastrophic short-lived reform'.

As its numerous drafts might indicate, 'Persephone' becomes one of Longley's most formative lyrics, going so far as to generate the two-step snowbound shapes of some of the elegies in *The Weather in Japan* (*Poems*, 36). While on the one hand, it obviously initiates a lifelong progress whereby Longley lays his elegiac footsteps 'Into the reluctant soil / And with the legendary dead' – beginning with his father and his literary forebears, Edward Thomas and Dr Johnson – 'Persephone' is still careful to remain essentially above ground. Although Longley is all the time coming closer to the 'exploded view' of life and death that will give its name to his next volume, the young poet is not yet ready – as his drafts substantiate – to 'put the world out' of his head. With its pared-down distichs, 'Man Friday' finally takes *No Continuing City* out to meet the liminal spaces of the 'furthest strand' – most powerfully in its first positioning on the very threshold of the original volume. Instead 'Persephone' works for an art dually capable of 'Finding leisure for fiction, room for grief.' Longley's comment that this lyric encapsulates 'the state of being in two minds' builds upon another draft reference to the poet's 'mind divided' between elegy and celebration, and the experience – as also recorded in its drafts – of lying agonisingly 'awake...learning to imagine/the time between snow and last leaf' devises its figurative world.[63] While winter ransacks life, it conversely releases the creative forces – a dichotomy encapsulated in Longley's first concrete adoption of part rhymes: 'numbskulled'/ 'skilled'...'winter leaf'/'aloof'. Warm-blooded animals, however, that live both above and below the ground instruct the artist how to combine security with freedom, hearth with heath. The ground rules they lay down are applied at a technical level to Longley's sound and metrical system when, with a literal borrowing of 'silence from the snow', his poetics succeed in both incorporating and consuming mortality. Initiating Longley's lifelong experimenting between what he refers to as Robert Frost's 'strict iambic and loose iambic', the new compromise calls, in this instance, for the full restoration at the last moment of the iambic pentameter's 'footsteps': 'I can tell how softly their footsteps go – / Their footsteps borrow silence from the snow.'[64] Analysing the prosody of Yeats, whom he called 'a vigorous counter of syllables', Longley quantified that 'syllables are added to or subtracted from the decasyllabic line as music and meaning dictate'.[65]

In order to completely insure against the 'Freeze-up' as explored in the neighbouring lyric of that name, *No Continuing City* is now ready to take its greatest, most durable step back towards the complexity of 'summer country'. With the hindsight of its intervening formal ventures upon the 'Atlantic's Premises', it does so through the long cumulative poem Longley wrote in 1964 – 'The Hebrides'. In Longley's revised ordering, it completes the artistic voyage of the volume's first half (*Poems*, 40–3). Like the warm-blooded creatures bobbing about the poem's drafts, the husband has now been thoroughly assimilated within the artist. Whereas the poet banishes the somewhat passive seals that 'slip over the cockle beds', the creatively 'effervescent otters – /On bridal pools' celebrate the homecoming of a poet-husband.[66] Significantly, Longley already senses the otter's potential as his work's Virgilian guide as fully realised in his later homecoming volume *Gorse Fires*. Like the progress of this first volume towards 'all harbours wrecked' – mirroring Larkin's abyss of 'no ships and no shallows' – the arduous drafting processes so evidently involved in the making of 'The Hebrides', suggests how literal was the difficult process of vacating his 'safe-as-houses commonwealth'.[67] A contemporary draft poem 'Beside the Seaside' employs a similarly littoral language to emblemise a new landscape of the imagination. Here, turning away from the secure holdings to follow down where 'pier and promenade embark' leads on to the more 'submarine / Hearsay' of poetry. Such literal sacrificing of the draft's 'cottages / Byres and stables' in 'The Hebrides', will find recompense through a simultaneous reclamation of those pejorative traces of 'broken wood' that the earlier domestic homecomings had sought to destroy. Ironically, it is such fragments that will constitute the building blocks of the poet's more enduring spiritual voyage. In the light of another Protestant archetype – that of the struggle of the Israelites to come home – this tendency of destroying in order to build augments the ameliorative building plans of one of Longley's forebears, John Hewitt.

It is important that the positioning of this poem should suggest that Longley has come 'home' to the Hebrides on his own steam. Yet the 'massive shambling incongruity in that desolate landscape' of Dr Johnson to whom two later poems of the original volume pay homage, and to whom the incongruous Wellington-clad figure of *Gorse Fires* will again allude, undoubtedly haunts 'The Hebrides'.[68] The voyage of the lexicographer, who 'had hitherto shown no interest in wild nature, who delighted in London, a crowded room and the security of home', inspires the Northern poet's expedition to get into the uncharted territory of 'his own head'. Unlike Herbert then, who desires only rest in 'Peace' – the poem which provided Longley with the stanzaic template of 'The Hebrides' – Longley fervently demands such Johnsonian flux for his art. The resulting double sway between this poem's long nostalgic lines and the shorter lyric ones that mine the subconscious, is mirrored by the volume's vacillation between Boswell-like efforts to compose itself amid 'terrifying circumstances', and a Johnson-like tranquillity.

There is of course another father figure guiding Longley home. The phrase '[a]cross the Minch' occurs in his copious drafts by which Longley gestures in his own move into his 'Irish seas', towards the sense of loss MacNeice registered in the travel book of this name. 'For the tripper', the inveterate poet-wanderer from Carrickfergus decides from *his* time in the Hebrides, 'the island means isolation'.[69] Yet exhibiting how extensively he has learnt to extend his metaphors, Longley's mapping of his new contours becomes a means of staking out his artistic rather than cultural identity. His own 'Nightcrossing' – one of the projected titles of the book – is a voyage into the isolating conditions of lyric heights, as the poem's concluding arrival at a lyricist's 'privilege / Of vertigo' demonstrates. Rather than merely seek a new plural identity from his English/Irish/Northern roots, this poem has a poetic expression as transcendental as the space between 'air and sea' in its sights. Its highly-wrought imagery of stasis and flux on the one hand, and stone and water on the other, may indeed echo the basic coordinates of MacNeice's early 'Carrick Revisited'. Yet whereas the antinomies of darkness and stasis on the one hand and Hesperian light and movement on the other, remain irreconcilables in MacNeice's figurative world, here Longley begins his lifelong and self-conscious process of reconciling them through the mechanics of his aesthetic world. Whereas the older poet longs to 'cancel' his 'city interlude', Longley thoroughly celebrates his humble beginnings in terms of his poetic rather than familial inheritance. He is proud that nothing he writes can now 'hide / That water line' where his art began. The city neighbourhood and domestic realm as charted through the figurative language of his juvenilia and earliest of published work, is as 'continuing' as it has been absorbed. While MacNeice traces any shortcomings in his art to the silence of his exilic 'belated rock', Longley's sea-colluding 'orphaned stone' conversely becomes a new stronghold of art. Longley's rhymes 'on my own' and 'so far from home' stress how resolute and independent his poetic calling. From here, Michael Longley, the poet 'In whom the city is continuing', as an emphatic stanza opening declares, can finally begin.

Chapter 11

'Snipping lyric leaves off the old narrative boughs': Seamus Heaney and the Book as Expressive Form

Colleen McKenna

In the spring of 1977, Seamus Heaney and Derek Mahon toured Northern Ireland presenting a joint poetry reading, entitled 'in their element', which was accompanied by a booklet of the same name, featuring twelve of Heaney's poems followed by fourteen of Mahon's. The title and organising theme of *in their element* are taken from a quotation by Michael Longley that characterises Heaney as the poet of 'water and earth' and Mahon as the student of 'fire and air'.[1] The cover of the collection, designed by Cathal Caulfield, shows the four elements – air, water, earth and fire – layered and enclosed in a circle. In terms of content and style, the illustration is reminiscent of that by Althea Gyles for W. B. Yeats's *The Wind Among the Reeds*, which also depicts the elements, as does the verse inside.[2] The pattern of the water and wind on the front of *in their element* resembles the woven reeds and water on Yeats's volume, and flames of fire dance upward on the bottom of both covers. Where the design of *in their element* differs from *The Wind Among the Reeds* is in the presence of a tree growing up through the centre of the illustration. With its root intermingled with the fire, the trunk extends skyward through the earth and water finally branching out into leaves suspended in the air. The cover of *in their element* also bears a similarity to the cover of Yeats's *The Secret Rose,* also illustrated by Gyles, which contains an ornate tree whose interwoven branches meet in two heads, and the roots of which are intermingled with a skeleton lying at the base of the image.[3] In all three volumes, highly symbolic cover art establishes a context through which the poetry gains meaning and contributes to the overall production of the book. Moreover, the cover of *in their element* (and the inclusion of the same image in the main body of the booklet) indicates an awareness of what D. F. McKenzie saw as the book's 'expressive form'.[4] McKenzie, writing about William Congreve's *Works* (1710), argues that bibliographic design and textual content are inseparable: '[it is] quite impossible...to divorce the substance of the text on the one hand from the physical form of its presentation on the other. The book itself is an expressive means.'[5] Features of the book, such as the cover, illustrations, typography, page formatting, footnotes, dedications, and so on contribute fundamentally to the meaning of the text therein.

The cover design of *in their element* also showcases a pivotal and protean symbol in Heaney's work – the tree – much like the eponymous tower on Yeats's 1928 volume. Heaney's private press (and early Faber) editions often reveal a

Yeatsian preoccupation with both production and the use of illustration to construct meaning. Examples of Heaney collections in which aspects of the book form extend and mediate poetic meaning include *Ugolino*, with Louis le Brocquy, which incorporates woodcuts; *Gravities*, which includes Noel Connor's graphical interpretations of poems; and *Towards a Collaboration* with Felim Egan in which Egan's abstract painting faces Heaney's 'Clearances 8'.[6] Furthermore, in early Faber editions of *Field Work,* the map illustration on the book jacket locates Heaney's Glanmore both topographically and symbolically and reinforces the positioning of Glanmore as a centralising space in the volume; in terms of œuvre, it signals graphically the shift of both poet and verse to a new place of writing, following *North*.[7]

The text in which the dialogue between book form and poetry is most knowingly and richly realised is *Sweeney's Flight*, a collaboration with photographer Rachel Giese,[8] in which Heaney revisits his original translation of *Buile Suibhne*.[9] *Buile Suibhne* is the legend of Sweeney, the seventh-century king of *Dal Araidhe*, who was exiled to the forest following a transgression against St Ronan. The story recounts Sweeney's penitential life as a bird-man amongst the trees, particularly his flights across Ireland, his ensuing madness, his relationship to the forest and his ultimate redemption. Heaney's translation of *Buile Suibhne*, *Sweeney Astray*, was first published in 1983 by the Field Day Theatre Company and in 1984 by Faber and Faber. His version draws on J. G. O'Keeffe's *Buile Suibhne (The Frenzy of Suibhne [Sweeney])*, an Irish–English edition, based on a seventeenth-century manuscript, published in 1913 by the Irish Texts Society.[10] Heaney's interest in the piece is both poetic (he was drawn to its 'bareness and durability', 'its double note of relish and penitence') and topographical. He had lived 'on the verges' of Sweeney's territory, and, having moved to Wicklow just before he began work on the translation, he was near to Sweeney's final resting place (*SA*, unpaginated introduction). The work is also an exploration of the literary tree and forest (particularly the forest as a site of social and mental instability) as well as the construction of the 'man of the wood' in the shape of Sweeney himself, all of which are preoccupations of Heaney. In 1992, Heaney collaborated with Giese to publish a new volume containing sections of verse from *Sweeney Astray* integrated with photographs. *Sweeney's Flight* is both the title of the entire book and the name of this particular interpretation of *Buile Suibhne*. (The book also contains the full, revised *Sweeney Astray* translation by Heaney as an appendix.) Significantly, *Sweeney's Flight* offered Heaney an opportunity to select and modify verse from the *Sweeney Astray* translation, a 'pleasure' that he 'desired' the first time around but rejected in favour of retaining the entire narrative (*SF*, vii). The new text is sparer, containing only poems (often excerpts of longer pieces from *Sweeney Astray*) and none of the prose from the earlier publication. The verse is re-ordered, interspersed with photographs and grouped into sections which do not correspond to those of *Sweeney Astray*. Significantly, Sweeney is the only named presence in *Sweeney's Flight*, the figures of St Moling, Lynchseachan, Eorann, the Hag, etc. having been omitted. However, in a few instances, the discourse of the absent characters is retained (most notably in the case of Moling, which is discussed below), and their words are spoken by an authorial figure. This change in speaking subjects in *Sweeney's Flight* has a profound impact on the development of voice in the new text, and, as I will argue, on the relationship between Heaney and Sweeney.

Buile Suibhne has been a discernible presence in the Heaney œuvre ever since Heaney began translating the piece in 1972 for the eventual publication of *Sweeney Astray* in 1983. Consequently, the Sweeney narrative forms an intertext in poems such as 'Exposure', 'The King of the Ditchbacks', 'The Strand at Lough Beg', 'Station Island' and 'The Flight Path', as well as in the 'Sweeney Redivivus' section of *Station Island*. The Heaney–Sweeney dialogue intensifies with the publication of *Sweeney's Flight* in which Heaney uses aspects of the book form – including the introduction of photographic illustration, the omission and repositioning of text, and the use of shifts in typography and white space to create a narrative frame – to produce a more secular reading of the *Buile Suibhne* legend and to interrogate further the poet–subject relationship. Taking *Sweeney's Flight* as its primary focus, this essay will consider the insertion into Sweeney's story of an authorial presence; the impact on the narrative of the interplay between text and image, the re-presentation of Sweeney's place of writing, and the reconfiguring of the relationship between Sweeney and Heaney. Specifically, it will consider how the 'semiotic function of bibliographic materials' is exploited by Heaney in this edition.[11]

To begin, the physical properties of *Sweeney's Flight* help to establish its identity. Reassuringly oversized, the dimensions of this large hardback edition (29 × 23 cm), the glossy pages, atmospheric black and white photographs and the generous use of white space (both on the page and through the inclusion of blank pages) combine to signal authority and to differentiate this text from the standard Faber format (20 × 12 cm) of *Sweeney Astray*. After a new preface, the reader encounters *Sweeney's Flight,* its status as a discrete literary work indicated by its enclosure in a series of pictorial, typographical and contextual frames. In terms of graphics, *Sweeney's Flight* sits within a photographic border: on either side of the new text there is a photograph of an old wooden door in a brick wall which bounds an external space, perhaps a deserted orchard. Through the door, the reader encounters a typographical frame: Heaney has italicised the first and last poems of *Sweeney's Flight*, in manner reminiscent of Yeats's *Responsibilities* (in which 'Introductory Rhymes' and 'Closing Rhymes' operate as a textual frame, set apart by typeface and, in the case of the Cuala Press edition, colour.)[12] The italicised opening poem is 'The King of the Ditchbacks', originally published in *Station Island*. The piece explores the process of translating *Buile Suibhne*, and, in particular, Heaney's developing relationship and self-association with Sweeney who is identified as 'small dreamself in the branches' (*SF,* 5). Although appearing under its own title in *Sweeney's Flight*, the poem is integrated into the new translation visually and typographically, and it articulates the poetic process of entering into an artistic space, a process which is, in part, being enacted by the reader:

> As if a trespasser
> unbolted a forgotten gate
> and ripped the growth
> tangling its lower bars
>
> (*SF*, 4)

This forgotten gate seems to correspond to the wooden door of Giese's photo and positions the reader as a sort of literary 'trespasser' while also reinforcing the metaphor of the piece as a walled, contained space.

Moreover, Heaney's use of framing inverts the paradigm of the forest as margin and defining boundary of society as suggested by cultural commentators such as Robert Pogue Harrison in *Forests: The Shadow of Civilization*:

> However broadly or narrowly one wishes to define it, Western civilization literally cleared its space in the midst of forests. A sylvan fringe of darkness defined the limits of civilization, the margins of its cities, the boundaries of its institutional domain; but also the extravagance of its imagination...the governing institutions of the West – religion, law, family, city – originally established themselves in opposition to the forests.[13]

Although *Buile Suibhne* is not set exclusively in the forest, it does rely heavily on many of the tropes associated with the literary forest which is traditionally the site of the outlaw, mental and civic instability, the forest scribe, irrationality, poetry, paganism and the man of the woods. Furthermore, in *Buile Suibhne* and *Sweeney Astray*, the forest is the primary locus of struggle, transformation and redemption: it is in the forest that the physically and mentally unstable, dispossessed Sweeney (the transgressor of rules agreed in the dominant civilised space) acts out his penance and both endures and celebrates his place. In their explicit use of framing techniques in *Sweeney's Flight*, Heaney and Giese reverse the forest as 'sylvan fringe' motif by visually and textually bounding a largely wooded landscape and consciously defining it as the primary (rather than a peripheral) space of poetic interest.

In narrative terms, *Sweeney's Flight* represents a more significant reshaping of Heaney's previous translation. Most obviously, Heaney removes much of the expository discourse of *Sweeney Astray*. The original account of Sweeney's transgressions, his subsequent goading of and by his tormentors, and his emotional exchanges with his family have been stripped away, leaving him the only named presence in *Sweeney's Flight*. (The most conspicuous absence, as previously suggested, is the voice of St Moling.) As a consequence, point of view is streamlined, and, with a few exceptions, the descriptions of events and places are spoken by Sweeney's singular voice. Heaney also prunes back the pagan–Christian dialogue foregrounded in the original version, and as a result, the narrative focus shifts from a chronicle of the protagonist's misdemeanours, expiation and salvation to a series of poems detailing Sweeney's struggle and celebration of the Irish landscape, particularly the forest. By privileging images of trees and woodland, the photographs reinforce Heaney's re-centering of the piece.

Moreover, through typographical variation, selective omissions, and the addition of 'The King of the Ditchbacks', Heaney inserts an authorial presence into this version that did not exist in *Sweeney Astray*.

As mentioned earlier, 'The King of the Ditchbacks' (a sequence which contains both prose and verse) is, in part, a metapoem about Heaney's initial translating of *Buile Suibhne,* which articulates his developing relationship with the character Sweeney:

> I was sure I knew him. The time I'd spent obsessively in that upstairs room bringing myself close to him: each entranced hiatus as I chain smoked and stared out the dormer into the grassy hillside I was laying myself open. He was depending on me as I hung out on the limb of a translated phrase like a youngster dared out on to an alder branch over the whirlpool. Small dreamself in the branches.[14]

> (*SF*, 5)

By introducing 'The King of the Ditchbacks' at the beginning of this edition, Heaney opens *Sweeney's Flight* with a prologue voiced by an authorial presence, and closes the text with the same voice speaking an epilogue, composed of stanzas of the blessing originally spoken by Moling in *Sweeney Astray*. Again, such a reading is possible due to the re-editing of the text and the use of typeface to help to construct voice: both 'The King of the Ditchbacks' and the epilogue are in italic script. In terms of a consideration of voice, the excision of the character Moling from *Sweeney's Flight* is especially significant. In *Sweeney Astray,* Moling presides over Sweeney's conversion, and it is Moling who secures and records Sweeney's history, making him the de facto poet of the piece:

> You shall leave the history of your adventures with us and receive a Christian burial in a churchyard. Therefore, said Moling, no matter how far you range over Ireland, day by day, I bind you to return to me every evening so that I may record your story.

> (*SA*, 76)

When a few sections later in *Sweeney Astray*, Sweeney lays dying, it is to Moling he repents and makes his confession, and it is from Moling that he receives communion. *Sweeney Astray* closes with Moling's eulogy delivered at Sweeney's grave. Although he is absent from *Sweeney's Flight*, five of the seven stanzas from Moling's final blessing in *Sweeney Astray* are included, and these stanzas close the edition and complete the italicised frame that opened with 'The King of the Ditchbacks'. So *Sweeney's Flight* begins with the authorial persona of 'The King of the Ditchbacks' and finishes with the following words of remembrance originally spoken by Moling:

> *I am standing beside Sweeney's grave*
> *remembering him. Wherever he*
> *loved and nested and removed to*
> *will always be dear to me.*

Because Sweeney loved Glen Bolcain,
I learned to love it too. He'll miss
all the fresh streams tumbling down,
all the beds of watercress.

I ask a blessing, by Sweeney's grave.
His memory rises in my breast.
His soul roosts in the tree of love.
His body sinks in its clay nest.

                                        (*SF*, 78)

In the context of the structural and typographical frames of *Sweeney's Flight*, this speaking voice seems to be continuous with the 'I' of 'The King of the Ditchbacks', an 'I' with which Heaney has associated himself. This new 'I' both positions Heaney as a speaking subject occupying a narratorial role, and collapses the distance between the poet and Sweeney.

There is also an italicised poem midway through *Sweeney's Flight*, which, in *Sweeney Astray* (and earlier versions) was spoken by the mill-owner Lynchseachan, who like Moling, is not present in the new text:

VIII

Woods and forests and wild deer –
things like these delight you more
than sleeping in your eastern dun
on a bed of feather-down.

Near a quick mill-pond, your perch
on a dark green holly branch
means far more now than any feast
among the brightest and the best.

                                        (*SF*, 25)

As before, the italicised font visually aligns this utterance with the authorial voice that opens and closes the textual frame. The lines are also set apart by the point of view: all other poems in the collection (within the italicised frame) are spoken in the first person, as if by Sweeney himself. Poem VIII, however, represents the only instance in which the second person is used in *Sweeney's Flight*. Furthermore, this is the only time when two separate poems or sections (indicated by roman numeral headings) are placed on facing pages. This combination of typographical difference, poem placement and shift in point of view invites a dialogic reading of the two pieces. Such a dialogic interpretation also holds at a semantic level: in the first of the paired poems, the speaking subject laments the loss of his past existence:

Fugitive, deserted, mocked
by memories of my days as king,

> no longer called to head the troop
> when warriors are mustering,
> no longer guest of honour
> at tables anywhere in Ireland...
>
> (*SF*, 24)

In poem VIII, the 'authorial' speaking subject responds directly to these despairing comments, observing that 'woods and forests and wild deer – / things like these delight you more'. Beyond the dynamic of these two facing poems, the interjection of the authorial voice strengthens the sense of the dialogic relationship between speaker-poet and Sweeney. These edits and additions, whose meaning is emphasised by typography and layout, create an intimacy between writer and subject in this edition that the 1984 text never attains.

Sweeney's Flight also differs thematically from *Sweeney Astray*, particularly in terms of the Christian–pagan dialectic that is foregrounded in the earlier text. For example, Heaney not only excises the saint, Moling, from *Sweeney's Flight* but he also drops the following two stanzas from what remains of his eulogy:

> I waited long but knew he'd come.
> I welcomed, sped him as a guest.
> With holy viaticum
> I limed him for the Holy Ghost...
>
> Now, if it be the will of God,
> rise, Sweeney, take this guiding hand
> that has to lay you in the sod
> and draw the dark blinds of the ground.
>
> (*SA*, 84)

The following prose conclusion is also omitted: 'His spirit fled to heaven and his body was given an honourable burial by Moling' (*SA*, 85). Thus, rather than presiding over Sweeney's conversion and ascension to heaven, *Sweeney's Flight* closes with a secular prayer which reverses the clear Christian ethos of the original ending. Although elements of the original Christian discourse are retained in this text, thereby preserving the Christian–pagan dialectic, Heaney's editing and reorganisation of Sweeney's story unpicks much of the Christian fabric of *Buile Suibhne* and interweaves sections that are more obviously a celebration of nature and the forest. One is reminded of his comments on an unnamed seventh-century poem that shares many of the exaltations of Sweeney, particularly those from his praise poems:

> And so it goes on, the hermit's rhapsody, full of the primeval energies of the druid's grove. And that word 'druid', of course, calls up a world older and darker and greener than the world of early Christian Ireland, although some authorities would have it that the role of the *file*, the official poet in historic times, was continuous with the role of the druid in archaic times. I like that possibility a lot because the root of the word 'druid' is related to *doire*, the oak grove, and through that the poet is connected with the

mysteries of the grove, *and the poetic imagination is linked with the barbaric life of the wood, with Oisin rather than with Patrick.* (Emphasis added.)[15]

This final statement, in which Heaney (like Yeats before him) sides with Oisin, and, by association, the forest, the heathen, the mysterious and the slightly irrational, perhaps explains the governing aesthetic principle of *Sweeney's Flight*, in which a construction of Sweeney as Man of the Wood, exile and tree-dweller, is privileged.[16]

In essence, Heaney's revision of *Sweeney Astray* was motivated and in part achieved by his collaboration with Rachel Giese, whose pictures 'convinced me that [she] was the person to *look again* at Sweeney's places as they are identified in *Sweeney Astray* and to represent them from her own particular perspective' (emphasis added, *SF*, vii). And, he might have added, 'my own particular perspective', because the collection of images accentuates Heaney's added pantheistic emphasis in the project. There are no trappings of Christianity, no images of country churchyards or verdant crosses; all the photographs are of unpopulated landscape, the bulk of them displaying trees. Furthermore, Giese's photographs lend a certain immediacy to *Sweeney's Flight* that the original translation does not contain. As with poet-narrator and subject, the historical distance between reader and subject is partly collapsed, because through her use of perspective, Giese's pictures signify by forcing the reader into an intimate relationship with the landscape and particularly the tree. Trees are rarely viewed straight-on or centred on the page. Rather the imagined viewer is positioned (like Sweeney) underneath or above the tree, so that the eye is drawn up through the branches from ground level, or down on them with from an aerial perspective: only trunks are visible in some photos; only canopies in others. Sometimes the image emphasises the fruit of the tree and one particular picture captures the utter abundance of an apple tree in full yield; this photo faces Sweeney's description of working through the windfalls on the forest floor:

> Every night I glean and raid
> and comb the floor of the oak wood.
> My hands work into leaf and rind,
> old roots, old windfalls on the ground,
>
> they rake through matted watercress
> and grope among the bog-berries,
> cool brooklime, sorrel and damp moss,
> wild garlic and wild raspberries,
>
> apples, hazelnuts and acorns,
> the haws of sharp, jaggy hawthorns,
> the blackberries, the floating weed,
> the whole store of the oak wood.
>
> (*SF*, 70)

The poem communicates a sense of plenitude and fertility which is constructed without effacing the struggle of Sweeney's existence. He must still 'raid', 'comb', 'work', 'rake' and 'grope' the forest floor, but after the first six lines, the speaking presence and his activities modulate into a catalogue of the fruits of the forest that are yielded up to him: 'the whole store of the oak wood'. The photograph captures this sense of excess in an image fit to accompany Keats's 'To Autumn'. Given the context, this naming of things equates to a form of possession (albeit temporary) for Sweeney, a brief respite against the general chaos, dispossession and material penury of the forest.

Through the Heaney and Giese collaboration, a text-altering dialogue between image and poem is achieved. One thing that poetry struggles to deliver, which a painting or photograph allows the viewer, is a sense of simultaneity. John Barrell has written persuasively in *The Idea of Landscape and the Sense of Place* and in *Poetry, Language and Politics* on John Clare's use of syntax to effect a sense of vista.[17] Barrell argues that Clare's phrases are grouped in such a way that the reader hurriedly moves through a collection of images (often arranged in paratactic dependent clauses) in an attempt to meet a completing grammatical construct (often a main verb or direct object or complement), thereby coming as close as possible to reading and thus visualising the entire scene at once. Interestingly, Heaney himself analyses Clare's work in a visual idiom, using the metaphor of sketch-making to describe the process articulated by Barrell: 'The couplets hurry in upon themselves as fast as pencil-strokes in an excited drawing and, as in the act of drawing, there is no anxiety about lines repeating and intersecting with the trajectory of other lines.'[18] Although Heaney does not use the closure-driven syntax of Clare, there is some similarity in his attempt, through the work with Giese, to effect a visual and simultaneous sense of Sweeney's place (including landscape, texture, seasons and point of view). In contrast to Clare, however, the impact of the integration of photography into *Sweeney's Flight* is a disruption of the overall narrative flow: the pictures force a slower reading while the reader considers the relationship between text and image and shifts between acts of reading and viewing. Furthermore, the construction of the book, which tends to use the pattern of one image facing one short section of verse, both of which are surrounded by plenty of white space, draws the attention to the visual, shaped nature of the poetry itself.

Giese's images foreground place, augmenting the depth and complexity of landscape which is already written into the poetry. Through mimesis, Giese's photos admit the reader, who adopts Sweeney's visual point of view, thereby entering into a shared experience with the protagonist. Giese demarcates a bounded, topographical space with the paired photos of walls, and by naming many of the places in the pictures, she attempts to sketch out a particular journey. The book jacket that details Giese's project, reinforces the idea that her work represents a visual mapping of Sweeney's place:

> Inspired by Seamus Heaney's poems...Rachel Giese has produced a stunning portfolio of pictures of the northern Irish landscape, covering the boundaries of Mad Sweeney's original kingdom of Dal-Arie. She has

resourcefully followed the clues to topography and the natural world in Sweeney's wanderings.

(*SF*, jacket)

Like Heaney and Giese, Sweeney undertakes a poetic mapping of place, and given that in places he is treated as the author of short bursts of verse, the forest might even be read as an inchoate place of writing. The forest is a space for madness, the place of the outsider, and the entire piece is predicated on the paradoxical condition of simultaneously belonging and being exiled. Sweeney is banished to woods and is condemned to restlessness and homelessness, yet he also maps out and names a place for himself, eventually making Glen Bolcain his own sacred space.

While not exclusively of forest, most of Giese's pictures depict trees, thus developing the iconic symbol that Heaney so cherishes. The use of landscape photography also helps to construct the place of writing. It enables what Heaney has called elsewhere a 'wide-lensed attentiveness' to the poetic subject.[19]

In his preface to *Sweeney's Flight*, Heaney refers to the editing process as 'snipping lyric leaves off old narrative boughs', but, in fact, the volume represents much more than a literary pruning: *Sweeney's Flight* is a new interpretation of *Buile Suibhne* which is arrived at through the repositioning, revision and omission of text as well as a reliance on 'material signs' (such as typography and layout).[20] Heaney's collaboration with Rachel Giese enables him to impress his own mark upon the poetic material through disrupting and reshaping the narrative and integrating image, text and medium. In the process, he has stamped the legend of Sweeney more obviously with his own signature by shifting the narratorial voice (thus effecting a more intimate relationship between poet-speaker and subject), privileging a pantheistic reading of *Buile Suibhne*, and foregrounding the sense of place.

In *The Textual Condition*, Jerome McGann argues that the 'object of the poetical text is to thicken the medium as much as possible' in order to exhibit 'processes of self-reflection and self-generation'.[21] One obvious sense in which such thickening occurs in *Sweeney's Flight* is through the foregrounding of extra-linguistic elements such as photography, blank white pages and italic typefaces; another is through the inclusion of the full text of the *Sweeney Astray* translation, which sits outside the typographic and photographic frame of Part I but within the volume as Part II, a structure which itself encourages a dialogic reading of the new version. In this sense, there is a process of self-reflection occurring at the level of œuvre as Heaney enacts a Yeatsian retrospective editing of previously published writing. Furthermore, this thickening of the text, particularly the inclusion and typographical integration of 'The King of the Ditchbacks' (and the excision of St Moling as a speaking presence) enables Heaney's insertion of the authorial self into the poem. This self-conscious edition (which opens with sixteen lines of the Irish version, thereby drawing attention to the act of translation) also highlights Heaney's engagement with bibliographic and textual processes: he is translator, collaborator, editor, reader, poet and narrator as well as de facto man of the wood.

Little has been written about *Sweeney's Flight*, and it frequently does not appear in bibliographies of Heaney's primary works, perhaps omitted through the false assumption that it simply represents a coffee table version of a previously published text. Yet editing is an interpretive act and the production of editions is commensurate with the construction of literary meaning.[22] *Sweeney's Flight* is a work in its own right – a volume which sees Heaney exploiting the potential of the book as expressive form.

Chapter 12

Light Enough and Time: Derek Mahon and the Literary Marketplace

Stephen Enniss

The competitive market for Irish literary manuscripts – which has been driven in large part in recent years by my own institution's collecting[1] – has provided a welcome subsidy to Irish writers who, in some instances, may make more from the sale of their manuscripts than they do from the initial publication of the work itself. This peculiar feature of the contemporary Irish literary market, however, is by no means a recent development. In the early decades of the twentieth century, the American collector and patron of the arts John Quinn provided similar support to Yeats, Synge and Joyce, at times purchasing manuscripts even before the work had appeared in print.[2] In the 1960s the Humanities Research Center at the University of Texas purchased manuscripts of Austin Clarke and Louis MacNeice, while more recently the University of Tulsa, SUNY Buffalo, and Boston College have each provided welcome support to Irish writers through the purchase of other literary archives.[3]

This subsidy of literary publishing has left a complex legacy. A story sometimes heard in Ireland describes one particular poet who in the 1960s is said to have manufactured a new set of manuscript drafts for sale to an American library whenever he was pressed for money. The tale sounds apocryphal, but it nevertheless says a great deal about Irish resistance to the overpowering wealth of American institutions. Of greater interest than the economics of this exchange, however, is the impact of collecting not simply on Irish book history, but on writing itself. Implicit in collecting is a conferral of cultural worth that publishing alone may not convey. As Ciaran Carson expressed it when he visited Emory soon after the library had acquired his own papers, 'I feel half dead already.'[4] Collecting shifts the immediate audience for a new work from that small circle of poetry readers to a more distant reader – often an American one – engaged in formal academic study. In such an environment what may be of greater interest is not the achieved poem at all but the record of its many indirections.

The following essay considers Derek Mahon's evolving stance towards audience and the way his position has been shaped by publishers, by the literary marketplace, and, most recently, by the presence of his literary archive. Over the course of his career, Mahon has demonstrated a persistent disinterest in the stable fixity of print. He has chosen to revise his poems long after the ink has dried. Familiar titles change, lines are altered and entire stanzas reworked. On occasion he has been known to deny any knowledge of early poems when the poem is one that no longer rises to his own present standard.[5] This pattern of ongoing revision suggests not a building up of a body of work so much as a distillation of that work down into its most essential elements, a notion that is confirmed, I believe, by the revisions and omissions of his *Collected Poems*.[6]

Even as Mahon has been engaged in a distillation of his work, he has also been engaged in shaping an audience as well. One of the features of his poetry is the large number of poems addressed to specific readers. Opening his early collections one finds a procession of names that have at one time or another helped to call the poem into being. As he expressed it in his recent *Paris Review* interview, 'I invoke a circle of friends, a reading society. I didn't realize that in the beginning, but I was creating a circle of readers.'[7] That circle has come to dominate Mahon's own sense of audience. Nowhere is that more apparent than in his decision to curtail public readings (he gave only three readings in the USA from *The Hudson Letter* and none at all for *The Yellow Book*) and, more recently, in his decision not to allow distribution of review copies of his *Collected Poems*.

Over the years the circle of readers to whom his poems are aimed has indeed taken the shape of 'a reading society'. While publication plays an essential role in the relation of poet to audience, it has become in recent years an increasingly interim one. The larger movement includes the literary archive and finally is aimed towards a more distant end. This stance towards audience that I am describing has been encouraged by our culture's antipathy towards poetry, by Mahon's own exacting art, and more recently, I believe, by his self-consciousness towards his own archive. It is worth examining the way Mahon came to this position both for what it reveals about the nature of his verse and for what it reveals about the conditions for poetry in Ireland in the last half of the twentieth century.

Mahon's first published poem appeared in the 1958 Christmas issue of the *School News* when he was still a student at the Royal Belfast Academical Institute. Over the next seven years, he published poems in a number of literary magazines, largely in the Trinity College literary magazine *Icarus* and in *The Dubliner*, before his first pamphlet appeared as the third title in the 'Festival Publication' series issued by Queen's University in 1965. This new series had been established earlier that year and had already issued pamphlets by Michael Longley and Seamus Heaney. On the strength of their respective pamphlets, Mahon and Longley shared the Eric Gregory Award (along with John Fuller and Norman Talbot) in 1965, an award intended to support the work of promising British poets under 30. This shared prize further reinforced the closeness of the two poets' collaborative friendship (Fig. 12.1). Mahon has commented that when he first began writing he wrote for 'a few friends . . . the crowd who were running *Icarus* at the time. That was the first audience, a little nucleus of people.'[8]

Later that same year Mahon travelled to Canada and the US where he moved between odd jobs and short-term teaching assignments. His letters to Michael and Edna Longley, which survive among the Longley papers at Emory, make clear that publication in the States was also very much on his mind. While Longley watched for publishing opportunities in Ireland, Mahon sought them abroad. During this period the Grolier Bookstore in Cambridge, Massachusetts, published his second pamphlet, *Design for a Grecian Urn*, under the Erato Publishing Company

Figure 12.1 Derek Mahon and Michael Longley in a 1965 photograph shortly after receiving the Eric Gregory Award. (Robert W. Woodruff Library, Emory University.)

imprint. Mahon's pamphlet was only the second title published by Erato,[9] which would issue two more titles before folding by the end of the year. Writing to Michael and Edna Longley from Toronto, Mahon announced the news with feigned nonchalance:

> By the way, my pamphlet 'Design for a Grecian Urn' is out in Boston, though I haven't seen a copy yet. I'll send you one as soon as my copies arrive. The poems are printed on rough light-grey paper, very pop-arty, and the cover, at my request, is of the 'Greek blue' Joyce wanted for the cover of *Ulysses*, if you see the connection (between me and Joyce, that is) – I think it's the same blue as the clock-faces in Trinity...[10]

Design for a Grecian Urn appeared in the autumn of 1966 in an edition of seventy-five numbered copies, twenty of which were signed by Mahon (Fig. 12.2). In a 1991 interview with William Scammell, Mahon was dismissive of the book, stating 'the less said about that the better'.[11] The small limitation was most certainly due to Mahon's own anonymity and the marginal nature of Erato's efforts. Yet the form – seventy-five numbered copies, twenty signed by the author – suggests a much desired rarity. It was certainly not the first or last time a book largely without an audience was offered to the public in the guise of a prized collectible. That strategy, however, is itself revealing and points to one of the unspoken assumptions about literary publishing: that is the paradoxical notion that what is outside the marketplace may indeed be its greatest prize. That notion informs our view of art to this day and lies behind the subsidy of the arts in Ireland as in the US.

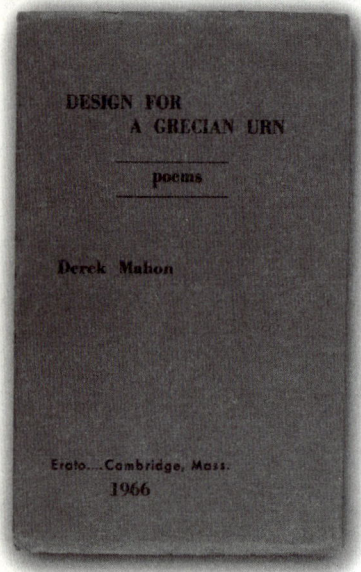

Figure 12.2 Derek Mahon's *Design for a Grecian Urn*, no. 31 of seventy-five numbered copies, published by Erato Press in Cambridge, Massachusetts in 1966. (Robert W. Woodruff Library, Emory University.)

During his stay in Canada and the States, Mahon continued to seek other publishers for his and Longley's poems. Plans to publish a second pamphlet under the Pym-Randall Press imprint came to nothing, however,[12] as did efforts to gain the attention of the larger publishing houses in New York and Boston. In Ireland Longley was encountering similar difficulties. A disaffected Mahon wrote to Longley in the autumn of 1966:

> Too bad about the publishers – why do they never recognize the real thing when they see it? America, however, is not the answer. For pamphlets and things, yes – but the big firms in Boston and New York are too busy turning out the well-wrought droppings of tightassed literocrats who teach in the right places. It's all part of the Great Society, from which god save us. Better a real fish in a real pond than in a vast aquarium kept alive by central heating and artificial light.[13]

In a follow-up letter soon after, he reiterates, 'America will solve nothing for you that you can't solve on the home stomping ground. I'm thinking of publication, of course.'[14]

While the early pamphlets failed to reach a wide audience, they nevertheless served an important role in validating Mahon's writing and in giving him a mechanism to reach editors. Jon Stallworthy, poetry editor at Oxford University Press in the mid-1960s, recalls admiring poems Mahon was publishing during this period in the *Dublin Magazine*; however, Mahon and Longley were leaving nothing to chance but instead were using their early pamphlets to actively promote their work. 'Have you sent off to OUP yet?' Mahon writes from Toronto. 'If not, do so. I wrote to Stallworthy telling him I'd get you to send him our pamphlets – that kind of thing is always a help, I should think.'[15] The following December Mahon writes about the new collection he is putting together. 'There are 37 poems there, which is enough for a book, so if and when I resurrect a few oldies and perhaps write another one or two, I'll be in a position to approach Jon Stallworthy again. If he says no this time,' he adds, 'I'm going to start my own printing press.'[16]

Though Mahon was being facetious, the latter comment suggests something of poetry's position outside the marketplace. There is a long tradition of going to just such lengths to secure publication. Peter Fallon's unlikely-named Tara Telephone Publications, Hayden Murphy's *Broadsheet*, and Frank Ormsby's Ulsterman Publications come immediately to mind. To the extent that poetry remains commercially unviable, all poetry publishing is vanity publishing. More often than not it is subsidised by the personal generosity of individuals, the Arts Council, or other external support. It exists in defiance of commercial values and economic realities.

The limited market for poetry in Ireland has certainly contributed to the flight of Irish writers abroad. Mahon's own opportunity came with acceptance by Stallworthy of *Night-Crossing* (originally titled *Night Train Journey*), which was published in 1968 as a Poetry Book Society Choice. Mahon did not, however, abandon small-press publication but instead began the practice of alternating pamphlets – *Beyond Howth Head* (Dolmen 1970), *Ecclesiastes* (Phoenix Pamphlet Poets, 1970), *Light Music* (Ulsterman Publications, 1977), *A Kensington Notebook* (Anvil Press, 1984) – with major collections issued by Oxford: *Lives* (1972), *The Snow Party* (1975), *The Hunt by Night* (1982).

Liam Miller's publication of *Beyond Howth Head* likely came about through Mahon's position on OUP's poetry list with Thomas Kinsella.[17] Over the next few years other interim works appeared under the imprint of Harry Chambers' Phoenix Pamphlet Poets series, the Poem of the Month Club, and Frank Ormsby's Ulsterman Publications. 'I note with interest that you hope to *pay* pamphleteers,' he wrote Ormsby in the mid-1970s, 'let us bear this in mind!'[18] Such publication, however, could offer little in the way of monetary compensation. Copies of *Light Music*, for example, sold for a mere 20p. What such presses could offer was more timely publication and a figurative repatriation, at a time when his primary collections were being issued from

England. Perhaps most importantly, however, pamphlet publication also preserved Mahon's connection to that intimate circle of readers that his work had always been pitched to.

The 1979 publication *The Sea in Winter* marked a significant turning point in Mahon's publication history. Up to this point interim publications had been soft-cover pamphlets, often no more than folded and stapled sheets, but the Deerfield/Gallery edition of *The Sea in Winter* was issued in hardcover, on high quality paper, with a frontispiece by the artist Timothy Engelland. If Peter Fallon was hoping to secure Mahon's later work for his Gallery Press, he certainly began well. The publication of *The Sea in Winter* also coincided with Mahon's own growing dissatisfaction with Oxford. The publication of *Poems, 1962–1978* had been a particular disappointment to him. The collection, Mahon's first selected, was riddled with typographical errors introduced by the printer, as well as inconsistencies in design that are visually distracting. In a handwritten note laid into Emory's copy of this volume, Mahon writes, 'It was chiefly the appalling shambles OUP made of this book which convinced me to leave them. Good riddance.' In matters of production, editorial control, and management Oxford was simply not as responsive to Mahon's own wishes as the smaller, less commercial, Gallery Press.

In hindsight, the publication of *The Sea in Winter* seems to have anticipated the break that was to come with Oxford. This long poem is in part a meditation on art and its marginal status in our time. In a stanza present in the 1979 printings of the poem but cut from later printings, Mahon writes:

> . . . all the time I have my doubts
> About this verse-making. The shouts
> Of souls in torment round the town
> At closing time make as much sense
> And carry as much significance
> As these lines carefully set down.
> All farts in a biscuit tin, in truth–
> Faint cries, sententious or uncouth.[19]

This questioning of art's significance is a familiar element of Mahon's poetry (and one of the central themes of his 1997 collection *The Yellow Book*). His customary position is that of a witness to time's steady assault on all man's constructs. One thinks of the boilers resting on the seabed in 'A Refusal to Mourn', the tins awash in the surf in 'The Apotheosis of Tins', the growing pile of scrap metal in 'Gipsies', or the keyhole slowly rusting in 'A Disused Shed in Co. Wexford'. Mahon's poems are meditations on our fleeting presence here, and expressions of longing for some permanence beyond our reach.

Contributing to his state of mind is his own distance from the inhabitants of Portstewart, the poem's seaside setting, where one meets no welcoming face but only 'roving gangs' and 'the cool gaze of the RUC'. In such surroundings, the poem is the means of evoking the presence of his friend, one who, like Mahon, has known 'the curious sense of working on the circumference'. The verse letter establishes that bond between poet and reader that he envisions for the larger body of his work at some future time.

> [. . .] One day,
> Perhaps, the words will find their mark
> And leave a brief glow on the dark,
> Effect mutations of dead things
> Into a form that nearly sings [.][20]

In his own working copy of *Poems, 1962–1978* Mahon is unable to leave this expression of hope for a future audience without some check and has added to the stanza, 'Scrap paper left to indicate / Our long day's journey into night.' Often in his poems Mahon chooses to waver between art's relevance and its irrelevance; he takes a position where any disturbance causes a tilt in one direction or another. More than any other factor, what determines which way he tilts is the presence or absence of some receptive reader.

In the early years of his association with Gallery, Mahon took an active stance towards promoting his work, as well as that of other Gallery authors. He was working for the *New Statesman* at the time, and he was able to use that platform to review Gallery books.

> I'll get the Clifton poem into the NS [*New Statesman*] in the next few weeks; and we'll list some Gallery books in our forthcoming Autumn Books supplement. Do you circulate your catalogue to all the London journals? You should, you know: let them know you're there, like Salamander in Edinburgh. Poetry publishing is decentralizing to some extent, and why shouldn't you take advantage of the fact?[21]

Even as he hoped to see his new publisher expand its market, he was also able to admit how little money was, in fact, in such a venture, as we see from a 1982 letter in which he negotiates terms for his translation of Nerval's *Les chimères (The Chimeras)*. 'Dough. I honestly forget what we did the last time; but this time let's agree on some modest sum . . . and if, as I said on the phone, you find even that difficult, consider money irrelevant.'[22]

The history of poetry publishing is a history of such magnanimity. Such gestures indicate again the degree to which literary publishing in Ireland occupies a position outside the marketplace altogether. For his part, Peter Fallon has often returned that generosity either financially or through his patient accommodation of round after round of textual revisions. These changes typically progress up to proof stage and beyond. Even after publication, poetry readings serve as occasions to depart from the printed text and incorporate 'up-to-the-minute changes', as Mahon did at his Emory reading from *The Hudson Letter*.[23]

In contrast to Gallery's accommodation of such changes, OUP chose in 1986 to reissue *Poems 1962–1978*, against Mahon's wishes and without his recent revisions.[24] That decision, more than any other, prompted Mahon to end his association with Oxford. 'Many thanks for the reissued *Poems* and *Hunt*', he wrote to his editor in March:

I now have a difficult letter to write . . . you will think me crazy, but I would
like at this point to be released from all contractual obligations with OUP
so that I may publish in future with Gallery Press . . . Furthermore all rights
to all my work should revert to me; and finally you should let all my
Oxford books go out of print as from now.[25]

It is an extraordinary request. Immediately following the reissue of *Poems* and
Hunt by Night, Mahon asks that both be allowed to go out of print. As he put it to
Peter Fallon two months later, 'I am dismayed by the thought that OUP might go
on reprinting that awful Brown Book every two years in perpetuity.'[26]

This exchange is important not simply for the break it marks in Mahon's
publication history, but more importantly, for the glimpse it gives us of his attitude
towards his work. The conflict with OUP was fundamentally a disagreement over
the nature of art and who that art belonged to. From a publishing perspective, Oxford
was fulfilling the terms of its contract having, as his editor put it, 'taken the early
risks with a writer'.[27] But for Mahon, the reissue of 'that awful Brown Book' was a
kind of artistic theft that froze the further development of his poems in time. As Peter
Denman has pointed out, revisions are a way for Mahon to 'assert his continuing
right as the author of the poems'.[28] OUP, however, approached the 1979 printing of
his poems as a fixed and stable text and denied him the option of ongoing revision.
Mahon's own working copy of *Poems* includes entire stanzas that have been
reworked, and deletions of entire poems (Fig. 12.3), but OUP gave him no means of
incorporating these changes in the 1987 reissue. What had long been economically
marginal now seemed artistically suspect, and the combination proved fatal to any
continued relationship with Oxford. It is worth noting one additional feature of this
exchange with his Oxford editor; that is, how Mahon turned this statement about
textual integrity into a statement about repatriation. 'The point is,' he wrote to
Simms, 'I want to be published from Ireland henceforth . . . '[29] While we may be
tempted to read this return to an Irish publisher as a political gesture, I would suggest
it was a return to that reading society that had supported his earliest work.

The break with OUP contributed to Mahon's diminished productivity in the late
1980s and early 1990s. When he finally wrote his way out of that blocked time
with *The Hudson Letter* and *The Yellow Book*, he took as a central theme the
elusive nature of artistic creativity and the imperiled state of art in our time. In *The
Hudson Letter* the poet seeks to recover his lost voice while all around him art is
in decline as expressed by a fading radio signal, a tropical bird that will not survive
the New York winter, or a hurricane that threatens 'any structure presumed
permanent'. *The Yellow Book* advances that theme further. In this volume the
consolations of art remain fleeting and the poet has withdrawn from that
previously expansive world of London and New York and inhabits figuratively 'a
secret garden in a locked park'.[30] With the shrinking dimensions of this world goes
a corresponding shrinking of audience. Here we learn:

> *real* books like vintage wines survive
> among the antiquities, each yellowing page
> known only to astrologer and mage.[31]

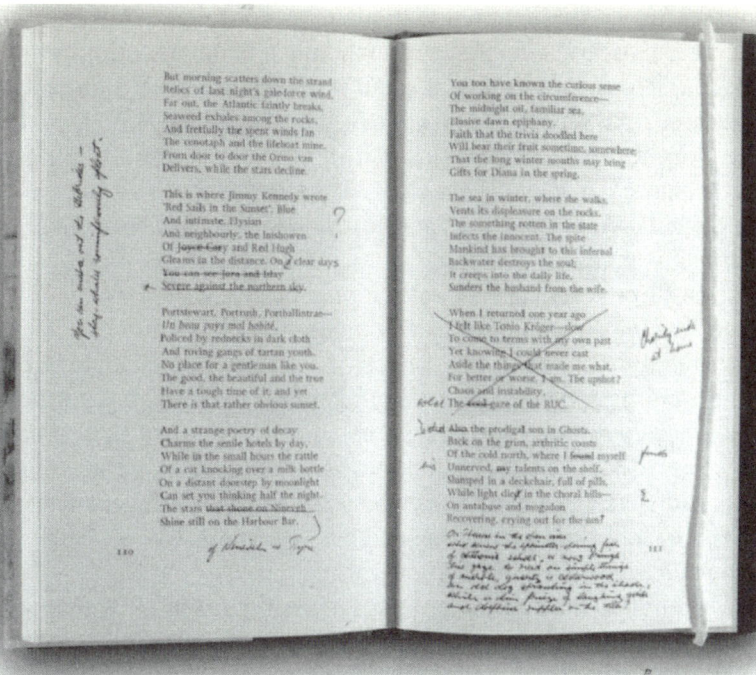

Figure 12.3 Derek Mahon's working copy of *Poems, 1962–1978* (open to 'The Sea in Winter') with numerous revisions in his hand. (Robert W. Woodruff Library, Emory University.)

This constricted view of art's audience is, I would suggest, a logical outcome of Mahon's forty-year struggle with art and audience. After his split with OUP – which coincidentally coincided with Emory's collecting of Mahon's work – there is a progressive contracting of the audience posited by his work.

His *Collected Poems* were published in November 1999 with the instructions that no review copies were to be distributed. The decision to issue that volume without the promotion that would normally accompany the publication of a collected poems is only the most visible sign of his self-imposed withdrawal from the public sphere. With this effacement of his own work has gone a corresponding effacement of the self. When asked what advice he would offer young poets, Mahon once replied, 'Publish posthumously',[32] and in recent years it has sometimes seemed like he was indeed trying to follow just such advice. A letter written a few months before the publication of his *Collected Poems* is quite revealing of his new stance. In March, after receiving a standard information request, Mahon replied, 'Thank you for yours of 24th Feb. I would be grateful if you would omit me altogether from the new edition of *Who's Who in Ireland*.'[33]

The stance that Mahon has taken towards his *Collected Poems* should not, however, be construed as an abandonment of audience altogether, nor should these gestures of personal self-effacement be overstated. The *Collected Poems* were published after all and, more importantly, so is new work. Instead Mahon's refusal to promote himself or his work marks a conscious rejection of the commercialisation of art and the corresponding commodification of the artist himself. Mahon, it seems, would be content if his picture never hung in a Dublin pub or peered out from a postcard rack on Grafton Street. He is content, rather, to produce the work for that reader (often named at the start of each poem) willing to seek out the particular rewards his poetry has to offer. Such a stance is in sharp contrast to the self-promotion that more often characterises contemporary Irish writing, and that is precisely the point.

Over the past forty years, Mahon has not only been shaping a body of work, he has also been seeking an audience for whom that work truly matters. While some would undoubtedly condemn the selectivity of such a stance, we should acknowledge that it is a logical outcome of our culture's antipathy towards poetry which Mahon has confronted over the course of forty years of publishing. It is a return in a sense to that small circle of readers that he first wrote for when he imagined his audience as a few friends who were writing for *Icarus* at the time. If that circle of readers does not seem enough, we misjudge the large role the appreciative reader has played in Mahon's work.

Even as Mahon has taken deliberate steps to restrict his work within the public sphere, he has also been taking steps to insure that the most full record of that work is preserved. Shortly after his *Collected Poems* were published, revised drafts of these poems arrived at the Emory archive. What the archive offers in addition to a willing accommodation of that still-changing text is the very real prospect of some reader that his work may reach in the future. In *The Sea in Winter* he expresses the hope that his words will one day 'find their mark / And leave a brief glow on the dark'.[34] Elsewhere, in 'An Image from Beckett', he imagines willing his work to some future reader if only 'they have time, / And light enough, to read it'.[35] Ultimately Mahon's largest audience may be found not among a contemporary book-buying public at all but instead out there in that still unformed future. The characteristic posture of Mahon's best poems is a posture of yearning for that still unrealised future. In the end the circumstances that I describe are less about economics or about Ireland than they are about the rarefied nature of art in our time.

Chapter 13

Blackstaff Press: Publishing 'a local row'

Anne Tannahill

That was the year of the Munich bother. Which
Was more important? I inclined
To lose my faith in Ballyrush and Gortin
Till Homer's ghost came whispering to my mind
He said: I made the Iliad from such
A local row. Gods make their own importance.[1]

(Patrick Kavanagh, from 'Epic')

Parochialism and provincialism are opposites. The provincial has no mind of his own; he does not trust what his eyes see until he has heard what the metropolis – towards which his eyes are turned – has to say on any subject...The parochial mentality on the other hand is never in any doubt about the social and artistic validity of his parish...Parochialism is universal; it deals with the fundamentals.[2]

(Patrick Kavanagh, from *Collected Pruse*)

Blackstaff Press was founded in 1971. It is almost contemporaneous with the Troubles – and our publishing has reflected a conflict that has attracted international interest. We are nevertheless 'parochial' in Kavanagh's sense, profoundly convinced of the social and artistic validity of our region. We are entirely comfortable with the term 'regional publisher' – that is who we are and where we are, whatever the difficulties and constraints.

In 1971, with the help of the first Bass Carrington/Arts Council of Northern Ireland Bursary Award, Jim Gracey, a librarian, and his wife Diane, who had been an editor at Hodder and Stoughton, started Blackstaff Press with £400 capital. There had been no serious commercial book publishing in the north of Ireland for several decades, and little in the south, with the exception of Mercier, Dolmen and Gill and Macmillan, plus of course Irish University Press, but, as I said, very little commercial publishing. There was to be an extraordinary renaissance of Irish publishing in the 1970s; it is interesting to speculate as to why a northern publisher was in the vanguard of that development. There are a number of factors, not least the remarkable vision and commitment of Jim and Diane Gracey. And given that, as Michael Longley says, 'Northern Ireland is a province twice over: an Irish province and a province of the United Kingdom', there was undoubtedly also a useful creative tension between Jim's Irishness and Diane's Englishness.[3]

It was a time of extreme political and social ferment after decades of stagnation, with as yet no inkling that the balloon was about to go up for three decades of shocking violence. Questions about identity, nationality and culture were being debated openly, not least by the young men and women from working-class backgrounds – Protestants as well as Catholics – who had been the first to benefit from the 1944 Education Act. W. R. Rodgers speaks of 'the creative wave of self-consciousness which occurs wherever two racial patterns meet'; in the early 1970s this 'wave' had become a tidal wave that was generating new thinking, new writing and new publishing.

A factor that can not be overstressed in the Blackstaff story is the support of the Arts Council of Northern Ireland, from the initial bursary right down to the present day, where the Council continues to fund our literary titles. In those early start-up years and indeed up to 1991 the key figure was Michael Longley, the Arts Council's Literature Officer: his benign, non-interfering but passionate interest in Blackstaff – he saw his job as helping us to prepare 'healthy and receptive soil' to receive 'the seed corn' of local writing – was a model of enlightened arts administration.

That is certainly part of how we see our role as regional publishers – as discoverers and nurturers of local talent. We also see ourselves as holding the ring, providing a forum, for political and historical debate. Over the years, we have published almost all shades of the political spectrum in the north – I say 'almost' because our liberalism is not absolute, and from the personal conviction of the Graceys and later of myself and Michael Burns, owner of the company from 1980 to 1995, we have not so far published work from the paramilitary extremes (although we have published books *about* the paramilitaries – examples are Padraig O'Malley's book about the hunger strikes, *Biting at the Grave* (1990), and a book about loyalist prisoners and the impact of the criminalisation policy in the late 1970s, *Defenders or Criminals?* by Colin Crawford, which we published in 1999). In recent years some of our politics and history titles have been subvented by the Cultural Traditions Group of the Community Relations Council, a body which promotes cultural diversity and mutual understanding in ways that mirror our own ethos.

I joined Blackstaff as an editor in 1976 and when Michael Burns bought the company in 1980 he made me managing director (I felt a bit like a corporal who finds himself promoted to colonel in the aftermath of a battle, and I had to grow into the job). While Michael Burns and myself are both secular liberals, I feel that his Catholic background and my Protestant one gave the list an interesting balance.

Patronage has played some part in our work, and indeed has determined the survival of the Press. When Michael Burns bought Blackstaff he did so against the advice of his accountants; he proceeded to work tirelessly for fifteen years as an unsalaried chairman. The W & G Baird Group bought us in 1995 for our perceived social and cultural worth rather than our financial lustre, and have been very supportive ever since.

Profits have proved elusive, as accountants say; there are a number of reasons why this is so. First of all, the very regionalism that we are so committed to brings its own constraints. Our home market, the one we know best and can supply most economically, is *tiny*. Northern Ireland has a population of under a million and a half and I dread to think how many of them are serious readers, let alone book buyers, let alone buyers of local books. Well actually I do have a pretty good idea about how many buyers of local books there are – going by our local sales of all but the most popular titles, there must be somewhere under a thousand of them.

With these sorts of numbers, the diseconomies of scale are frightening – dependence on exclusively local sales would long ago have been the death of us and we have worked hard to build up what is now an increasingly effective overseas network of distributors, agents and co-publishers. We have had particular success recently in selling our literary fiction via our American distributor Dufour Editions. Excellent reviews of several of our books – including Professor Bob Welch's fine novel *Groundwork* – in, for example, the *New York Times*, *Library Journal*, *Kirkus* and *Publishers' Weekly* – generated so much demand in 2001 that we had to reprint several times just for the American market. This is particularly encouraging as we have sometimes found that America, especially Irish-America, seems to want what we call 'shamrock and shillelagh books' rather than books that try to express the complex realities of modern Ireland, north and south. We have also greatly increased the number of translation rights we sell, and have recently completed deals with publishers in Germany, France, Poland, Sweden, the Czech Republic, and Greece.

Apart from its smallness, our home market of Northern Ireland is also remarkable for – and it pains me to have to admit it – its residual philistinism. Dating from the north's heyday as one of the industrial hubs of the British Empire, there is still a hard-headed suspicion and lack of respect for the arts which shows itself not only in low sales of our books, but in the attitude of, for example, the business and banking worlds. I may be wrong, but I believe that the automatically higher social status that, say, a Dublin publisher enjoys gives him that bit more rope with a bank manager when cash is tight. Blackstaff certainly noticed an immediate improvement in our bank's general tone towards us once we were acquired by Bairds, a group that makes its money in a solid, sensible activity like printing rather than an airy-fairy, high-risk one like publishing. I referred to *residual* philistinism, and there is no doubt that it is now dwindling fast. On my more optimistic days, I like to think that Blackstaff has played some part in building a wider, less elitist and more inclusive cultural community in the north, one that is at last squeezing out these dinosaur attitudes.

Other constraints arising from our regional position include the lack of local book publishing expertise – with few exceptions, Blackstaff has had to train its own editors, proofers, publicists and so on from scratch. The tight margins have also meant that we have been chronically understaffed; one side effect is that it takes us too long to assess submitted scripts, and we have lost some good authors because of our delays. Our relative distance from the Dublin and London media is also a problem. By and large, we have good support from our local journalists and broadcasters, but, notwithstanding the fact that *The Sunday Times* voted us UK Small Publisher of the Year in 1992, it is difficult to get reviews, articles and author reviews in the two capitals.

One of our most painful problems – and it is common to all Irish publishers – is the depressing regularity with which we lose writers to the London publishing houses. Since the publishing renaissance of the 1970s, new Irish writers have a much better chance of being published at all, but the more effectively their work is published and promoted in Ireland, the more likely they are to be spotted by a London publisher or agent who whisks them away just when they might have started yielding substantial income for their Irish publishers.

The situation is complex and difficult, and you can not really blame an author who is tempted by the cash and indeed the cachet offered by famous houses, but it has tended to keep a ceiling on the development of Irish publishers. Some ways have been found around the problem – for instance, Blackstaff Press managed to negotiate the Irish rights for Bernard MacLaverty's work when Jonathan Cape accepted his second book *Lamb* in 1978 (*Lamb* has just been listed in *The Modern Library* as one of the fifty best novels in the English language since 1950). This arrangement with Cape still continues, largely thanks to Bernard's loyalty. Increasingly, Irish publishers like Lilliput have been selling on rights to London publishers (Penguin recently bought the paperback rights of Michael Viney's *A Years Turning* from Blackstaff, for example). But the situation is still a thorn in our side, especially now when Irish writing is so trendy, with astronomical advances being paid. Even British editors remark that the frantic buying up of Irish talent by London publishers has the scent of plunder and pillage.

As for the pleasures of regional publishing, they are – in spite of everything – many, and far outweigh the pains. It is actually quite useful being both an Irish and a British publisher – we can be a big fish in the small Irish pond – for example at the Frankfurt and London Book Fairs – or a small one in the big British ocean as and when it suits us. For example, the same year that we were named UK Small Publisher of the Year we also received a Bank of Ireland Better Ireland Communications Award, and the previous year, 1991, we received a Special Citation from the judges of the Christopher Ewart-Biggs Memorial for 'producing books which have genuinely added to a greater understanding between the peoples of Ireland and Britain'. Our books have also won a fair number of Irish Book Awards and *Irish Times* Literature Prizes, as well as production and design prizes from the British Federation of Printers and the *Bookseller*.

There is also the pleasure of working with some of the most interesting and impressive people of our place and time – Blackstaff has published over 650 titles now, and the list of authors and artists is too long to recite, but I count myself privileged to have worked with people like Sam Hanna Bell (his *December Bride* is also listed in *The Modern Library*), John Hewitt, Helen Lewis, Jonathan Bardon, Raymond Piper, Michael and Edna Longley, A. T. Q. Stewart, David McKittrick, Paul Durcan and Bernard MacLaverty. Like the speaker in Kavanagh's 'Epic', Blackstaff – the company and all its workers over the years – has 'lived in important places, times when great events were decided' and the last three decades of conflict have undoubtedly given our work added edge, added resonance. But the social and artistic validity of our parish was there before this 'local row' and will be there after it ends – and that is what we will continue to publish.

Chapter 14

The World of Irish University Press

Michael Adams

The rise and fall of the Irish University Press was one of the most dramatic events in Irish publishing in the twentieth century. In the annals of publishing history it cannot, of course, be given pride of place. For one thing, there existed right through the period the subculture of schoolbook publishing, an area of the business which is like a closed book to the outside world – and one responsible for a large part of Irish publishing turnover. For another thing Irish University Press had a notoriously short life (1967–74). But dramatic it was, and its achievement abides, notably in the form of its publications but also in its influence on numerous careers in Irish publishing in the last thirty years. Old IUP hands, myself among them, have threatened, at times, to write it all down.[1] No doubt, some researcher will in due course tackle the job in greater detail. In the interim, this essay sketches the story; it is based somewhat on archival material which is held at the Four Courts Press.

Immediate background

The *éminence grise* behind the Irish University Press was a Scot, James Hamilton Grieve MacMahon, who was an executive in the business world of the Canadian tycoon Lord Thomson, and who was actively involved in acquisitions on behalf of the Thomson Organization. In the course of this, MacMahon fronted the takeover of Thomas Nelson & Co., the Scottish publishers and printers, whose main shareholder was Ronnie Nelson, a man whose interests lay outside publishing and who, after the sale, readily accepted overtures from James MacMahon to reinvest much of his cash gains. MacMahon then left the Thomson Organization and proceeded to establish his own, a company called Trinity Holdings, whose capital came from Ronnie Nelson, and which had three directors – Nelson, MacMahon and Gerry Wall, a friend of MacMahon.

For some years Nelson was effectively sidelined. MacMahon projected himself as the person who mattered, and acted with style as an entrepreneur in his own right. He proceeded to spend and invest the Nelson money – in a hotel, a printing school, a printery here, a bindery there, a publishing house, book shops (I cannot recall the full list, if ever I knew it); and soon his attention turned to Ireland. Here he acquired the Cahill Group, which comprised a huge printing house (it took on large commissions for the government), the educational publisher, C. J. Fallon, and publishing imprints, including the Mellifont Press. (Mellifont, during the war, published cheap classics, all cut down to fit economic printing modules.) The principal hands-on publisher in that group was Martin J. McManus, who had worked his way up from office boy to senior executive. In McManus, MacMahon found an obedient servant – a man of considerable charm, dedicated to his work, and ungreedy. Soon MacMahon and McManus were attracted by the tax-free status of the Shannon Industrial Estate in the west of Ireland, near Limerick, where they established a state-of-the-art printery. It is difficult to say whether the original intention was a printing press, or a publishing house with a printery. In all probability it was the need to feed the planned presses at Shannon that led to the creation of Irish University Press as a publishing imprint in 1967. The vast presses at Shannon were greedy for work – and the entire Irish publishing industry of the time would not have kept them busy for more than 10 per cent of their capacity: by 1969 the highly efficient printery, presided over by Robert Hogg (previously a Nelson printer), could produce forty 640-page folio volumes per month (in runs of 2000) – the equivalent of some 600 demy monographs.

THE HEYDAY OF REPRINTING

It was a good time for reprinting. New universities, well endowed with public and private funds, were springing up, most notably in the USA but indeed world wide (Japan deserves a special mention) – and their libraries had a seemingly insatiable appetite for books and microfilm. Good new academic writing was of course difficult for a publisher (especially an untried publisher) to come by, but no such difficulty applied to reprints. These were the days of Kraus Reprint, Readex, Oceana, and Gale. Reprinting provided a fast-entry system for up and coming would-be publishers – most of them quite unskilled in the niceties of copy-editing and book production but highly motivated and indeed masters in the sphere of selling. The reprint was a commodity; seemingly every printed book since Caxton was at risk.

To head up the publishing division of the newly incorporated Irish University Press, McManus first suggested Dr T. P. O'Neill, the historian and biographer (with Lord Longford) of de Valera. O'Neill, an academic, demurred; and Tadgh MacGlinchey, an army officer and a knowledgeable book-collector, jumped at the chance of retiring, in his early forties, and starting a new career as a publisher. T. P. O'Neill recommended to McManus the idea of reprinting some of the British Parliamentary Papers (BPP) of the nineteenth century, particularly those of Irish interest such as the Famine papers. Tadgh MacGlinchey confirmed that this was a good idea and, additionally, quickly came up with many other reprint ideas based on his knowledge of antiquarian books. Other publishers were dipping into the BPP corpus at this time, notably Frank Cass (in London), in whose house MacMahon also had a minority interest. When Frank Cass, already an active reprinter, was told by MacMahon of IUP's more modest BPP plans, he reportedly told MacMahon to back off. This nod of confirmation about the validity of BPP reprints was enough to convince MacMahon that Parliamentary Papers were the very thing to feed his Shannon presses and that IUP should embark on a huge

BPP reprint programme that would scare off all competitors, Cass included. In fact, in 1967 or 1968 IUP bought Cass's stock (some ten reprints) of British Parliamentary Papers, or 'Blue Books', to console him for being squeezed out of the BPP race.

On 21 July 1967 Thomas F. Turley, newly appointed editor, wrote the following letter to HMSO:

> We are engaged in reprinting fundamental source material of high academic standard for scholars and students. We would very much appreciate your permission to reprint in particular the titles included on the attached list. We would also like to know if you would be prepared to grant us general permission to reprint the Series of 'Blue Books' published between 1825 and 1840 on New Zealand, Australia, Africa, Upper and Lower Canada and the Slave Trade.[2]

It was an unnecessary application, for HMSO's reply of 1 August pointed out that the material was out of copyright.

THE 1,000-VOLUME SERIES OF BRITISH PARLIAMENTARY PAPERS

The rest is history. IUP announced some 10 BPP reprints, then 102, then 250, then 750 and was eventually prevailed upon by its American salesmen to STOP at the magic number of 1000 on the grounds that university libraries, no matter how rich, would not sign up for an open-ended series. When I joined IUP, shortly after the first few 'Blue Books' were printed, the print run was 2000; the order book stood at 55 (standing orders for the then open-ended set). In 1968 a new case-bound monograph was expensive at £4 4s retail; BPP volumes sold at about £25.00 – a lot of money (especially when multiplied, as it soon would be, by the magic 1,000 volumes in a full set). The BPP scheme, of course, had burst its 'Irish' banks: the only Irish set, really, was the eight-volume Famine one. The series ran to 82 subdivisions (called 'subject-sets'), the largest of which was the ninety-five-volume Slave Trade set. A thousand folio volumes, replete with facsimiles (which often meant five or six colours) of folding maps etc., sometimes as many as thirty tip-ins in a volume, printed on laid acid-free paper, real head-bands, gilt-tops, quarter bound leather and buckram cases, was a huge printing and publishing programme; and yet within two years plans were being laid which would cause the 1000-volume series to pale into insignificance.

The 1,000-volume series was no mere reprint: apart from the editorial work of selection, which meant that in some cases a single IUP volume could contain tens of Parliamentary Papers, originals had to be found, borrowed, disbound, photographed, repaginated (sometimes), and rebound. The series was confined largely to home and colonial papers; it was, moreover, highly selective as against the entire 7,000-volume corpus of 'Blue Books' produced by Westminster in the nineteenth century. New series were projected – the eighteenth-century BPP; the 'foreign' papers – consular reports, etc. covering the United States (sixty volumes);

China and Japan (fifty-two volumes); Russia; Central and South America. Completely new fields would be ploughed – the India Office records, the Secret Archives of the Vatican, the Archives of the Indies in Spain. IUP executives – salesmen turned would-be editors and publishers – hobnobbed with distinguished librarians and academics in a search of more and greater projects.

OPEN FOR BUSINESS

Coming to the fledging IUP from a small Dublin-based publisher with a staff of two, I was stunned by the size of the 1,000-volume project and by the other goodies that IUP planned to bring out. When I learned that the print run was 2,000 on my first day, 2 October 1968, I thought to myself that the world was not big enough to buy even that output. Much, much later, the print run was reduced to 1000 and eventually (c.1972) to 400, as it turned out, the realistic figure. Figure 14.1 is an edition of an IUP 'invoice progress sheet' in the company's first active year of publishing. It focuses on BPP; but the fact is that the company was doing very little outside of that area. So sizeable was the overhead at that time and so puny its turnover, that Martin McManus was provided with a daily record, not only of invoicing (for the year to date) of books dispatched but also of invoices raised in advance of production. It will be remembered that there were some fifty-five standing orders at the time; some for technical reasons had not as yet been supplied with all published titles. Note the especially high sales figure for Index volumes 2 and 3 (these were facsimiles of the official nineteenth-century indexes to the BPP). Only 1596 BPP volumes have been invoiced. This document was produced by Mr Laurence Shelly who operated an IBM typewriter; he raised one-line invoices and spent his spare time typing invoices for books that did not yet exist. 'Cramps' is a reference to the Cornwall bindery which did work for IUP prior to the commissioning of the bindery at Shannon; 'Cahill's' is the printery in Dublin, the anchor of the Cahill Group.

In 1968 IUP had no salesmen of its own in the field. To promote itself and the Parliamentary Papers it relied on advertising and direct mail, and attendance at academic and library conferences. IUP's catalogues were elegant, not to say lavish, by the standards of the time; its mailings, cooperative ones with other firms such as Blackwells, Richard Abel, Erasmus, Dawsons; its advertising designed to show that here was a new publishing force to be reckoned with – witness a full page in the *Times Literary Supplement*. The number of executives to appear at such events as the American Library Association were very few – MacGlinchey, Tom Turley, and Commander John F. Standish, who came to the company in 1968 from Routledge, where he had gained experience of academic publishing at a senior level. Most of the already considerable publishing staff was burrowing away at 141 Thomas Street, Dublin, hoping that it would all work out. 'Oh!' said Jeremy Addis on my first day there, 'have they managed to fool you too [into abandoning my previous job]?' 'Maybe,' I thought, 'maybe.' Maybe I had been beguiled by McManus, and especially by Standish, with his grandiose talk about

			above line	below line
Total volumes invoiced			1596	375
Value of invoices			£25,079	£6,434
Value per volume			£15	£17
Volumes dispatched			1237	NIL

[Date: *c.* October 1968]

	SBN	TITLE	EX BINDERS	CHARGED	REMAINING	INVOICED	VALUE	DESPATCHED
+	0092 2	Slave Trade 8	395	90	305	86	£1129	75
	0083 3	Index 2		180		176	£2218	152
	0082 5	Index 3		159		155	£3124	156
	0171 6	Health General 1		57		55	£1331	51
+	0103 1	Child Employ 8	395	87	308	84	£1406	84
+	0084 1	Text [iles]7	396	82	314	78	£738	76
	0189 9	Tobacco 1	43	54		50	£823	41
	0090 6	Australia 2				1	£17	1
	0114 7	Text iles 6		60		57	£932	45
	0124 4	Aborigines 2	104	54	50	50	£567	61
+	0089 2	Canada 2	409	82	337	77	£1265	42
	0181 3	Iesign 2		54		49	£872	
+	0177 5	Bribery [at Elections]	362	46	316	45	£954	
	0184 8	W Indies 1	63	60	3	50	£1071	51
	0134 1	N Zealand 1	41	63		53	£900	54
	0172 4	Colonies [General] 1		56		48	£595	45
	0176 7	Famine [Ireland] 1		57		48	£564	38
	0106 6	Agriculture 3		60		51	£730	50
	00183 X	Poor Law 2		72		62	£999	61
	0123 6	Aborigines 1		62		52	£1100	58
	0190 2	Drunkenness 1		57		47	£586	51
+	0159 7	Emigration 3		64		53	£587	
	0179 1	Poor Law 1		74		64	£1003	
	0111 2	Agriculture 8		62		52	£714	
	0156 2	Industrial Relations 3				53	£854	

INVOICED BUT NOT RECEIVED FROM BINDERS

	SBN	TITLE				INVOICED	VALUE	
	0085 X	Child Employ 6				74	£869	
+	0087 6	Transportation 2				61	£1224	
	0164 3	Text 5				47	£1063	
	0188 0	Prisons 1				53	£765	
	0135 X	Health Mental 1				48	£750	
	0198 9	Explosives 1				44	£584	
	0199 8	Child Employ 1				48	£1169	
						375	£6434	

GENERAL BOOKS

	SBN	TITLE	EX BINDERS	CHARGED	REMAINING	INVOICED	VALUE	DESPATCHED
	0030 2	Kenney	79	29	50	28	£224	25

Notes:
1. Col. 4 includes Requisition and consignment notes as well as invoices
2. Col. 8 shows only those despatches as reported by binders.
3. * indicates volume not yet released by Production Department.
4. + indicates bound stock held at Cramp's (items unmarked held Cahill's)

Total standing orders in hand: 45   [Signed:] L. Shelley

Figure 14.1 An early Irish University Press 'invoice progress sheet'.

'we publishers' and 'the Polish Academy of Sciences' (whom IUP planned to distribute in the west), and Matthias Corvinus, the subject of a delicious book he had just bought from Corvina Press, Budapest, and the three-volume *Byzantine Wall Paintings in Asia Minor* (soon to be out in an English edition). This was publishing. This was where I was meant to be, saved (I thought) from the job I had applied for as MD of C. J. Fallon: to be alive in IUP as a sales manager would be very heaven.

Soon there *was* a sales force – three men covering the UK; an IUP Inc. at White Plains, NY, controlled by Michael Glazier and Bob Davis; Gustave Pairoux (who came from Desclée) swanning around the Continent; Dr Ghosh reportedly living like a prince in a New Delhi enclave and dutifully reporting on his visits across India to enthusiastic but penniless libraries. Soon the Scottish-based sales rep, ecstatic over the very concept of the 1,000-volume series, was making the world his oyster, flying off to Japan and Canada and sending back reports that Maruzen (or was it Kinokunya) wanted an exclusive for fifty sets. Orders did indeed pour in as the interest stirred up by advertising was pinned down by hard-nosed representatives. These were men who had done their apprenticeships in reprint houses (Kraus, mainly). The primary market was, of course, US academic libraries.

John Standish speedily sought to impose administrative order on the sales and production aspects of the business and his counsel also contributed to the company's editorial planning. But his career in Dublin was short-lived, for he was replaced in 1969 when he was moved to London as editorial director, a position which he soon resigned in order to start his own company, the Curzon Press, specialising in Asian and African studies. Standish probably always regarded Ireland as something of a backwater, but his disillusionment was also inspired by the roles which McManus and MacMahon were now playing, staying in the background and very much expecting lower-level directors to be courtiers. His successor, Liam Carroll, was replaced by George Prior, who came to IUP from Penguin. IUP sales reps with editorial briefs were constantly on the move. However, library budget cutbacks soon put paid to these ambitions.

Figure 14.2 reproduces IUP's invoice progress sheet of November 1972. It is a record of *invoicing*, not sales; therefore, the figures are as much a function of new book production (mainly BPP) as of new sales. Most of the BPP full set standing orders were bagged by 31 March 1970 – the end of the 69/70 year – but they did not produce turnover until the Shannon presses actually printed the volumes ordered. At its height, Shannon was producing up to forty 'Blue Books' per month; in the year 69/70 it reached a peak of 391. The reader will observe that IUP turnover for non-BPP (that is, General Titles and Sales of Editions), was really quite small; the Parliamentary Papers (i.e. what is called in the progress sheet 'British Parliamentary Papers' and which should properly include Area Studies – Parliamentary Papers that supplemented the 1,000-volume series) accounted for 95 per cent of Press turnover. From this perspective, it has to be admitted that IUP was a book-factory rather than an academic publishing house. 'Cuala Press' – mentioned bottom right – was the IUP facsimile reprint of the eighty-two hand-printed volumes that had been issued prior to 1950 by the Yeats family private press. Sets of these sold for about £400 and made a considerable contribution to turnover in the year of production (1971/72). Note also the figure for 'Trade work'. This progress sheet does not contain figures for invoicing of printing work done by Shannon for companies outside the Cahill Group, but it is fair to say that

IRISH UNIVERSITY PRESS

Mr Adams / Mr Hogg
Mr Caffrey Mr C Gore-Grimes
Mr Turley Mr McGarry

Invoice progress sheet covering despatches up to and on (date): 30 November 1972

BRITISH PARLIAMENTARY PAPERS

	Inv.Sales '68/'69	Inv Sales '69/'70	Inv.Sales '70/'71	FINAL Inv.Sales '71/'72 15 months	Inv.Sales '72/'73
Tot vols inv in period	10,498	47,961	58,506	23,423	4,232
Value of invoices	£163,566	£1,031,268	£1,360,631	£580,625	£102,147
Value per volume	£15.58	£21.50	£23.33	£22.50	£21.50
No.new titles inv/des	141	391	373	95	
FSO still effective	43	46	19	3	2
Avge. vols inv per title published	74	110	129	140	

GENERAL TITLES

...t vols inv in period	1,862	8,164	20,855	29,507	7,884
Value of invoices	£5,683	£21,459	£75,051	£67,136	£24,589

SALES OF EDITIONS

Tot No.titles sold	7	10	9	14	4
Value of invoices	£5,425	£16,524	£10,632	£38,569	£1,431

AREA STUDIES	A.S.O.	U.S.A.	J.S.O.	R.S.O.		
Tot vols inv in per.					2,984	3,665
Value of invoices					£50,044	£59,275
...titles inv/des	1	56	60	1	51	57

TOTAL: 1.2.3.4. above:	£174,674	£1,069,251	£1,446,314	£736,374	£187,442

INFORMATION RE CURRENT MONTH	Volumes	Value
Blue Books:	1,312	£35,583
General Books:	1,632	5,339
Sales of Editions:	520	734
Area Studies:	169	2,859
		£44,515

New Area Studies Invoiced : 3

Signed:

Date: 30 November 1972

*NOTE: Tel Aviv FSO Figures appear in IPS

CUALA PRESS
Total sets sold: 214
Total value: £64,149
Total paid: £30,842

TRADE WORK
Fig to 30.6.72   £20,602
July 1 - Nov 30   £19,022

Figure 14.2 'Invoice progress sheet', November 1972.

little such work was done and that really the Shannon presses were dedicated to and dependent on IUP publishing in Dublin. When (from 1971 onwards), Shannon, in a struggle for survival had to seek outside 'trade' work, it proved quite incapable of obtaining it (£19,022 worth in July–Nov. 1972).

Changes of ownership

Some of IUP's finance came from First National City Bank, Dublin, and the Bank of Ireland, but the main funds for the group of which the Irish companies formed part came from the original Nelson loans. Ronnie Nelson had in the meantime married and come to live in Ireland with his wife, Elizabeth. The story goes that their bank manager, to Elizabeth's surprise, announced that there was 'no money left'. Where was the money? Without much difficulty, the Nelsons, with the banks' support, managed to oust MacMahon from control of Trinity Holdings, and proceeded to dismantle the empire that MacMahon had built up. In mid 1971, at a time when most of the 1000-volume series had been published, the Shannon printing operation was severely cut back by its Nelson controllers. At the same time, the US operations of IUP Inc. were starved of funds. The Nelsons had no great interest in saving a troubled IUP, and a search for a buyer began. In December 1971 William G. Stern (of Stern Family Holdings) acquired the Cahill Group, which included IUP. Stern, essentially a property developer, was fascinated by the IUP 1,000-volume series. He put Mark Matthews, an aide with a PR background, in charge of IUP. In an early report to the board, Matthews outlined his opinion of the company:

Figure 14.3 A promotional shot of volumes in the Irish University Press series of British Parliamentary Papers.

Figure 14.4 In addition to vast direct mail promotion, media advertising and sales representation to libraries, IUP travelled far and wide to promote its publications at academic meetings and book fairs. Attendance at such meetings was grant-assisted by the Irish Export Board. (Photo by Sunbeam Photo, Margate.)

The size and dominance of [the 'Blue Book' project] has left the organization unprepared for the more normal flow of a variety of projects and the greater co-ordination and flexibility needed. The traumatic experiences of the last year [1971] have left their impact in various ways and which is the most important only time will tell. The recession in the USA has severely cut back the sales turnover. This fact, the financial problems associated with it, and the drastic remedies implemented, have left obvious problems. A suspicious attitude towards top management, a sense of insecurity and above all a loss of the excitement and challenge of a thriving on-going situation. Additionally the harsh cuts [in mid 1971] have left at Shannon an uneconomic and resentful production unit: in the USA a disbanded sales organization, lost records and rumours; in Dublin a weakened and de-energized team; and in London, a feeling of impending closure. The power struggle for control in the midst of the above difficulties opened the door to political in-fighting, confused lines of control and further deepened the clefts in the organization which had arisen from the previous divide and (sometimes) rule philosophy of management.

In essence the present situation is that of a skeletal organization which can be viewed negatively or positively. On the present evidence there are no clear indications. In terms of publications it has the prestigious 'Blue Book' project, the ancillary Area Studies and a miscellaneous selection of smaller projects and monographs. The forthcoming projects are, with some exceptions, neither over-exciting nor of sufficient demand to create the income required to sustain an international publishing organization. In the main the staff at all levels appear extremely willing both in terms of effort and flexibility. It is only necessary to create a suitable environment and opportunities. In conclusion it would seem that the acquisition of the organization by Stern Family Holdings, is seen internally in favourable terms and not as a further stage in the financial gyrations of top management.[3]

But unfortunately the Stern takeover caused no lasting improvement to IUP's fortunes.

Figure 14.5 Dr Edward MacLysaght and the poet Austin Clarke at an IUP reception. Ned MacLysaght, writer, geneaologist, farmer, politician, market gardener, was director of the Irish Manuscripts Commission in the days of IUP. The Press published for the Commission, whose offices were a few doors away from 81 Merrion Square, where the 'Doc' was a regular visitor for an elevenses glass of Guinness. In his youth he had come to the rescue of Maunsel, the prolific Dublin publishing house in the teens of the century. (Photo by PR Fotoservice, Dublin.)

Figure 14.6 Captain T. MacGlinchey, IUP Publisher, presenting a copy of the final volume of the 1,000-volume series to Quincey Mumford, Librarian of Congress, in the presence of the Irish Ambassador to the United States, William Warnock. (Photo by deKun, Washington.)

During the Stern period, the company did manage to complete production of the 1000-volume series (with prestigious presentations of the set to the Library of Congress and the House of Commons Library), and two out of four ancillary Parliamentary Papers projects (Area Studies: USA, and Area Studies: China and Japan); it also completed the eighty-two volume Cuala Press series (a successful project, but not big enough to impact greatly on the company's future). The period also saw the publication of the first volumes in the series entitled *Documents of the American Revolution*, a collection of documents, calendars and transcripts which were expertly edited by K. G. Davies, who was to become Professor of Modern History at Trinity College Dublin. This series – which was completed by Irish Academic Press in 1981 – eventually ran to twenty-one volumes and was described in 1974 as 'one of the most important published sources for the history of the Revolution' and 'a "must" purchase for all graduate research libraries'.[4]

In April 1973 Stern presided over the closure of the Shannon plant, which now became a warehouse for unsold stock – bound, sewn and flat-sheet – and containing the makings of perhaps a million 'Blue Book' volumes. At a board

Figure 14.7 Shannon, 1975. After the collapse of IUP, its stocks were housed in 37,000 sq. ft of warehouses at a rental of 50p per square foot.

meeting in late 1973, when I proposed to Stern a huge cut-price sales programme for the material (against the backdrop of a severe recession in the academic libraries market), Stern turned to Paul Caffrey, the accountant and then MD of IUP, and asked, 'Mr Caffrey, how much do my warehouses cost me?' He replied,

'£25,000' a year or some such figure. Stern's comment was: 'Then I can leave the "Blue Books" there, and in ten years' time have the libraries of the world come knocking on my door' – very much the thinking of a property-owner and one not strapped for cash. The problem was that cash was precisely what Stern did not have; and the following year (1974) saw the collapse of the Stern empire, with IUP its Achilles' heel, the first segment of it to be put into receivership. William Stern subsequently went personally bankrupt for a record sum (in excess of £100,000,000, as I recall).

IUP was once again a publisher in search of an owner, and its receiver, Laurence Crowley (appointed in 1974), put it on the market as a going concern with a price tag of £1,000,000. The following is an extract from the receiver's briefing to potential buyers.

Main Products and Structures

The company's best known achievement is the publication of the IUP Series of British Parliamentary Papers ... Apart from internally generated publicity, the importance of the Papers has been reinforced by such material as the Japanese annotated catalogue of the Papers prepared by the major Japanese Book Importers Maruzen in association with IUP. Sets of the British Parliamentary Papers are in the Library of Congress, the Diet Library in Tokyo and of course the completion of the Series was marked, in February 1973, by the presentation of a Set to both Houses of Parliament ...

The Markets

McKinsey estimated in 1970 that the main market potential for the British Parliamentary Papers in the near term was about 200 Sets in the North American market. Distribution through non-IUP sources and access to a number of smaller institutions could materially accelerate the timing and extent of sales. The UK and Japan have always been sizeable markets for the company's products. Recent market investigations lead the company to believe that significant expansion is possible in the Japanese market. The company is also cultivating the Eastern European Market. Progress here is necessarily slow but there is no doubt that in due course appreciable sales will be achieved in the Soviet Union, Poland, East Germany and to a lesser extent Hungary and Czechoslovakia.

Sales

In the period from first publication (May 1968) to June 1974 the Press' total turnover from the sale of books has been approximately £4,150,000 which breaks down as £3,800,000 from Parliamentary Papers and £350,000 from other publications. The bulk of the Parliamentary Papers revenue (all but approximately £150,000) has come from the 1000 volume series. Of this series some 130 full sets are located in Libraries throughout the world and a further 40 set-equivalents are held in subject set or single volume form.[5]

There was no queue to buy IUP on the receiver's terms, and he did not delay in making almost the entire staff redundant. It was not a year to go looking for work in Dublin – particularly work in publishing. IUP had been a colossus in a very small industry.

At the time I was sales director of the company, along with two other executive directors – Tom Turley (editorial) and Paul Caffrey (MD and accounts). Tadgh MacGlinchey had already moved out to establish himself at the Museum Bookshop (a hand bindery owned by IUP) and create the Malton Press imprint. I proposed to the banks that they let me run the company back into financial health, that is, effectively make me receiver with a two- or three-year brief. The 1974 collapse was not, in fact, the collapse of IUP; in its already trimmed down form IUP was viable as a business. It failed on account of its exposure as part of a hugely unviable Stern empire. The banks seemed to believe that the Stern collapse meant that suddenly, at the same time, the market for IUP materials had dried up: the world would not, could not, buy another 'Blue Book'. Events proved them quite wrong.

The prospect of buying IUP as a going concern did not prove attractive; but many were interested in buying the firm's assets. Microfilmers reckoned that they could part-finance a purchase by selling 'Blue Book' printed stock for c. £100,000 (that was correct, but the erratic market for pulp was soon to collapse). No one seemed interested in searching for yet another millionaire: millionaires with no publishing experience had failed us before. The natural buyers of the IUP assets were publishers – particularly those with experience in the world of reprinting. Crowley, the receiver, received three main offers. The first was a bid of $500,000 ($c$. £200,000) from Philip Cohen of Oceana, whom John Burn and I brought on board; this bid was heard by Crowley but he was holding out (or thought he was) for more. The second was from a consortium made up of Frank Cass and Littlefield Adams, the New Jersey publisher and owner of the Barnes and Noble imprint, and other investors; but their bid, though substantially more, involved staged payments (not attractive to a receiver installed by banks who wanted to be *out*). Cohen had given Crowley a deadline – which ran out. He therefore withdrew his bid; the very next day Crowley informed me that the Cohen bid was acceptable – but Cohen and his entourage had returned to the USA from Europe and were not recoverable. The third bid came some weeks later and was put together by a consortium consisting of Cass, Littlefield Adams, a UK printer, and myself. It matched the Cohen bid, was accepted and led to the formation of Irish Academic Press, to catch the IUP assets. This was November 1974. Irish University Press continued to be used as an imprint of Irish Academic Press; but as a company name it was retained by the receiver.

In a sense, Irish Academic Press was a continuation of Irish University Press. At the very least it ensured the continuity, the survival, of the 1,000-volume series. For the first seven or eight years of its existence (1974–81), IAP was largely a bookselling, rather than a publishing company. Its owners were very aware that the real profitability of the company lay in selling existing stock; such new publishing as was done (including the *Documents of the American Revolution* series) was designed to convey the impression that this was a bona fide publishing house rather than a huge remainder operation with a skeleton staff. It succeeded in installing some fifty sets of the Parliamentary Papers in libraries across the world; but by 1981 we had run out of libraries or run out of worlds. It was at this juncture that IAP moved into Irish legal publishing in the form of the Round Hall Press, a largely IAP-owned subsidiary which soon made a huge impact on local legal publishing. By 1995, Round Hall was sold off to the Thompson Organization, ironically the very people whose purchase of Nelson had started the whole IUP ball rolling. In the post-1981 period, when British Parliamentary Papers came to take a back seat, Irish Academic Press did some useful Irish academic publishing, but its best energies went into the Round Hall Press.

I am sure that there are IAP stories to be told, too. Another day's work...someone else's?

GAZETTEER: THE PEOPLE OF IUP AND WHERE THEY WENT

Adams, Michael: Author of *Censorship: The Irish Experience* (Dublin, 1968) who ran Scepter Publishers, a fairly active theology publisher in Dublin 1959–68. Joined IUP as sales manager; became a director in 1970 with broad administrative responsibilities; sales director from 1972 to the demise of the company. In 1972 he established Michael Atteridge Ltd as a small press, which did no publishing outside of poetry and theology; in 1971 that company became Four Courts Press which Adams ran alongside Irish Academic Press from November 1974. Four Courts gradually expanded from theology into Mediaeval and Celtic niches and was able to catch IAP's staff when Irish Academic Press was restructured in 1996. (In the period 1981–96, IAP developed a highly successful law-publishing house, the Round Hall Press, which was bought in 1996 by Sweet & Maxwell, a unit of the Thompson Organization. In the decade 1986–96 Round Hall greatly outstripped its parent in terms of turnover and production.)

Addis, Jeremy: One of the few IUP Irish executives with publishing experience, having been with Browne and Nolan, Dublin; he joined the company in 1968 and stayed until 1974. He was, first, production manager (involved on the publishing side with the design and standards of the 'Blue Book' production); under Stern he became publicity manager. In 1976 he went on to found *Books Ireland*, which he has run successfully ever since. In association with the Kilkenny Design Centre (where he worked for a while in the late 1970s), he was responsible for the operation of the Kilkenny Design Book Awards.

Adolphus, Lalit: An Indian, he worked in an editorial capacity at IUP's London office, and subsequently did some work for Irish University Press. He died at a young age.

Bing, Geoffrey: Queen's Counsel, former Attorney General of Ghana, Labour politician; journalist; an advisor to IUP during the Stern period.

Browne, Sean: Editor at IUP; tried to organise a bid with the owners of the Dublin microfilm company, Memo Ltd, to buy IUP assets, hoping to finance same by a massive pulping programme. Started Academy Press *c.*1975 (not to be confused with Irish Academic Press), but it did not survive.

Burn, John: Book dealer and library rep; produced some of the earliest US full-set orders for the British Parliamentary Papers. He repatriated to London from the USA, and worked out of the IUP London office until the fall of MacMahon. He supported the Oceana/Adams bid for IUP assets in 1974. He went on to run Unifo Inc., a government documents sales and publishing company in the US.

Byrne, Philomena: Headed up the unit at Merrion Square designed to produce indexes to the contents of the IUP series. A few index volumes were produced but the project was later judged non-viable. Philomena is now head of public affairs at the Irish Museum of Modern Art, Dublin.

Caffrey, Paul: An accountant and gifted musician, he was managing director of IUP in the latter half of the Stern period. Now financial controller, Institute of Technology, Tallaght, Co. Dublin.

Carroll, Liam: An Irishman, based in Edinburgh, he had a teaching background; became a UK sales rep. for IUP in early 1969; replaced John Standish as sales director; soon left for health reasons.

Cashman, Seamus: Editor at IUP 1968–74, surviving all but the last cut; toured the US libraries during the main sales of 1969–70. He created Wolfhound Press which he ran until he retired in 2001.

Cass, Frank: London bookseller and publisher; part-financed by MacMahon (q.v.); he later became a leading (and eventually the only) shareholder in Irish Academic Press and went on to develop his own publishing company specialising in scholarly journals and monographs.

Clancy, Julitta: An indexer; later a professional law indexer.

Craven, Claire: An editor; later co-founder of Gifford and Craven (see Lewis).

Davis, Robert (Bob): Had a Kraus background; with Michael Glazier (q.v.), was responsible, for a short time, for IUP Inc. in the period beginning April 1969. He subsequently ran his own sales company.

Dickens, Homer: A book importer at Barnes and Noble (in succession to John Mladnich). He imported editions of many IUP 'general' titles into the USA.

Ghosh, Dr K. K.: Ran a New Delhi office for IUP.

Gillen, Patrick: With Gifford Lewis (q.v.), a designer at IUP, Merrion Square. He later became very active in left-wing politics.

Glazier, Michael: Joined IUP Inc. on its inception, with a mainly editorial brief – involving Mellifont Press Inc. and Scholarly Resources Inc., the latter being developed by him mainly after his separation from IUP. He subsequently published successfully under the Michael Glazier imprint.

Gore-Grimes, Christopher: A distinguished Dublin solicitor of the firm Gore and Grimes; an adviser of the Nelsons in their successful attempt to gain control of Trinity Holdings, he became non-executive chairman and managing director of IUP in the period prior to the Stern takeover. Michael Adams, his personal assistant and a director, was meant to be de facto controller of the company; this did not happen.

Hanratty, Lelia: Secretary to Tadgh MacGlinchey, 1967–74, and later copy-editor. She married Gerry O'Flaherty (1974). Still does occasional editorial work.

Harvey, Max: A printer based in Cornwall, married to Sue MacAlpine: an investor in Irish Academic Press in its early years.

Hogg, Robert: A hugely experienced Nelson printer, who became 'Printer' at

Shannon, to Tadgh MacGlinchey's 'Publisher' – titles borrowed from the OUPs and CUPs of this world. He oversaw the commissioning of the plant, which he ruled over as lord.

Jerman, William (Bill): An American, editor at Thomas Street, responsible for Ecclesia Press, a theology imprint of IUP, which published some titles, mainly in 1969.

Kavanagh, Paddy: Bookbinder; later a partner in Museum Bookbinders.

Kenna, Claire: Accounts executive and later linchpin at Irish Academic Press.

Lanz, Phyllis: She had a background in McGraw Hill publishing and ran the Madison Avenue offices in the Stern period.

Lewis, Gifford: Designer at IUP, 81 Merrion Square. Migrated with Claire Craven to Ballydehob, Co. Cork, to establish Gifford and Craven, a tiny house with its own handpress, which survived for a while. Gifford Lewis subsequently married Thomas Charles-Edwards and became prominent for her work on Somerville and Ross. She lives in Oxford.

Logue, John: The IUP estimator at Merrion Square. He worked in pencil until at long last he acquired a very large and noisy calculating machine. A gentleman. He died in 1995.

Lorimer, Robin: A scion, I think, of the family that contained J. G. Lorimer of *Gazetteer of the Persian Gulf* fame, was already a publisher (with Oliver and Boyd) when he was cajoled by MacMahon and others to join Scottish University Press, a MacMahon entity designed to do for Scotland what IUP had done for Ireland. Lorimer's first projects were to be reprints; few books were published under this imprint because SUP was never properly funded.

Lundberg, Nick: Senior proof-reader at Merrion Square. He was later, for a time, editor of the *Irish Catholic*.

MacGlinchey, Tadgh M. (1923–75): Served in the Irish Army, 1944–67. A book man and book collector, appointed publisher at IUP in 1967, he was the public face of IUP publishing during its most active period. In 1973(?) under Stern he left the company, being given use of the Museum Bookshop, Kildare Street, Dublin, as a base. He published reproductions of Malton and Brocas prints and some few books at the Malton Press, Dublin. He died tragically in a road accident in 1975.

MacLysaght, Edward: Director of the Irish Manuscripts Commission, for whom IUP acted as publisher. Author of successful IUP books on geneaology.

MacMahon, James: After his ousting from Trinity Holdings he started a rival IUP (International University Press), and tried to interest backers in some of the projects that Irish University Press had nosed out – especially the India Office records. But, presumably for want of financial backing, International University Press never got off the ground.

Matthews, Mark: Stern aide who was for over a year the managing director of IUP.

McCreadie, William (Bill): An early IUP rep. who travelled in the UK and further afield; he later was sales director at Andre Deutsch and is now managing director of Aurum Press.

McGarry, Noel: Second-in-command in accounts.

Mellor, David: A former Cassell director who was an IUP rep in the UK in 1969.

Mladinich, John: A Croat in origin, he was a highly experienced book man, who worked for many years at Barnes and Noble's downtown bookstore in Manhattan. He eventually moved with the imprint to Littlefield Adams & Co. and was for many years a director of Irish Academic Press.

Moore, Colin: Bookbinder; later a partner in Museum Bookbinders.

Nelson, Elizabeth: Much of the vigour behind the Nelson recovery of control over Trinity Holdings is to be credited to her – her husband, Ronnie, delegating most of his authority to her. Despite debilitating illness, she has managed to oversee the development of the huge Jury's Hotel Group in which the Nelsons have a substantial stake.

Nelson, R. I.: The source of most of the finance behind the group that owned and developed IUP.

Nordstedt, Marilyn: An American with a library background, she was already a trained editor by the time she joined IUP in 1969. She brought great professionalism to IUP's liaison with its (relatively few) live authors.

O'Cathain, Brian: Ran IUP'S publicity department for some two years until replaced by Jeremy Addis. His next-in-command was Barbara Redmond.

O'Flaherty, Gerry: PA to Tadgh MacGlinchey, 1969–72, then an IUP editor; worked at Irish Academic Press to see out the *Documents of the American Revolution* series, and then joined Ireland's Department of the Environment as an editor and speech-writer. He is now a director of Four Courts Press.

O'Kelly de Gallagh, Count Donal: Had considerable publishing experience in the Cahill Group; was an editorial executive at IUP, 141 Thomas Street (its location prior to 81 Merrion Square) and was responsible for copyright clearance of the Cuala Press imprint. He retired on a small pension, which did not survive the IUP collapse.

O'Meara, John J.: Professor of Latin at University College, Dublin; vice-chairman of IUP during the days of Nelson control (1971); one of the few who sought to develop the bona fides of IUP as a scholarly, if not strictly speaking university, press; he headed up an editorial advisory board, which included academics from all Irish universities, the Dublin Institute of Advanced Studies, and the Chester Beatty Library; two of them were Fellows of the Royal Society.

Pairoux, Gustave: A Belgian with a Desclée background; was IUP sales executive and editorial scout in Europe.

Parsons, Michael: Second in command to Robert Hogg and his successor; he later ran a print factory at Shannon under Elsevier, and eventually became an independent printer.

Prior, George: His background was in sales (especially at Penguin): he joined IUP as sales director after Liam Carroll and lasted until replaced by Michael Adams. He relocated to the USA to help shore up IUP Inc. in the Stern period. He subsequently published/sold under the title of George Prior Publishers. He died at a comparatively young age.

Raff, Gilbert: An accountant, chief executive officer of Littlefield Adams, a US quoted company involved in sports goods, printing and scholarly publishing including the Barnes and Noble imprint (an important importer of scholarly editions into North America). He led Littlefield Adams to take a 40 per cent interest in Irish Academic Press when the consortium that created it was established. Littlefield Adams was eventually the victim of a raid, which resulted in the selling-off of most of the company's assets. Retired and now lives in California.

Roxburgh, Toby: Editor at Millington Books, an IUP subsidiary. Larger than life, he now raises large Scottish cattle on an island off Scotland.

Sadlier, Muriel: Secretary, junior editor; went on to be secretary to Professor Theo Moody and the Modern History department at Trinity College Dublin.

Slowey, Brian: Was an accountant at IUP and the Cahill Group in 1968/69. He soon moved on, no doubt unhappy with the management style in the group. He later became chief executive of Guinness Ireland.

Smith, Des: Bookbinder.

Soskice, Oliver: Son of sometime Labour Attorney General Sir Frank (later Lord) Soskice, joined IUP, Merrion Square, as an editorial trainee. Also worked with Robin Lorimer (q.v.). Went off to paint; is married to a noted professor of theology.

Tessier, Thomas: IUP's sales manager, 1970–72, who had moved to the company's Russell Square office to develop (under Stern) the IUP trade publishing subsidiary, Millington Books (named after John Millington Synge). He found a new owner for that company in 1974. He subsequently retired from publishing to write novels. He lives in Connecticut. His wife Alice, sometime PA to Allen Figgis of Dublin publishers and booksellers, Hodges Figgis, is now a successful local newspaper editor.

Turley, Thomas F.: Editor and subsequently editorial director of IUP until its demise. Went on to establish the imprint of the Blackwater Press, which was absorbed by Folens & Co., educational publishers, when Tom joined that press.

Zaidner, Michael: An executive director of Frank Cass and Company and a director of Irish Academic Press.

IRISH UNIVERSITY PRESS LOCATIONS

1967–68: Across the street from 77 Marlborough Street, Dublin, where the C. J. Fallon showrooms were located.

1968–70: 141 Thomas Street, Dublin; near Guinness's brewery. There it enjoyed the aromas wafting from the brewery and from O'Keeffe's, the knackers.

1968–71: A management site on Westmoreland Street, Dublin – M. J. McManus's base.

1970–74: 81 Merrion Square, Dublin.

1967–74: Shannon Industrial Estate, Co. Clare.

1968–72: The Museum Bookshop, Kildare Street, Dublin (opposite the Oireachtas buildings). This was the location of a second-hand book shop, an IUP showroom and, soon, a hand bindery, which Irish Academic Press sold off to the craftsmen in early 1975 and which became Museum Bookbindings, Lower Baggot Street, Dublin. In 1972–75 Captain Tadgh MacGlinchey operated as the Malton Press from the Kildare Street address.

1969 and earlier: James MacMahon had a London base at Furnival Street. This was c.1969. Moved to a mansion on Russell Square (near the British Museum), with adjoining showrooms at 109 Southampton Row; the latter rooms were also used by Millington, the IUP trade imprint started c.1972.

1969–70: IUP Inc., 2 Holland Avenue, White Plains, New York State.

1972–74: IUP Inc. at Madison Avenue and 51st Street, New York.

Notes

INTRODUCTION

1 In agreement with W. B. Yeats, John Butler Yeats used the phrase 'literary principality' to describe the Dun Emer Press. See Joseph Hone (ed.), *J. B. Yeats, Letters to his Son W. B. Yeats and Others, 1869–1922*, 2nd edn (London, 1983), 98. The first prospectus of the Dun Emer Press, which speaks of reviving book printing 'as an art' is reproduced in Liam Miller, *The Dun Emer Press, later the Cuala Press* (Dublin, 1973).

2 W. B. Yeats, 'Ireland after Parnell', *Autobiographies* (London, 1955), 200.

3 W. B. Yeats to T. Fisher Unwin, 10 April [1895], Eric Domville and John Kelly (eds), *The Collected Letters of William Butler Yeats: Volume 1 1865–1895* (Oxford, 1985), 462.

4 Yeats, 'Ireland after Parnell', 203.

5 I. R. Willison, 'Remarks on the History of the Book in Britain as a Field of Study within the Humanities, with a Synopsis and Select List of Current Literature', *Library Chronicle of the University of Texas*, 21 (1991), 95–122 (98); see also Lucien Febvre and Henri-Jean Martin, *L'Apparition du Livre*, trans. by David Gerard as *The Coming of the Book* (London, 1976).

6 D. F. McKenzie, 'History of the Book', in Peter Davison (ed.), *The Book Encompassed: Studies in Twentieth-Century Bibliography* (Cambridge, 1992), 290–301 (296).

7 Roger Chartier, *On the Edge of the Cliff: History, Language and Practices*, trans. Lydia G. Cochrane (London, 1997), 81.

1: CREATING AN AUDIENCE

1 Eamon Ó Ciosáin, *An t-Éireannach: Páipéar Sóisialach Gaeltachta* (Dublin, 1993); Fionnuala Uí Fhlannagáin, *Mícheál Ó Lócháin agus An Gaodhal* (Dublin, 1990); Caoilfhionn Nic Pháidín, *Fáinne an Lae agus an Athbheochan (1898-1900)* (Dublin, 1998).

2 Brian Ó Cuív, 'Irish Language and Literature, 1845–1921', in W. E. Vaughan (ed.), *A New History of Ireland, VI: Ireland Under the Union, 1870–1921* (Oxford, 1996), 419.

3 Ibid., 427–30; Philip O'Leary, *The Prose Literature of the Gaelic Revival, 1881–1921: Ideology and Innovation* (Pennsylvania, 1994).

4 D. McGuinne, *Irish Type Design: A History of Printing Types in the Irish Character* (Dublin, 1992), 124–8.

5 S. Ó Cuív, *Fiche Duan: A Selection of Gaelic Poems from the Best Modern Authors* (Dublin, 1919).

6   Eoghan Ó hAnluain, 'Irish Writing: Prose Fiction and Poetry, 1900–1988', in *The Field Day Anthology of Irish Writing*, 3 vols (Derry 1991), vol. 3, 814–17, quote on 814.

7   Nic Pháidín, *Fáinne an Lae*, 196.

8   Ó Cuív, 'Irish Language and Literature', 409; Seosamh Laoide, *Post-sheanchas, ina bhfuil Cúigí, Conntaetha agus Bailte Poist na hÉireann* (Dublin, 1905), 8.

9   Ó Cuív , 'Irish Language and Literature', 410.

10   Ó hAnluain, 'Irish Writing: Prose Fiction and Poetry, 1900–1988'.

11   O'Leary, *Prose Literature of the Gaelic Revival*, 1; Seamus Deane (ed.), *The Field Day Anthology of Irish Writing*, 3 vols (Derry, 1991), 814; F. S. L. Lyons, *Culture and Anarchy in Ireland* (Oxford, 1979), 35.

12   Maurice O'Sullivan, *Twenty Years A-growing* (Oxford, 1953), v. See Niall Ó Ciosáin, review of Blasket Island literature, *Irish Economic and Social History*, 20 (1993), 129–32.

13   Ó Cuív, 'Irish Language and Literature', 393; Risteard de Hae, *Clár Litridheacht na Nua-Ghaeilge, 1850–1936*, 3 vols (Dublin, 1938–40); Nic Pháidín, *Fáinne an Lae*, 2–13.

14   Eiluned Rees, *Libri Walliae: A Catalogue of Welsh Books and Books Printed in Wales, 1546–1820*, 2 vols (Aberystwyth, 1987).

15   Victor Durkacz,*The Decline of the Celtic Languages* (Edinburgh, 1983), chaps 1 and 3; P. H. Jones, 'A Golden Age Reappraised: Welsh-language Publishing in the Nineteenth Century', in P. Isaac and B. McKay (eds), *Images and Texts: Their Production and Distribution in the Eighteenth and Nineteenth Centuries* (Winchester, 1997), 121–41; Kenneth Morgan, *Wales in British Politics, 1868–1922* (Cardiff, 1970), 8–9. For Caernarvon and Bangor, see the newspaper holdings in the British Library. The production and circulation of newspapers, periodicals and books in Wales in the nineteenth century is tabulated in Dot Jones (ed.), *Statistical Evidence Relating to the Welsh Language, 1801–1911* (Cardiff, 1988), 499–518. The relationship between Welsh and industrialisation is discussed by Brinley Thomas, 'A Cauldron of Rebirth: the Industrial Revolution and the Welsh language', in his *The Industrial Revolution and the Atlantic Economy* (London, 1993), 208–31. For the Reformation and printing in Welsh see Ieuan G. Jones, 'The Nineteenth Century', in Philip Henry Jones and Eiluned Rees (eds), *A Nation and Its Books: A History of the Book in Wales* (Aberystwyth, 1998), and Glanmor Williams, *Religion, Language and Nationality in Wales* (Cardiff, 1979), chaps 1 and 6.

16   Michel Lagrée, 'La littérature religieuse dans la production bretonne imprimée: aspects quantitatifs' in M. Lagrée (ed.), *Les Parlers de la Foi: Religion et langues régionales* (Rennes, 1995), 85–94; Jean-Louis Le Floc'h, 'Les cantiques bretons de l'évêché de Quimper et de Léon (1800–1950): approche d'étude historique', *Bulletin de la Société Archéologique du Finistère*, 124 (1995), 375–90. For the Catholic Church's increasing support of regional languages during the nineteenth century, see Gérard Cholvy, 'Régionalisme et clergé Catholique au XIXe siècle', in *Région et Régionalisme en France du XVIIe siècle à nos jours* (Paris, 1977), 187–201.

17   Durkacz, *Decline of the Celtic Languages*, 131–3; Donald McLean, *Typographica Scoto-Gadelica* (Edinburgh, 1915).

18   Gearóid Ó Tuathaigh, 'An Chléir Chaitliceach, an Léann Dúchais agus an Cultúr in Éirinn, 1700–1850', in Pádraig Ó Fiannachta (ed.), *Léachtaí Cholmcille XVI* (Maynooth, 1986), 110–39.

19   Niall Ó Ciosáin, *Print and Popular Culture in Ireland, 1750–1850* (London, 1997), chaps 7 and 9.

20   Examples of priests' disapproval of their parishoners possessing books in Irish occur in the folklore of the 1930s and 1940s: for examples see Grace Neville, '"He spoke to me in English; I answered him in Irish": Language Shift in the Folklore Archives', in J. Brihault (ed.), *L'Irlande et ses Langues: Colloque de Rennes 1992* (Rennes, 1993), 19–32 (27), and Dáibhí Ó Cróinín, *The Songs of Bess Cronin* (Dublin, 2000), 23–4.

21   Breandán Ó Conchúir, *Scríobhaithe Chorcaigh, 1700–1850* (Dublin, 1982); L. M. Cullen, 'Patrons, Teachers and Literacy in Irish, 1700–1850', in M. Daly and D. Dickson (eds), *The Origins of Popular Literacy in Ireland* (Dublin, 1990), 15–44, (32–3).

22   L. M. Cullen, 'Filíocht, Cultúr agus Polaitíocht', in Máirín Ní Dhonnchadha (ed.), *Nua-Léamha: Gnéithe de Chultúr, Stair agus Polaitíocht na hÉireann c.1600–1900* (Dublin, 1996), 170–93. In *Love Songs of Connaught*, Hyde was also inclined to see the songs as anonymous folk songs rather than as compositions by recognised poets; see Cathal Ó hÁinle, 'Ceo Meala: an Craoibhín agus na hAmhráin Ghrá', *The Irish Review,* 14 (1993), 33–47.

23   Joep Leersen: *Remembrance and Imagination: Patterns in the Historical and Literary Representation of Ireland in the Nineteenth Century* (Cork, 1996), 1.

24   P. P. (ed.), *Aighneas an Pheacaig Leis an mBás, commonly known as 'Eachtra an Bháis'* (Waterford, 1899), 3.

25   This distinction was elaborated by Rolf Engelsing, who postulated a transition from intensive to extensive reading among more affluent readers in the late eighteenth century. See R. A. Houston: *Literacy in Early Modern Europe: Culture and Education, 1500–1800* (London, 1988), 195.

26   [Séamus Ó Dubhghaill], 'Gluaiseacht na Gaeidhilge – a tosach agus a fás', *Misneach*, 18 December 1920; Seamus Fenton, *It All Happened: Reminiscences of Seamus Fenton* (Dublin, 1948), 8. For the *Pious Miscellany*, see *Aighneas an Pheacaig*, 3 (for Waterford); Alf Mac Lochlainn, 'John M. O'Cahill of Templeglantine and Pentwater, Michigan', *The Old Limerick Journal*, 26 (1989), 36–41 (for Limerick); Seán Mac Giollarnáth, *Annála Beaga as Iorrus Aithneach* (Dublin, 1941), 175 (for Galway); *Cuimhne Cholmcille or the Gartan Festival, being a record of the celebration held at Gartan on the 9th of June 1897* (Dublin, 1898) (for Donegal).

27   For examples, see Ciarán Dawson, *Peadar Ó Gealacáin, Scríobhaí* (Dublin, 1992), 71, 96; Neil Buttimer, 'Gaelic Literature and Contemporary Life in Cork, 1700–1840', in N. Buttimer, P. O'Flanagan and G. O'Brien (eds), *Cork: History and Society* (Dublin, 1993), 585–653; Pádraig Ó Riain, 'Lámhscríbhinní Gaeilge i gCill Chaoi', *Éigse,* 13 (1969–70), 33–49.

28   W. Wheeler, 'The Spread of Provincial Printing in Ireland up to 1850', *Irish Booklore*, 4 (1978), 7–19.

29   *Wexford Independent*, 3 April 1844; *Belfast Vindicator*, 26 June 1844; *Kerry Examiner*, 8 March 1844.

30   Ó Ciosáin, *Print and Popular Culture*, 158–62.

31   Traolach Ó Ríordáin, *Conradh na Gaeilge i gCorcaigh, 1894–1910* (Dublin, 2000).

2 : THE BOOK IN THE IRISH ARTS AND CRAFTS MOVEMENT

The author gratefully acknowledges the assistance of the following individuals: Aiden Heavey, Fonsie Mealy, Jo McDonnell, the late Vincent Kinane, Warwick Gould, Robert

Rust, Sive Coffey, the late Anne Yeats, Peter Figgis, Peter Lamb, Adrian Le Harivel and the late Dolly Robinson.

1   From the private collection of Anne Yeats. The prospectus is quoted in full by Liam Miller, *The Dun Emer Press, later the Cuala Press* (Dublin, 1973), 29.

2   John Kelly (ed.), *The Collected Letters of W. B. Yeats*, 3 vols (Oxford, 1985–), III: 1901–1904 (pub. 1994), 495.

3   T. W. Rolleston, 'Art and Industry in Ireland', *Journal and Proceedings of the Arts and Crafts Society of Ireland* (Dublin, 1901), 232.

4   See Jeanne Sheehy, *The Rediscovery of Ireland's Past: The Celtic Revival, 1830–1930* (London, 1980), chapter 4; also Cyril Barrett and Jeanne Sheehy, 'Visual Arts and Society, 1850–1900', in W. E. Vaughan (ed.), *A New History of Ireland, VI: Ireland under the Union II, 1870–1921* (Oxford, 1996).

5   See Richard Ormond and John Turpin, *Daniel Maclise, 1806–1870* (London, 1972), cat. nos. 88 (A) and (B), and pp. 79–80.

6   Ernest A. Boyd (ed.), *Standish O'Grady: Selected Essays and Passages* (Dublin, 1917), 7; W. B. Yeats, *Collected Letters of Yeats*, III, 168n; foreword, 'A Celtic Christmas', *The Irish Homestead*, 8 December 1900, 1. See also Nicola Gordon Bowe, "The wild heath has broken out again in the heather field': Philanthropic endeavour and Arts and Crafts achievement in early 20th-century Kilkenny', *Irish Architectural and Decorative Studies: The Journal of the Irish Georgian Society* 2 (1999), 66–97, for the dramatic impact of O'Grady's ideas in rural Ireland. Sadly only the 1892 T. Fisher Unwin edition of *Finn and His Companions* included any complementary visual material, and then a frontispiece engraving from a conventional line illustration by John Butler Yeats.

7   Editorial annotation to Standish O'Grady, 'The Mountain Gates of Ulster', *The Irish Homestead*, Christmas number, December 1899, 9.

8   'A Tribute by A.E.', in Hugh Art O'Grady, *Standish James O'Grady, The Man and The Writer* (Dublin, 1929), 63–75.

9   Phillip L. Marcus, *Standish O'Grady* (Cranbury, N.J., 1970), 87, referring to Russell's 'Standish O'Grady', *Irish Literature*, (ed.) Justin McCarthy (Chicago, 1904), VII, 2737–40.

10 W. B. Yeats, 'Ireland after Parnell', *Autobiographies*, (London, 1955), II, 220.

11 Alice L. Milligan in *Standish James O'Grady*, 77–8. The archaeological collection of the Royal Irish Academy, which excelled in recently discovered Early Christian artefacts, was transferred to the National Museum of Ireland premises nearby in 1891. George Coffey, Curator of the Museum's Irish Antiquities from 1897, 'borrowed Celtic gold ornaments from the Museum' for performances of W. B. Yeats's *The Countess Cathleen* two years later, in which he acted with the writer, critic and revivalist T. W. Rolleston, Lady Constance Lytton, Lady Betty Balfour and Lady Fingall (Pamela Hinkson (ed.), *Seventy Years Young: Memories of Elizabeth Countess of Fingall* (London, 1937), 235).

12 Henry Holiday, *Reminiscences of My Life* (London, 1914); see biographical and catalogue entries under Coffey in Nicola Gordon Bowe and Elizabeth S. Cumming, *The Arts and Crafts Movements in Dublin and Edinburgh* (Dublin, 1998), 107–9.

13 T. J. Cobden-Sanderson, 'Bookbinding' in *Arts and Crafts Essays by Members of the Arts and Crafts Exhibition Society, with a Preface by William Morris* (London, 1893), states that the forwarder should perform all stages leading up to the work of the finisher 'who decorates and letters the volume'. 'Forwarding' included folding,

collating and sewing. Cobden-Sanderson, a lawyer, had started binding books at the suggestion of Morris's wife, Jane. In 1893, he set up the Doves Bindery, and in 1900 the Doves Press, both in Hammersmith. It was he who originally coined the term 'Arts and Crafts' in 1888 to describe architectural and applied arts in the exhibitions of the society formed with that name.

14 Colin Smyth (ed.), 'The Changing Ireland', chapter XIX in *Seventy Years: Being the Autobiography of Lady Gregory* (Gerrards Cross, 1974), 306. Parnell had died in 1891.

15 See Dermot Wyndham, 7th Earl of Mayo, (Founder and President of the Society), 'Inauguration of the Arts and Crafts Society of Ireland', in *Journal and Proceedings of the Arts and Crafts Society of Ireland*, vol. 1, no. 1, (1896), 2–11.

16 See Elizabeth Cumming and Wendy Kaplan, *The Arts and Crafts Movement* (London, 1991); Paul Larmour, *The Arts and Crafts Movement in Ireland* (Belfast, 1992); Nicola Gordon Bowe, 'A Contextual Introduction to Romantic Nationalism and Vernacular Expression in the Irish Arts and Crafts Movement *c*. 1886–1925', in N. Gordon Bowe (ed.), *Art and the National Dream* (Dublin, 1993); and Bowe and Cumming, *Arts and Crafts Movements*.

17 T. W. Rolleston, 'Art Work in Irish Exhibitions', *Journal and Report of the Arts and Crafts Society of Ireland* (Dublin, 1906), 280–6. Rolleston, a brilliant scholar, writer and contemporary of Oscar Wilde at Trinity College Dublin, became the manager of the Irish Industries Association, having been secretary of the Irish Literary Society in London. See Bowe and Cumming, *Arts and Crafts Movements*, 180–1.

18 See catalogue entry under Sullivan in Bowe and Cumming, *Arts and Crafts Movements*, 194–6.

19 Thomas V. Lange ('The decorated bookbindings of Sir Edward Sullivan, Bart.', *Long Room*, no. 40, 1995, 41–7) notes that 'the bindings decorated by Sullivan fall into three distinct categories: new bindings he commissioned and decorated, publishers' bindings he decorated, and old bindings he acquired and decorated'.

20 Cobden-Sanderson, 'Bookbinding', 1893, 147-8. This collection of essays was listed as recommended reading for 'Students and Workers in Artistic Handicrafts' at the end of the Society's first Journal (1896).

21 *Journal and Proceedings*, (1896), 57–9.

22 Sir Edward Sullivan, Bt., 'The Queen's Album', *Journal and Report of the Arts and Crafts Society of Ireland*, vol. 1, no. 2 (1898), 167–9. The album was also exhibited in the Department of Agriculture and Technical Instruction's Irish Pavilion at the 1901 Glasgow International Exhibition. In 1914 Sullivan's best-known book , 'one of the most interesting and beautiful manuscripts which has yet come from the hands of man', his seminal study of *The Book of Kells*, was first published. Sir Edward Sullivan, Bt., *The Book of Kells*, second edition (London, 1920), Introduction, 2.

23 In 1904 his detailed record of fifty of what his brother described as 'probably the most majestic series of bindings in the world' (in Fergal McGrath, SJ, *Father John Sullivan, SJ*, (Dublin, 1981), 18) was advertised for publication: 'They were MS. Journals of both houses of the Irish Parliament from 1613–1800. From 1707 on, they were triumphs of the bookbinder's art, of great size, about 53.3 cm. tall, full-bound in crimson morocco with vellum inlays and green title pieces.' Despite a fine Quaritch prospectus in 1905, the volume never reached publication, and Sullivan's complete set of rubbings was sold to the National Library in 1926, four years after the bindings were lost during the Civil War, when Dublin's Four Courts were destroyed. Sullivan's similarly knowledgeable interest in the history of Irish printing had been exemplified

in his discussion of 'Early Irish Printers and their Work', published in the Report of the Retrospective Section of the Irish Arts and Crafts Exhibition, *Journal and Proceedings of the Arts and Crafts society of Ireland*, vol. 1, no. 1 (1896), 43-6.

24 Lange, 'Decorated bookbindings', 42.

25 Sir Edward Sullivan, Bt. (writing as His Oddship Brother 'Bookbinder'), 'Decorative Book-Binding in Ireland', a paper read on 28 February 1911 to Ye Sette of Odd Volumes in London, and issued to members, privately printed as number LXVII of their Privately Printed Opuscula in a limited edition by the Arden Press, Letchworth, 1914.

26 See Bowe and Cumming, *Arts and Crafts Movements*, 25-7, 97.

27 The establishment by Joseph Maunsel Hone and George Roberts, player and master printer, of Maunsel & Co. in 1905 provided a new standard of excellence in Irish printing.

28 'Regulations', *Catalogue of the Third Exhibition of the Arts and Crafts Society of Ireland* (Dublin, 1904), v-vi.

29 As early as 1894, Yeats selected the Anglo-Irish Althea Gyles, 'very tall with dusty red-gold hair and a voice of commanding music' (a 'skin-deep' Golden Dawn occultist according to Clifford Bax), for what he saw as the 'visionary beauty' of her eclectic drawing, to design a cover and spine for his *Poems* (1895), then to produce designs for *The Secret Rose* (1897), *Poems* (1899) and *The Wind among the Reeds* (1899), all published in London, in various trade editions. Gyles also illustrated a privately circulated Mathurin Press imprint of Oscar Wilde's *The Harlot's House* (1904). See W. B. Yeats, 'A Symbolic Artist and the Coming of Symbolic Art', *The Dome*, I (October 1898), 233-5; Ian Fletcher, 'Poet and Designer: W. B. Yeats and Althea Gyles' in R. O'Driscoll and L. Reynolds (eds), *Yeats Studies*, I (Galway, 1971), who writes: 'Miss Gyles's work seems - if we discount the Celtic element in her lettering - not typically Pan-Celtic or *art nouveau* or Art[s] and Craft[s].' For an overview of the broader Irish context, see Nicola Gordon Bowe, 'Symbolism in Turn-of-the-Century Irish Art', *Irish Arts Review Yearbook* 1990/1, 133-44. Yeats, his brother Jack, Æ, Synge and Lady Gregory were among the contributors to *The Green Sheaf* (1903-4), a strongly visual periodical, hand-coloured and printed on handmade paper in London, incorporating original texts and illustrations, edited and published (and illustrated) by the American-born artist Pamela Colman Smith.

30 See Miller, *The Dun Emer Press*; Sheila Pim, 'Dun Emer - The Origins', *Irish Arts Review*, vol. 2, no. 2 (Summer, 1985), 18-22; William M. Murphy, *Family Secrets: William Butler Yeats and his Relatives* (Dublin, 1995); and Gifford Lewis, *The Yeats Sisters and the Cuala*, (Dublin, 1994); also catalogue entries under Dun Emer, Cuala, Gleeson, Yeats, Fitzpatrick in Bowe and Cumming, *Arts and Crafts Movements*.

31 First prospectus of the Dun Emer Press, 1903. Gifford Lewis points out her feat in establishing a press with no Irish commercial standard of fine printing to serve as a model, and her achievement in maintaining a consistently high standard of simple excellence in publishing important contemporary authors' texts, some for the first time (*The Yeats Sisters*). Emery Walker and William Morris had set out the principles of 'well-designed type, due spacing of the lines and words, and proper position of the page on the paper', in 'Printing', Cobden-Sanderson, *Arts and Crafts Essays*, 133. See also Vincent Kinane, 'Some Aspects of the Cuala Press', *The Private Library*, vol. 2:3 (Autumn, 1989), 119-29.

32 The integrity of her printing was maintained even after her death in 1940 by Esther Ryan, Eileen Colum and Maire Gill, whom she trained at Dun Emer.

33 Robin Skelton in Peter Faulkner, *William Morris and W. B. Yeats* (Dublin, 1962), 30.

34 Lewis, *The Yeats Sisters*, 181.

35 Particularly advised by the expert printers, Emery Walker and Sydney Cockerell, both of whom were involved with the running of Morris's Kelmscott Press. In New York, Yeats's attention was drawn to the publications of Elbert Hubbard's private press, The Roycroft Shop, at East Aurora, New York, perhaps because the young Irish emigrant sculptor, Jerome Connor (signing himself 'St. Gerome') had decorated a heavily Kelmscott-influenced edition of Olive Schreiner's *Dreams* in 1901. However, Yeats rejected as models for Dun Emer its generally 'eccentric, restless and thoroughly decadent' books (W. B. Yeats to Lily Yeats, December 1903, quoted in John Kelly and Ronald Schuchard (eds.), *The Collected Letters of W.B. Yeats 1901–1904*, vol. 3 (Oxford, 1994), 496.) I am grateful to Warwick Gould for clarifying Yeats's opinion of the Roycroft work, which Liam Miller (The Dun Emer Press, 35) interpreted as a positive influence, and to Robert Rust for showing me so much material produced by the Roycrofters.

36 Lewis (*The Yeats Sisters*, 56–9) illustrates pages from Norma Borthwick's *The Irish Alphabet* (1901) and *Irish Reading Lessons* (1902), published by The Irish Book Company in Dublin (1901/2) and illustrated by Elizabeth and Jack Yeats.

37 See Larmour, *Arts and Crafts Movement in Ireland*, for Braithwaite and the Belfast context.

38 T. W. Rolleston, 'Art Work at Irish Exhibitions', *Journal and Proceedings of the Arts and Crafts Society of Ireland*, vol. I, no. 4 (1906), 281, who bewails that Houston 'had lately to leave Ireland for want of work, while bodies supposed to encourage Irish art...were ordering replicas of eighteenth-century' artefacts. Her work, set amidst Lilian Davidson's embossed interlace, on the album cover, was reproduced in the Society's report of their 1904 exhibition and in *The Studio* magazine.

39 I am grateful to Emma Laws for drawing my attention to this 'buff morocco' binding, 'embossed design with brass studs, the title tooled in gold' (John P. Harthan, *Bookbindings* (London, 1985), 31, 48), collection Victoria and Albert Museum, London.

40 'The Art Movement: Bookbindings by Miss Mary Houston', *Magazine of Art*, vol. 23 (1899–1900), 375–6. See Larmour, *Arts and Crafts Movement in Ireland*, 105–7; in 1902 Houston designed a Christmas greetings card, depicting Emer steering a sailing boat, emblazoned with her own 'MGH' monogram for the Dun Emer Guild.

41 Austin Clarke, *Poems of Joseph Campbell* (Dublin, 1963), 1.

42 The pioneering, folksong-gathering sister of Alice Milligan, Carbery's fellow Ulster poet and co-founding editor of their nationalist monthly, *Shan Van Vocht* in 1896.

43 See Paul Larmour, 'John Campbell (1883–1962), An Artist of the Irish Revival', *Irish Arts Review Yearbook* (1998), 62–73.

44 Her contemporary, Sir William Orpen, recalled that she 'stood out' at the Dublin Art School, winning 'universal admiration' for her seemingly effortless and versatile skill in a variety of media (see Bowe and Cumming, *Arts and Crafts Movements*, 126–32).

45 See Joseph McDonnell, *Five Hundred Years of the Art of the Book in Ireland* (London, 1997), catalogue no. 1, for a superb example. The Tudor period in Ireland was perceived as the last in which the hereditary Irish chieftains were not in thrall to England. Kelly's perfectly crafted bindings were based on careful, often scholarly research, and emulated T. J. Cobden-Sanderson's seminal text, *Ecce Mundus – Industrial Ideals and the Book Beautiful* (1902), a copy of which she owned.

46 No attempts to trace the whereabouts of this volume in either the Royal or Aberdeen

collections have hitherto proved fruitful; like so much of the material described here, this ephemeral item may not be extant.

47　See N. Gordon Bowe, 'Percy Oswald Reeves, 1870–1967, Metalworker and Enamellist: forgotten master of the Irish Arts and Crafts Movement, *Omnium Gatherum*, Journal 18 of the Decorative Arts Society 1850 to the present (1994), 61–8; P. Larmour, 'The works of Oswald Reeves (1870–1967), artist and craftsman: an interim catalogue, *Irish Architectural and Decorative Studies*, vol. I, 1998, 34–59; N. Gordon Bowe, 'Evocative and Symbolic: Memorials and Trophies by Percy Oswald Reeves', *Irish Arts Review Yearbook 2000*, 131–8.

48　The Plunkett album was tragically destroyed when Sir Horace's purpose-built Arts and Crafts house in Foxrock, Co. Dublin was burnt down in January 1923 during the Civil War. See N. Gordon Bowe, *The Dublin Arts and Crafts Movement, 1885–1930* (Edinburgh, 1985), plate 4. 'Days to be Remembered', in *A Double Star,* is in a private collection.

49　Johnston taught writing and illumination at the Central School of Arts and Crafts in London from 1899, having been influenced by W. R. Lethaby, the School's co-director (1896–1901) and subsequent principal (1902), to study calligraphy and lettering. Johnston's key text, *Writing and Illuminating and Lettering*, was published in Lethaby's Artistic Crafts Series of Technical Handbooks in 1906. He is regarded as the 'father' of the early twentieth-century revival of lettering. See Bowe and Cumming, *Arts and Crafts Movements,* for details of Reeves and Atkinson, who actually studied under Johnston.

50　Sir John O'Connell, 'Foreword', *Catalogue of the fifth Exhibition of the Arts and Crafts Society of Ireland and Guild of Irish Art-Workers* (1917), 15–20.

51　Although the blocks for what would have been his first published book illustrations, for Coleridge's *Rime of the Ancient Mariner* (1913–15), had perished in the fire at Maunsel & Co.'s Abbey Street premises during the 1916 insurrection, Harrap's lavish production of his *Hans Andersen's Fairy Tales* had been published in London in 1916; see N. Gordon Bowe, *Harry Clarke, His Graphic Art* (Mountrath and Los Angeles, 1983) and *The Life and Work of Harry Clarke* (Dublin, 1989).

52　Reproduced: McDonnell, *Five Hundred Years*, cat. 71 (private collection). This binding was among five by Kelly included in the large *Exposition d'Art Irlandais*, held in Paris in February 1922 at the Galeries Barbazanges to celebrate the signing of the Irish Free State treaty; at this, Harry Clarke's book illustrations, particularly for Harraps's 1919 edition of E. A. Poe's *Tales of Mystery and Imagination*, were particularly eulogised.

53　Seumas O'Sullivan, the poet and subsequent editor of the *Dublin Magazine*, 'Joseph Campbell, an Appreciation', in *The Rose and the Bottle* (Dublin, 1946), 106. I am grateful to Julian Campbell for this reference.

54　As they are described in the catalogue of the *Fifth Exhibition of The Arts and Crafts Society of Ireland and Guild of Irish Art Workers*, printed by George Roberts (Dublin, 1917).

55　See Bowe and Cumming, *Arts and Crafts Movements*, under Geddes, who exhibited bookplate designs in both the 1917 and 1921 exhibitions.

56　Interlaced strapwork was adopted by Irish publishers as a favourite, instantly identifiable national source on book-covers, e.g. by The Educational Company of Ireland's Standard Library of Irish Authors, by M. H. Gill & Son, by The Talbot Press's Every Irishman's Library, and by the Dundalgan Press, who also prominently displayed the Irish trademark.

57 The Candle Press subsequently became the Three Candles Press, named after the 'three candles that light up every darkness – Truth, Nature, Knowledge'; one of the earliest Candle Press limited editions was Ella Young's collection of poems, *The Rose of Heaven* (1920), illustrated by Maud Gonne. O'Lochlain also adapted his name to the more obviously Irish 'O Lochlainn'.

58 As detailed in the six entries under Pender's name in the *Sixth Exhibition Catalogue of The Arts and Crafts Society*, printed by Maunsel and Roberts (Dublin, 1921), nos.116–21.

59 For the prolific McKee, see Larmour 1992, *Arts and Crafts Movement in Ireland*, 147–50; McKee made book covers in decorative leatherwork as well as in repoussé metals, using swirling Celtic interlaced designs.

60 Thomas Bodkin, 'The Arts and Crafts Society of Ireland', *The Studio*, vol. 82, (1921), 262.

61 This page was instrumental in O'Murnaghan's being invited to illuminate *An Leabhar na hAiserghe* ('The Book of the Resurrection'), an unfinished, unbound Irish Republican memorial meticulously and inventively painted in brushwork on vellum. After executing nine and a half pages between 1924 and 1927, O'Murnaghan executed a further sixteen between 1937 and 1951. The pages are presently housed in the National Museum of Ireland.

3: 'YOGIBOGEYBOX IN DAWSON CHAMBERS'

1 Richard Ellmann (ed.), *Letters of James Joyce: Volume II* (London, 1966), 230; Ann Saddlemyer (ed.), *The Collected Letters of J. M. Synge: Volume 1, 1871–1907* (Oxford, 1983), 136.

2 W. B. Yeats (hereafter WBY) to A. H. Bullen, 15 May 1905, The Kenneth Spencer Research Library, University of Kansas, Lawrence (hereafter Kansas). For lists of the books printed and published by Maunsel, see my 'Checklist of the Publications of Maunsel and Company, Irish Publishers, 1905–1925', *Publishing History*, 51 (Spring, 2002), 5–36.

3 James Joyce, 'Ivy Day in the Committee Room', *Dubliners*, ed. John Kelly (London, 1991), 148; George Roberts to James Joyce, 23 August 1912, in Ellmann, *Letters of Joyce, II*, 314. For the more complicated history of the *Dubliners* saga, see my 'Chapters of Moral History: Failing to Publish *Dubliners*', *Proceedings of the Bibliographical Society of America*, 97 (2003), 493–517.

4 See John P. Boland, 'How Ireland Got a National Trade-mark', *The World's Work*, March 1907, 593–6.

5 For a list of the books published by the Dun Emer Press, later the Cuala Press, see Liam Miller, *The Dun Emer Press, later the Cuala Press* (Dublin, 1973). Elizabeth Yeats preferred the elegant simplicity of Doves Press typography to the extravagant designs of 'Morris books' (Elizabeth Corbet Yeats to an unidentified subscriber to *In the Seven Woods*, 11 August 1903, Kansas).

6 The first prospectus of the Dun Emer Press, quoted in full by Miller, *The Dun Emer Press*, 29. W. B. Yeats contributed to the composition of this prospectus – there is a draft copy in his hand at the Ellen Clarke Bertrand Library of Bucknell University. The text has been reproduced in Mary Chenoweth Stretton (ed.), *Printing as Art: William Morris and His Circle of Influence* (Lewisburg, PA, 1994), 37.

7 John Carter to Lawrence Powell, 10 February 1954, Kansas; Elizabeth Corbet Yeats to P. S. O'Hegarty, 15 September 1939, Kansas. For a description of the outstanding O'Hegarty collection of Yeats first editions and Irish books of the revival period, see Wayne K. Chapman and James Helyar, 'P. S. O'Hegarty and the Yeats Collection at the University of Kansas', in *Yeats Annual*, 10 (1993), 221–38.

8 D. F. McKenzie, 'Typography and Meaning: The Case of William Congreve', in Giles Barber and Bernhard Fabian (eds), *The Book and Book Trade in Eighteenth Century Europe* (Hamburg, 1981), 81–126 (82, 99).

9 W. B. Yeats (ed.), *Selections from the Writings of Lord Dunsany* (Dublin, 1912), 'Preface', unpaginated.

10 In 'A History of the House of Maunsel and a Bibliography of Certain of Its Publications' (unpublished M.Litt. thesis, University of Dublin, 1969) Frances-Jane French gives the date as January 1905 (9). It is clear from John Kelly (ed.), *Collected Letters of Yeats*, 3 vols (Oxford, 1985–), III: 1901–1904 (hereafter *CL*, III) 635n that Roberts and O'Sullivan were planning their venture before this date.

11 Address from a blank sheet of headed paper inside the Bodleian Library copy of Seumas O'Sullivan's *The Twilight People*. The offices of *Dana*, a short-lived monthly periodical which ran from May 1904 to April 1905, were located at 26 Dawson Chambers, next door to Whaley and Company. Many of the individuals who were associated with this 'Irish Magazine of Independent Thought' – including Æ, Padraic Colum, John Eglinton, Stephen Gwynn, Seumas O'Sullivan, Frederick Ryan – were subsequently published by Maunsel.

12 Alan Denson (ed.), *Letters from Æ* (London, New York and Toronto, 1961), 274.

13 For a discussion of Yeats's reviews of this book, see Peter Kuch, *Yeats and Æ: The Antagonism that Unites Dear Friends* (Gerrards Cross, Buckinghamshire, 1986), 92–104. When he first encountered Æ's book, James Cousins declared that he 'went on fire with the realization that immortal poetry had been given to Ireland'. *We Two Together,* James and Margaret Cousins (Madras, 1950), 33.

14 'Obituary: C. A. Weekes', *BEAMA Journal for the Electrical Industry*, 53 (1946), 75.

15 Len Platt, *Joyce and the Anglo-Irish: A Study of Joyce and the Literary Revival*, Costerus New Series 119 (Amsterdam, 1998), 9; James Joyce, *Ulysses,* The Corrected Text, edited by Hans Walter Gabler (London, 1986), 157, 158.

16 George Roberts, 'A Meeting with AE: Memoirs of George Roberts, part 1', *The Irish Times,* 13 July 1955, 5.

17 *CL*, III, 566n.

18 *The Shadow of the Glen, The Well of the Saints* and *Kincora* were first produced at the Abbey on 28 December 1904, 4 February 1905 and 25 March 1905 respectively.

19 See Frances-Jane French, *The Abbey Theatre Series of Plays: A Bibliography* (Dublin, 1969) for a complete list of the plays in this series.

20 French, *The Abbey Theatre Series*, 13, 15, 17.

21 A. H. Bullen (1857–1920), an Elizabethan scholar and publisher. Works which Yeats published under Bullen's imprints included: *The Celtic Twilight* (Lawrence and Bullen, 1893), *The Secret Rose* (Lawrence and Bullen, 1897), *Cathleen ni Hoolihan* (A. H. Bullen, 1902), *The Celtic Twilight*, rev. edn (A. H. Bullen, 1902), *Ideas of Good and Evil* (A. H. Bullen, 1903), *Where There is Nothing* (A. H. Bullen, 1903), *The Hour-Glass, Cathleen ni Houlihan, The Pot of Broth* (A. H. Bullen, 1904), *The King's Threshold and On Baile's Strand* (A. H. Bullen, 1904), *Poems, 1899–1905* (A. H. Bullen, 1906), *The Shadowy Waters* (A. H. Bullen, 1907), *Deirdre* (A. H. Bullen, 1907), *The Collected Works* (8 volumes, Shakespeare Head Press, 1908), *Poems* (A.

H. Bullen, 1909), *The Green Helmet* (Shakespeare Head Press, 1911), *Plays for an Irish Theatre* (A. H. Bullen, 1911), *Stories of Red Hanrahan, The Secret Rose, Rosa Alchemica* (A. H. Bullen, 1913), and *The Tables of the Law and the Adoration of the Magi* (Shakespeare Head Press, 1914).

22 WBY to Augusta Gregory, 28 December 1901, *CL*, III, 141; WBY to Augusta Gregory, 1 July 1904, *CL*, III, 614; A. H. Bullen to WBY, 17 August 1904, *CL*, III, 635. See also Ian Rogerson, 'The Shakespeare Head Press', in Patricia Anderson and Jonathan Rose (eds), *British Literary Publishing Houses, 1820–1880*, Dictionary of Literary Biography, 106 (Detroit and London, 1991), 301–4.

23 A. H. Bullen to WBY, 17 August 1904, *CL*, III, 635.

24 A. H. Bullen to George Roberts, nd, NLI MS 13272 (14); dated in *CL*, III, 635 to November 1904.

25 WBY to Henry Davray, 19 March [1896] in Kelly (ed.), *Collected Letters of Yeats*, II: 1896–1900 (1997), 15 (hereafter *CL*, II).

26 WBY to A. H. Bullen, 15 May 1905, Kansas.

27 'Whaley and Company's New Books' (on the back cover of *Blátha Fraoich*, Whaley, 1905), claimed that a 'cheap issue' of the three works in question – *The Secret Rose, The Celtic Twilight, Ideas of Good and Evil* – was 'ready immediately'. I have not located any Whaley editions of these works.

28 The first editions of *The Secret Rose* and *Ideas of Good and Evil* appeared under Bullen's imprint in April 1897 and May 1903. A revised and enlarged edition of *The Celtic Twilight* appeared under Bullen's imprint in July 1902. According to Allan Wade, *A Bibliography of the Writings of W. B. Yeats*, 3rd rev. edn (London, 1968), Maunsel issued 400 copies of each book in the autumn of 1905. (Wade items 23, 48, 37 respectively.)

29 WBY to A. H. Bullen, 15 May 1905, Kansas.

30 WBY to A. H. Bullen, 22 June 1905, Kansas.

31 French, 'A History of the House of Maunsel', 10.

32 WBY to A. H. Bullen, 15 May 1905, Kansas and *CL*, *II*, 'Chronology', xlii.

33 French, 'A History of the House of Maunsel', 11. The company file is no longer extant; it was destroyed as a result of the bombing of the Public Record Office in the Second World War.

34 WBY to A. H. Bullen, 15 May 1905, Kansas.

35 A. H. Bullen to WBY, 21 May 1905, in Richard J. Finneran and George Mills Harper (eds), *Letters to W. B. Yeats*, 2 vols (London, 1977) I, 149–50.

36 A. H. Bullen to WBY, 21 May 1905, Finneran and Harper, *Letters to W. B. Yeats*, I, 150.

37 WBY to George Roberts, 18 May 1905, NLI MS 21, 946 (xiii).

38 Ibid.

39 WBY to A. H. Bullen, 15 May 1905, Kansas.

40 French, 'A History of the House of Maunsel', gives the sum as £2,000 (11). Yeats thought it was £1,000 (WBY to A. H. Bullen, 15 May 1905, Kansas; WBY to Augusta Gregory, 30 May 1905, in Allan Wade (ed.), *The Letters of W. B. Yeats* (London, 1954), 449. Hone refers to £500 (from his father) in his letter to Seumas O'Sullivan, 14 April 1905, Seumas O'Sullivan papers, Trinity College Dublin.)

41 Adrian Frazier, *Behind the Scenes: Yeats, Horniman and the Struggle for the Abbey Theatre* (London, 1990), 116.

42 WBY to George Russell, [April 1904], *CL*, III, 577.

43 WBY to A. H. Bullen, 15 May 1905, Kansas.

44 Padraic Colum published the following titles under the Maunsel imprint: *The Land*

(1905); *Studies* (1907); *Wild Earth* (1907); *The Fiddler's House* (1907); *Thomas Muskerry* (1910); *Broad-Sheet Ballads* (1913). Seumas O'Sullivan's Maunsel titles included: *Verses, Sacred and Profane* (1908); *Poems* (1912); *An Epilogue to the Praise of Angus and other Poems* (1914); *The Rosses and Other Poems* (1918), and *The Twilight People* (Whaley (subsequently Maunsel), 1905). Susan Mitchell's Maunsel titles were: *The Living Chalice* (1908); *Aids to the Immortality of Certain Persons in Ireland, Charitably Adminstered in Verse* (1913), and her study, *George Moore* (1916). There was only one Maunsel publication by Eva Gore-Booth, *The Egyptian Pillar* (1907), one by Thomas Keohler, *Songs of a Devotee* (1906), and one by Alice Milligan, *Hero Lays* (1908). This litany of names and titles suggests the extent to which Maunsel published a generation of minor revival writers; in most cases these writers would have been less successful had they been forced to find London publishers.

45 George A. Birmingham, 'The Literary Movement in Ireland', unpublished typescript (1908), Kansas.

46 Denson, *Letters from AE*, 269.

47 James Cousins, *We Two Together*, 49, and Denson, *Letters from AE*, 269.

48 A. H. Bullen to WBY, 21 May 1905, Finneran and Harper , *Letters to W. B. Yeats*, I, 150; James Joyce 'Gas From a Burner', in J. C. C. Mays (ed.), *Poems and Exiles* (London, 1992), 107–10 (108).

49 George Roberts, 'George Moore in Dublin: Memoirs of George Roberts, part 3', *The Irish Times,* 19 July 1955, 5.

50 Roberts, 'Meeting with Æ', 5.

51 They had two sons, Oliver (d. 1978), who became a Professor of Botany in University College Cork, and Ruairi, who became the Secretary of the Irish Trades Union Congress. According to his obituary in *The Irish Times*, 10 November 1953 (4), Roberts moved to London in 1926 after Maunsel and Roberts had discontinued business. He was appointed printing adviser to the London firm of Gollancz; he later joined the Western Typesetting Company and remained with this firm until retirement in 1951. Máire Garvey, from whom Roberts had separated, died in 1946; two years later Roberts married Patricia Allen.

52 William M. Murphy, *Prodigal Father: The Life of John Butler Yeats* (Ithaca and London, 1978), 292.

53 Frazier, *Behind the Scenes*, 123.

54 WBY to Katharine Tynan Hinkson, 1 September 1906, Houghton Library, Harvard University, Cambridge, Massachusetts.

55 'Our Scrap Book', *The Irish Book Lover*, August 1915, 18.

56 Padraic and Mary Colum, *Our Friend James Joyce* (London, 1959), 89.

57 John Quinn to Augusta Gregory, 24 July 1916, The Henry W. and Albert A. Berg Collection, New York Public Library.

4: EARLY SCIENCE AND LEARNED PUBLICATION

1 David Cabot, *The New Naturalist: Ireland* (London, 1998), 19–23.

2 Personal communication.

3 Gerard Boate, *Ireland's naturall history* (London, 1652), 176–7.

4 Samuel Hartlib, 'Dedicatory' [addressed to Oliver Cromwell and the Rt. Hon. Charles Fleetwood], in Boate, *Ireland's naturall history*, [iii–x].

5 Cabot, *New Naturalist*, 23.

6 Boate, *Ireland's naturall history*.

7 William Petty, the *Down Survey*, *c*.1654–56; this was a manuscript survey. The original maps were destroyed in the Record Office fires in 1711 and 1922. A set of manuscript parish maps (incomplete) copied from the Down Survey in 1786 is held by the National Library of Ireland, whilst the Public Record Office of Northern Ireland holds copies of the parish maps for Antrim and Tyrone. Manuscript barony maps are held by the Bibliothèque Nationale, fonds anglais 1 & 2. For further information on the Down Survey maps see Charles McNeill, 'Copies of Down Survey maps in private keeping', *Analecta Hibernica*, 8, (1938), 419–27; R. C. Simington, 'Origin of copies of the Down Survey maps', *Analecta Hibernica*, 8 (1938), 429–30; William Nolan, *Tracing the past: sources for local studies in the Republic of Ireland* (Dublin, 1982), 53–5.

8 Theodore K. Hoppen, *The common scientist in the seventeenth century: a study of the Dublin Philosophical Society, 1683–1708* (London, 1970), 13.

9 Moses Pitt, *The English Atlas*, 5 vols (Oxford, 1680–82). Of eleven projected volumes only five were published and the fifth consists of text only.

10 William Molyneux, *The case of Ireland's being bound by acts of parliament in England, stated* (Dublin, 1698).

11 William Molyneux, *Dioptrica nova: a treatise of dioptricks* (London, 1692).

12 John Locke, *Essay concerning human understanding*, 2nd edn (London, 1694).

13 Dwight Atkinson, *Scientific discourse in sociohistorical context: the Philosophical Transactions of the Royal Society of London, 1675–1975* (New Jersey & London, 1999), 17.

14 John K'eogh, *Botanalogia universalis hibernica, or A general Irish herbal* (Cork, 1735); John K'Eogh, *Zoologia medicinalis hibernica* (Dublin, 1739).

15 Caleb Threlkeld, *Synopsis stirpium Hibernicarum* (Dublin, 1727).

16 Cabot, *New Naturalist*, 29–30.

17 John K'Eogh, *A vindication of the antiquities of Ireland* (Dublin, 1748).

18 Charles Smith, *The antient and present state of the county and city of Waterford, being a natural, civil, ecclesiastical, historical and topographical description thereof...*, published with the approbation of the Physico-Historical Society (Dublin, 1746); Charles Smith, *The antient and present state of the county and city of Cork* (Dublin, 1750).

19 Cited by R. B. McDowell, 'The Main Narrative', in T. Ó Raifeartaigh (ed.), *The Royal Irish Academy: a bicentennial history, 1785–1985* (Dublin, 1985), 4.

20 John Rutty, *An Essay towards a natural history of the county of Dublin* (Dublin, 1772); Cabot, *New Naturalist*, 31.

21 Thomas Prior, *A list of absentees of Ireland... with observations on the present trade and conditions of that Kingdom* (Dublin, 1729).

22 Barbara Traxler Brown, 'Three Centuries of Journals in Ireland: The Library of the Royal Dublin Society, Grafton Street', in Barbara Hayley and Enda McKay (eds), *Three hundred years of Irish Periodicals* (Dublin, 1987), 14.

23 *Transactions of the Royal Irish Academy*, 1 (1787), preface, xv.

24 William Preston, 'Essay on the natural advantages of Ireland, the manufactures to which they are adapted and the best means of improving these manufactures', in *Transactions of the Royal Irish Academy*, 9 (1803), 161–428.

25 McDowell, 'The Main Narrative', 14.

26 G. F. Mitchell, 'Antiquities', in Ó Raifeartaigh, *Royal Irish Academy*, 95.

27 Richard Lovell Edgeworth, 'An essay on the art of conveying secret and swift intelligence', in *Transactions of the Royal Irish Academy*, 6 (1797), 95–139.

28 Gordon L. Herries Davies, 'The Geological Society of Dublin and the Royal Geological Society of Ireland' in *Hermathena*, 100 (1965), 67.

29 Gordon L. Herries Davies, *Sheets of many colours: the mapping of Ireland's rocks, 1750–1890* (Dublin, 1983).

30 The Geological Survey of Ireland has its origins in the fieldwork of the geological section of the Ordnance Survey and can be traced back to 1826. However, the official title, Geological Survey of Ireland, was adopted in 1845 when the Survey became a branch of the Geological Survey of Great Britain. The Geological Survey of Ireland continues in operation and is located at Beggar's Bush in Dublin. For the full history of the Geological Survey see Gordon L. Herries Davies, *North from the Hook: 150 years of the Geological Survey of Ireland*, (Dublin, 1995).

31 Jonathan Pim, 'Address delivered at the opening of the 8th session of the Society' [read 20 November 1854], in *Journal of the Dublin Statistical Society*, 1 (1855), 14.

32 Thomas Colby, *Ordnance survey of the county of Londonderry* (Dublin, 1835). This volume included the parish of Templemore and the city of Londonderry only and was published as a preprint. The most commonly known edition is that of 1837 which contains more information and was published under the title *Ordnance survey of the county of Londonderry, volume the first* (Dublin, 1837).

33 Angélique Day and Patrick McWilliams (eds), *The Ordnance Survey Memoirs*, 40 vols (Belfast and Dublin, 1990–98).

34 The Royal Irish Academy holds the original manuscript *Letters*, which are commonly referred to as the *O'Donovan Letters*. Typescript copies compiled by Revd Michael O'Flanagan in the 1920s are held by the Academy and other libraries. A limited number of county volumes has been published over the years.

5: *SALOME*: A TEXT UNVEILED

I must pay tribute to the pioneering work by William Tydeman and Steven Price in the Cambridge University Play series *Wilde: Salome* (1996). I hope I have added something to their own findings, for, though pioneering, their work is not exhaustive. Errors and omissions remain firmly my own.

1 Richard Strauss (1864–1949) German composer whose operas include *Elektra*, *Ariadne auf Naxos*, *Der Rosenkavalier*, *Arabella*, etc.

2 Richard Ellmann, *Oscar Wilde* (London, 1988).

3 These include Josephine Barstow, Hildegard Behrens, Inge Borkh, Montserrat Caballé, Olive Fremstad, Mary Garden, Christel Göltz, Karen Huffstodt, Marjorie Lawrence, Göta Ljungberg, Catherine Malfitano, Birgit Nilsson, Hildegarde Ranczak, Teresa Stratas, Astrid Varnay, Ljuba Welitsch, Marie Wittich.

4 C. Steven Larue (ed.), *International Dictionary of Opera* (London, 1993); Robin May, *A Companion to the Opera* (London, 1977); David Ewen, *The New Encyclopædia of the Opera* (London, 1973); Lesley Orrey (ed.), *The Encyclopædia of Opera* (London, 1976); Stanley Sadie (ed.), *New Grove Encyclopædia of the Opera* (Basingstoke, 1992).

5 1856–1931, Welsh/Irish journalist, short story writer and biographer.

6 1886–1968, English diplomatist, essayist and biographer.

7   1844–1896, French poet.

8   Harold Nicolson, *Verlaine* (Constable, n.d.) 202; J. Joseph Renaud, preface to Oscar Wilde, *Intentions* (Paris, 1905), xxiii; William Rothenstein, *Men and Memories, Recollections* (London, 1931) vol. 1, 88.

9   1849–1926, French dramatist, sometime lover of Sarah Bernhardt.

10   Elaine Aston, *Sarah Bernhardt, A French Actress on the London Stage* (Oxford, 1989), 75.

11   1861–1943, author, journalist and multiple biographer of Wilde.

12   1863–1915, American Parisian poet who subsequently became estranged from Wilde.

13   1864–1937, Paris American writer, perhaps the originator of the term 'free verse'. 'Le vers est libre' is a phrase in his anthology *Joies* of 1888, announcing the overthrow of the Alexandrine. Edmund Wilson says nastily, 'We are surprised to learn that Vielé-Griffin is still considered an important poet.' Edmund Wilson, *Axel's Castle: A Study in the Imaginative Culture of 1870–1930* (New York, 1940), 16. The novelist of New York life, Herman Knickerbocker Vielé (1856–1908), was his elder brother.

14   Vyvyan Holland, 1886–1967, Wilde's younger son: the family name was changed by Wilde's wife after his gaol sentence. Adolphe Retté, 1863–1910, French Symbolist poet; Pierre Louÿs, 1870–1925, French poet and novelist who subsequently became estranged from Wilde; Marcel Schwab, 1867–1905, French writer who subsequently became estranged from Wilde.

15   Oscar Wilde to Stuart Merrill, late 1891, Sir Rupert Hart-Davis (ed.), *More Letters of Oscar Wilde* (London, 1985), 102.

16   Vincent O'Sullivan, *Aspects of Wilde* (London, 1934), 169.

17   Robert H. Sherard, 'Notes from Paris', in *The Author*, 2 August 1892 (notes dated 22 July).

18   Jules Renard, *Journal* (Paris, 1935). Renard (1864–1910) was a French diarist and novelist who did not much care for Wilde. León Daudet (1867–1942), the elder son of Alphonse Daudet, was a reactionary politician, and a co-founder of the Action Française.

19   Robert Harborough Sherard, *The Life of Oscar Wilde* (London, 1906).

20   Oscar Wilde to Robert Sherard, December 1891, in Hart-Davis, *More Letters*, 103.

21   Hart-Davis, *More Letters*, 102n.

22   1870–1945, Wilde's lover and nemesis, known as Bosie.

23   London: The Folio Society, 1957, and London: William Heinemann & Co., 1957 respectively.

24   1844–1923, the leading French *tragédienne* of her day.

25   1858–1924.

26   1872–1911, English writer, contributor to *The Yellow Book*, and music critic.

27   Oscar Wilde to Stanley Makower, 21 October 1897, in Rupert Hart-Davis (ed.), *The Letters of Oscar Wilde* (London, 1962), 664.

28   Wilde also described a volume of poems by Ernest Raynaud as of a 'troublante beauté' (Oscar Wilde to Ernest Raynaud, 29 November 1891, in Hart-Davis *More Letters*, 101).

29   Oscar Wilde to Leonard Smithers, [10] December 1897, in Hart-Davis, *Letters of Oscar Wilde*, 695.

30   Oscar Wilde to Robert Ross, *c.*23 November 1897, in Hart-Davis, *Letters of Oscar Wilde*, 683.

31   Anita Roittinger, *Oscar Wilde's Life as Reflected in his Correspondence and His Autobiography* (Salzburg, 1980), 309.

32 1856–1925, leading portrait painter

33 1893. Private collection, California. Reproduced in Carter Ratcliff, *John Singer Sargent* (Oxford, 1983).

34 Ellmann, *Oscar Wilde*, 518.

35 For a comparison of Duse's Paula Tanqueray with that of Mrs Patrick Campbell, see Prince Serge Volkonsky, *My Reminiscences*, trans. by A. E. Chamot (London, 1925), vol. 1, 129–31.

36 William Weaver, *Duse, A Biography* (London, 1984).

37 1860–197, leading 'New Drama' actress.

38 1880–1957.

39 1862–1935, Dutch-born promotor of the New Drama.

40 1880–1948, a virulently chauvinistic MP.

41 1883–1956, dancer attacked for indecency, lesbianism and other *causes de scandale*.

42 b. 1895, theatre enthusiast who created the Cambridge Theatre Festival before turning to racehorses instead.

43 1880–1970, theatre director.

44 b.1926, better known as a film director.

45 1908–1992, the first man to play Wilde in the West End and on Broadway.

46 1898–2001, Irish founder of the Royal Ballet, her real name being Edris Stannus.

47 1905–1951, English composer.

48 1923–1999, German-born actress.

49 1903–1982, English man of the theatre domiciled in Dublin.

50 1869–1940, French experimental actor and director. I retain the diaresis in his name as this seems to be the general usage, although John Henderson has written that 'the second part of Lugné's name is often spelled Poë in reference works, though Poe seems more logical, in view of the connection with Edgar Allan Poe, and is the spelling adopted by Lugné's editors in his autobiography', John A. Henderson, *The First Avant-Garde, 1887–1894*, Sources of Modern French Theatre (London, 1971), 11n.

51 1869–1924, leading French actor.

52 Anon, *The Pretty Women of Paris* [1883], new edition introduced by Robin de Beaumont (Ware, 1996), 140.

53 1860–1919, French poet.

54 Christopher Innes, *Modern British Drama, 1890–1990* (Cambridge, 1992), 214, 354.

55 F. W. J. Hemmings, *Culture and Society in France, 1848–1898: Dissidents and Philistines* (London, 1971) 240–1.

56 1853–1917, English actor-manager. Lord Illingworth: a character in Wilde's *A Woman of No Importance*.

57 1858–1918, English actor-manager. Jack Worthing: a character in Wilde's *The Importance of Being Earnest*.

58 Lugné-Poë did direct two plays by Shaw (*The Doctor's Dilemma* in May 1922, and *Mrs Warren's Profession* in October 1924). His penultimate play was Maugham's *The Circle* in November 1928.

59 *Theatre and Art Review*, St Petersburg, 1906. Other details unknown.

60 Secretary of the Moscow Art Theatre. 'Lyki', as he was called, was said to be one-third Greek, one-third Russian, and one-third English.

61 1867–1942.

62 1885–1960.

63 1865–1936.

64 1879–1953.

65 Spencer Golub in Martin Banham (ed.), *The Cambridge Guide to the Theatre* (Cambridge, 1995), XX.

66 d. 1950.

67 Alexander Tairov, *Notes of a Director*, trans. William Kuhlke (Florida, 1969), 107, 120–1.

68 1873–1943, German director.

69 1858–1925, German painter who had studied in Paris.

70 1874–1915, German poet, a number of whose poems were set as songs by Strauss.

71 Published in 1903 in Leipzig by Insel-Verlag, with illustrations by Max Behmer.

72 Gary Schmidgall, *Literature as Opera* (New York, 1977), 250–1.

73 Ibid., 263.

74 This is covered in Elliot L. Gilbert, '"Tumult of Images": Wilde, Beardsley and Salomé', *Victorian Studies*, 26 (1983); Michael Morris, 'The Beardsley Illustrations for Salome', *Wilde about Wilde Newsletter*, Mount Airy, Maryland, October 1992; Joan Navarre, 'The Publishing History of Aubrey Beardsley's compositions for Oscar Wilde's *Salome*', Ph.D. thesis Marquette University, 1995.

75 Maureen Borland, *Wilde's Devoted Friend: A Life of Robert Ross* (Oxford, 1990), 103.

76 Or Ema Destinnová, 1878–1930.

77 1867–1957, Italian conductor who gave *Salome* its Milan premiere.

78 1913–196, Bulgarian soprano.

79 b. 1927.

80 b. 1937.

81 1879–1961.

82 1894–1981

83 b. 1944.

84 b. 1929.

85 1928–1999.

86 1903–1960.

87 1901–1990.

88 1910–1976.

89 1888–1965.

90 1893–1954.

91 b. 1936.

92 1853–1928.

93 1902–1958.

94 b. 1951.

95 b. 1946.

96 1912–1997.

97 1897–1970.

98 b. 1910.

99 O'Sullivan, *Aspects of Wilde*, 201–2.

100 1899–1977.

101 1883–1951.

102 1866–1944, influential French novelist and critic.

103 1875–1944.

104 1870–1958. Although the name is occasionally given as Schmidt (perhaps confused with Franz Schmidt) Grove correctly has Schmitt.

105 1869–1915.

106 1862–1934, British composer who lived in Paris in the 1890s.

107 1836–1932.

108 1885–1978. Karsavina is regarded as one of the greatest of the twentieth-century ballerinas.

109 David Escott, 'Florent Schmitt', in Lionel Carley (ed.), *Frederick Delius, Music Art and Literature* (Aldershot, 1998), 115. Loïe Fuller was not only painted by Toulouse-Lautrec, but most surprisingly also by Jean-Léon Gérôme, who was swept up in the enthusiasm and for once abandoned his vapid classicism and portrayed the dancer under her red and orange spotlights in a Whistler-esque swirl of draperies. Gerald M. Ackerman, *The Life and Work of Jean-Léon Gérôme, with a catalogue raisonné* (London, 1986), figures 413 and 414.

110 Anna, Comtesse de Brémont, *Oscar Wilde and His Mother, A Memoir* (London, 1911), 145. I have found no other reference to this curious occasion, which antedates Wilde's imprisonment.

111 Postgraduate work being carried out at Portland State University, Oregon; Queen's University, Belfast; Reiksuniversiteit Gent; Goldsmiths College, London.

6: FROM THE POINTED ONES TO THE BONES

1   W. B.Yeats, *Memoirs* (London, 1972), 156.

2   Samuel Beckett to Thomas MacGreevy, 27 March 1949 (TCD); all subsequent references to this correspondence will be as 'SB to TM' with omitted but known or probable dates in square brackets. Particularly severe judgements of Dublin are to be found in Beckett's letters of 1930 (after his return from Paris; e.g. 14 November [1930])and 1931, and it was not until 8 October 1935 that he could write 'perhaps after all I may find myself immune to Dublin now', which did not prove to be the case.

3   Samuel Beckett, *Disjecta: miscellaneous writings and a dramatic fragment*, (ed.) Ruby Cohn (London, 1983), 69, 82, 89 (SB to TM 9 June 1936: 'I compared him to Ariosto'), 93.

4   'Censorship in the Saorstat', *Disjecta*, 87.

5   E.g. Eoin O'Brien, *The Beckett Country* (Dublin, 1986); John P. Harrington, *The Irish Beckett* (Syracuse, NY, 1991); Mary Junker, *Beckett: The Irish Dimension* (Dublin, 1995).

6   *Proust and Three Dialogues with Georges Duthuit* (London, 1965), 101.

7   'Dante...Bruno.Vico...Joyce', *Disjecta*, 19.

8   Theo Dorgan, 'The Making of the Great Book Ireland', *Irish Studies Review*, 1 (Spring, 1992), 10.

9   Lawrence E. Harvey, *Samuel Beckett: Poet and Critic*, (Princeton, NJ, 1970), 249.

10 Harvey, *Samuel Beckett*, 301, n91.

11 SB to TM, 25 August [1930].

12 SB to TM, 14 July 1932.

13 SB to TM, 25 August [1930].

14 SB to TM, 6 January 1931.

15 SB to TM, either 17 or 24 July 1930.

16 SB to TM, 1 March 1930.

17 SB to TM, [?14 November 1930].

18   SB to TM, [?20 June 1930]; Beckett's mixed feelings about *transition*, which he was subsequently apparently quite content to publish in, presumably reflect Eugene Jolas's commitment to Joyce above all other writers, which sometimes ruffled feathers other than Beckett's.

19   SB to TM, 25 August [1930].

20   SB to TM, [27] August 1932.

21   The Leventhal material at the Harry Ransom Humanities Research Center (HRHRC) at the University of Texas at Austin, Texas, is particularly rich as regards poems, offering variant versions of 'Casket of Pralinen...', 'Hell Crane to Starling' and 'Text'. It includes a contents list for '*POEMS* by Samuel Beckett', listing twenty-seven poems; by March 1935, as a card to George Reavey (headed 6 March but postmarked 16 March) indicates, Beckett had scaled the project down, and changed the title to one he (if no one else) considered 'Plus modeste'.

22   SB to TM, first week of August 1930.

23   SB to TM, 7 July [sic; but on internal evidence almost certainly August] 1930.

24   SB to TM, 1 March 1930.

25   SB to TM, 25 July 1930. Beckett presumably sent a copy to Joyce – rather than giving it to him – because relations between them had been soured by Beckett's treatment of Lucia Joyce (as her father saw the matter); this was presumably intended as a kind of peace offering.

26   SB to TM, 7 July (=August) 1930.

27   Harvey, *Samuel Beckett*, 305, n.107.

28   SB to TM, either 17 or 24 July 1930. Beckett gave the poem to Henry Crowder on Bastille Day, 14 July 1930.

29   Deirdre Bair, *Samuel Beckett: a biography* (London, 1978), 109.

30   Beckett's letters to Charles Prentice of 14 October and 3 December 1930, which are part of the Chatto and Windus material held in the Archives department of the Library at the University of Reading, and contain important information about which poems Beckett was prepared to let Prentice see, in the hope that Chatto might be interested in publishing a volume, which they were not.

31   SB to TM, 14 November [1930].

32   SB to TM, 12 December 1932.

33   SB to George Reavey, 9 January 1936 (misdated 1935 by Beckett; HRHRC).

34   SB to TM, 18 October 1932.

35   SB to TM, [?29 September 1931].

36   SB to TM, 9 October 1931.

37   SB to TM, in mostly undated letters between August and October 1931; see my edition of *Beckett's 'Dream' Notebook* (Reading, 1999), where the items from Bérard are numbered 710–717, and item 712 reads: 'molu – antidote to Circe (moly)'.

38   Prentice's letter to Beckett of 27 August 1932 is part of the Chatto material held in the Archives department of the Library at the University of Reading.

39   SB to TM, 4 August and 18 August 1932.

40   SB to TM, 30 August 1932.

41   SB to TM, 13 [October 1932].

42   SB to TM, 4 August and 27 August 1932.

43   SB to TM, 8 October and 12 December 1932.

44   SB to TM, 30 August 1932.

45   SB to TM, 22 June 1933.

46   Harvey, *Samuel Beckett*, 221.

47 SB to TM, 29 May 1931.

48 SB to TM, [?12 September 1931].

49 SB to TM, [?29 September 1931].

50 SB to TM, 9 October 1931.

51 SB to TM, 8 November 1931.

52 SB to TM, 11 November and 21 November 1932.

53 SB to TM, 9 October 1931.

54 SB to TM, [?29 September 1931].

55 SB to TM, 18 October 1932.

56 SB to TM, 8 November 1931.

57 SB to Seumas O' Sullivan, 27 November 1931; TCD MS 4644/3322/2.

58 SB to TM, 20 December 1931.

59 SB to TM, 7 September 1933.

60 SB to TM, 9 October 1933.

61 SB to TM, 18 August and 28 August 1934.

62 SB to TM, 26 April 1935.

63 Bair, *Samuel Beckett*, 186.

64 Richard Admussen, *The Samuel Beckett Manuscripts: A Study* (Boston, 1979), 26, 119.

65 Harvey, *Samuel Beckett*, 77.

66 SB to TM, 18 October 1932.

67 Bair, *Samuel Beckett*, 91.

68 SB to TM, 5 October and 14 November 1930.

69 Prentice to SB, 27 July 1932 (Reading); SB to TM. 11 November 1932.

70 SB to TM, 9 October 1931.

71 SB to TM, 13 [September] and 8 October 1932.

72 SB to TM, 5 January 1933 and 18 October 1932.

73 SB to TM, 18 October 1932.

74 SB to TM, 23 [April] and 13 May 1933.

75 SB to TM, 5 January 1933.

76 SB to TM, 13 May 1933.

77 SB to A. J. Leventhal, 28 July [1934] (HRHRC).

78 SB to TM, 8 September 1935.

79 SB to TM, 8 October 1935.

80 Prentice to SB, 13 November 1933 (Reading).

81 SB to TM, 6 December 1933.

82 SB to A. J. Leventhal, 7 August [1935] (HRHRC).

83 SB to TM, 26 April 1935.

84 SB to TM, 8 September [1935].

85 Ibid.

86 SB to TM, 19 September 1936; 'Cascando' was published in *Dublin Magazine*, vol. XI, no. 4, October–December 1936, 3–4.

87 See James Knowlson, *Damned to Fame: the life of Samuel Beckett* (London, 1996), 225. More surprising, perhaps, in view of the information given by Knowlson to the effect that O'Sullivan 'promised to pay for all of the printing costs for three years', a very generous offer indeed, and – as my editor has reminded me – given O'Sullivan's editorship of the magazine for many long years after.

88 Prentice's rejection came in his letter to Beckett of 27 July 1932 (Reading). Prentice was, by his own admission (and as is clear from the authors he did encourage) much

more comfortable with prose fiction than with poetry, even when quite experimental work (if not quite as experimental as Beckett's *Dream*!) was put in front of him.

89 SB to TM, 12 December 1932 and 8 November 1931.
90 SB to TM, 31 December 1935.
91 SB to TM, 9 January 1936 (misdated by SB 1935).
92 See *Dublin Magazine*, vol. XI, no. 2 (April – June 1936), 78; *The Irish Times*, 25 July 1936, 7.

7: IRISH CENSORSHIP

1   W. J. McCormack, *Fool of the Family: A Life of J. M. Synge* (London, 2000), 312–24.
2   See Ruth Dudley Edwards, *Patrick Pearse, The Triumph of Failure* (London, 1977), 101–3.
3   Quoted in McCormack, *Fool of the Family*, 320.
4   See Catherine Forde's article on abortion in W. J. McCormack (ed.), *The Blackwell Companion to Modern Irish Culture*, rev. paperback edn. (Oxford, 2001), 7–9.
5   The conventional view is encapsulated in Tony Gray's casual but amusing biography of the great wartime *Irish Times* editor, *Mr Smyllie, Sir* (Dublin, 1991), 53–9.
6   Desmond Fitzgerald to Ezra Pound, 24 October [1928], and Ezra Pound to Desmond Fitzgerald, 16 August 1928, University College Dublin, Archives Department.
7   W. B. Yeats, 'The Censorship and St Thomas Aquinas', *Irish Statesman*, 22 September 1928.
8   Michael Adams, *Censorship: the Irish Experience* (Dublin, 1968), 17. See also Julia Carlson, *Banned in Ireland* (London, 1990).
9   W. B. Yeats, 'The Irish Censorship', *Spectator*, 29 September 1928, reprinted in John P. Frayne and Colton Johnson, *Uncollected Prose by W. B. Yeats*, vol. 2 (London, 1975), 480–5.
10 W. B. Yeats, *On the Boiler* (Dublin: The Cuala Press, 1939), 31.
11 Personal Communication.
12 Donal Ó Drisceoil, *Censorship in Ireland, 1939–1945: Neutrality, Politics and Society* (Cork, 1996), 77, 4.
13 For some remarks on this phenomenon, and its historical background, see W. J. McCormack, 'The Cult of the Contemporary in Ireland' in Peter Dávidházi and Judit Kárafiáth (eds), *Literature and its Cults; an Anthropological Approach* (Budapest, n.d.), 203–11.

8: BLACKLISTS AND REDEMPTIONS

1   *Aengus,* 4 (July 1920), 6.
2   I am indebted to Tom Clyde's *Irish Literary Magazines: An Outline History and Descriptive Bibliography* (Dublin, 2002) for this information.
3   A. Norman Jeffares, *A Commentary on the Collected Poems of W. B. Yeats* (London, 1968), 295.
4   Francis Stuart in Francis MacManus (ed.), *The Yeats We Knew* (Dublin, 1977), 36.
5   Allan Wade (ed.), *The Letters of W. B. Yeats* (London, 1954), 705.
6   David Krause (ed.), *The Letters of Sean O'Casey 1910–41* (London, 1975), 123.

7   H. Stuart, 'In the Hour Before Dawn', *To-morrow*, 1:2 (September 1924), 4.

8   Francis Stuart, *Lecture on Nationality and Culture* (Dublin, 1924), 6.

9   Seumas O'Sullivan, *Dublin Magazine*, November 1924, 5.

10 For Edward Garnett see George Jefferson, *Edward Garnett: A Life in Literature* (London, 1982).

11 Michael Howard, *Jonathan Cape, Publisher* (London, 1971), 137.

12 See A. A. Kelly, *The Letters of Liam O'Flaherty* (Dublin, 1996).

13 Information courtesy of Mike Bott, University of Reading Library.

14 James Devane, 'Is an Irish Culture Possible?' *Ireland Today*, 1:5 (October 1936).

15 Kelly, *The Letters of Liam O'Flaherty*, 185.

16 Ibid., 277.

17 Ian Norrie (ed.), *Mumby's Publishing and Bookselling in the Twentieth Century* (London, 1982), 64.

18 Scrapbook of reviews and articles collected by Iseult Stuart, Francis Stuart Collection, University of Ulster, 33.

19 Review, *Irish Press*, February 1932.

20 Kelly, *The Letters of Liam O'Flaherty*, 268.

21 Francis Stuart, *Black List, Section H*, 3rd edition (London, 1982), 231.

22 Dr. J.M. Bulloch, *Sunday Times*, October 1934.

23 *Irish Press*, 28 May 1935.

24 Kelly, *The Letters of Liam O'Flaherty*, 276.

25 Scrapbook, Francis Stuart Collection, University of Ulster, 57.

26 Francis Stuart Collection, University of Ulster.

27 Sean O'Faolain, *John O'London's Weekly*, 24 February 1939.

28 Brendan Barrington, *The Wartime Broadcasts of Francis Stuart* (Dublin, 2000), 7.

29 Ibid., 25.

30 These novels were the focus of a confrontation in the *Sunday Independent*, October 1999 when Conor Cruise O'Brien argued that an MA thesis by Raymond Patrick Burke, 'The Representation of Jews and Jewishness in the Novels of Francis Stuart', (NUI, Galway, 1999), provided conclusive proof of Stuart's anti-Semitism; a contention that was strongly rejected by Anthony Cronin, *Sunday Tribune*, November 1999, who accused O'Brien of failing to read the texts for himself.

31 Barrington, *Wartime Broadcasts*, 23.

32 Ibid., 26.

33 Stuart, letter in *The Irish Times*, 13 December 1938.

34 Scrapbook, Francis Stuart Collection, University of Ulster, 1.

35 Barrington, *Wartime Broadcasts*, 28.

36 Diary entry, December 1948, Notebook XIII, University of Ulster Library.

37 Francis Stuart, *Julie* (London, 1938), 158.

38 Barrington, *Wartime Broadcasts*, 28.

39 Diary entry, 20 August 1942, Notebook II, University of Ulster Library.

40 Ibid., 25 September 1942.

41 Ibid., May 1947.

42 Letter from Victor Gollancz, 19 March 1948, MS 5/2.5, Francis Stuart Collection, Southern Illinois University, Carbondale.

43 Ibid., 22 March 1949.

44 Ibid., 21 October 1948.

45 Ibid., 14 April 1953.

46 Ibid., 17 February 1960.

47 Publisher's archives for Victor Gollancz are in the University of Warwick.

48 Letters of rejection from David Higham Associates, 20 September 1967; McGibbon & Kee, 22 February 1968; A. P. Watt, 11 August 1969; Michael Gill, 4 November 1969; Andre Deutsch, 15 June 1970; Vernon Sternberg, 13 April 1972; Tom Stacey Ltd, 9 May 1972 and Wm. Heinemann, 19 July 1972. MS 27, Francis Stuart Collection, University of Ulster Library.

49 Timothy O'Keeffe published other Irish authors including Brian O'Nolan and Patrick Kavanagh. His papers are in the McFarlin Library, University of Tulsa.

50 Peter Fallon, 'Poetry in Action' *The Irish Times*, 6 June 1998.

9: THOMAS KINSELLA AND THE PEPPERCANISTER PRESS

1 John Haffenden, 'Thomas Kinsella', in *Viewpoints: Poets in Conversation with John Haffenden* (London, 1981), 105.

2 Thomas Kinsella, *A Technical Supplement* (Dublin, 1976).

3 Carolyn Rosenberg, 'Let Our Gaze Blaze: The Recent Poetry of Thomas Kinsella' (unpublished doctoral thesis, Kent State University, 1980), 209.

4 Ibid., 1–2.

5 Thomas Kinsella, *Fifteen Dead* (Dublin and Oxford, 1979), 9.

6 Robin Skelton, 'Twentieth-Century Irish Literature and the Private Press Tradition: Dun Emer, Cuala, & Dolmen Presses 1902–1963', in Robin Skelton and David R. Clark (eds), *Irish Renaissance: A Gathering of Essays, Memoirs, and Letters from the Massachusetts Review* (Dublin, 1965), 158–67, 162.

7 Thomas Kinsella, preface to Stephen Enniss (ed.), *Peppercanister 1972–1997, Twenty-five Years of Poetry: A Bibliography* (Atlanta, 1997), 1.

8 Enniss, *Peppercanister 1972–1997*, 6.

9 Kinsella, preface to Enniss, *Peppercanister 1972–1997*, 1.

10 John Montague, *The Rough Field* (Portlaoise, 1972, reprinted 1984), 63–70.

11 Seamus Heaney, *Field Work* (London, 1979), 29–30. In this edition Ó Riada's name appears neither in the English, as Reidy, nor the Irish, as Ó Riada, but in a hybrid of both: O'Riada.

12 Aidan Matthews, 'Modern Irish Poetry: A Question of Covenants', in Mark Patrick Hederman and Richard Kearney (ed.), *The Crane Bag Book of Irish Studies (1977–1981)* (Dublin, 1982), 380–9, 384.

13 Quoted from publicity produced by Peppercanister for their first four pamphlets.

14 Thomas Kinsella Papers, Woodruff Library, Emory University, box 8, folder 20.

15 Thomas Kinsella, *Fifteen Dead* (Dublin, 1979), 74.

16 Gisela M. A. Richter, *The Portraits of the Greeks* (London, 1965), vol. 2, 164–7. The cover image of *The Good Fight* and that facing part III come from a head in the National Museum, Athens (plate 21, figs. 957–8). The image facing the title page is held in the Fitzwilliam Museum, Cambridge (plate 16, fig. 946). The image facing part II comes from the Musée Granet, Aix-en-Provence (plate 14, fig. 939). The final image, facing the last page of the poem, is from the National Museum, Syracuse (plate 9, fig. 921). All plate and figure references are from Richter's *The Portraits of the Greeks*.

17 Thomas Kinsella, 'Notes from the land of the dead', *Poems 1956–1973* (Portlaoise, 1980), 132. The revised version of the poem in *Collected Poems* omits these lines.

18 Dennis O'Driscoll, 'Interview with Thomas Kinsella,' *Poetry Ireland Review*, 25 (spring 1989), 61.

19 Ibid., 61.

20 Enniss, *Peppercanister 1972–1997*, 18.

21 Ibid., 20.

22 Kinsella, *A Technical Supplement*, [13]–[17].

23 Enniss, *Peppercanister 1972–1997*, 24.

24 Maurice Harmon, '"Move, if you move, like water": The Poetry of Thomas Kinsella, 1972–1988', in Elmer Andrews (ed.), *Contemporary Irish Poetry: A Collection of Critical Essays* (London, 1992), 194.

25 Thomas Kinsella Papers, Woodruff Library, Emory University, box 17, folder 3, contains drawings by Kinsella of herons and bats, and of the images used for the cover, title page and last page of the Peppercanister edition. See also Enniss, *Peppercanister 1972–1997*, 26.

26 C. G. Jung, *Alchemical Studies,* trans. by R. F. C. Hull, *The Collected Works of C. G. Jung,* vol. 13 (London, 1967), 235.

27 Ibid., 223.

28 Kinsella's 'Preface' to Ennis, *Peppercanister* 1972–1997, 2.

29 Thomas Kinsella (ed.), *The New Oxford Book of Irish Verse* (Oxford, 1986), vii.

30 See also Elgy Gillespie's mention in 'Thomas Kinsella, the poet,' *The Irish Times,* 20 June 1981: 'He's just knocked off four new poems for Cecil King's print collection, commissioned by Monica Beck, and will be Peppercanistering the texts soon.'

31 Thomas Kinsella Papers, Woodruff Library, Emory University, box 62, folder 1.

32 Ibid., folder 2.

33 Ibid.

34 For a list of the poems chosen see the Thomas Kinsella Papers, Woodruff Library, Emory University, box 62, folder 2.

35 P. W. Joyce, *A Smaller Social History of Ancient Ireland*, 2nd edn (London, 1908), 294.

36 W. B. Yeats, *W. B. Yeats: Selected Poetry,* (ed.) Timothy Webb (London, 1991), 179.

37 Letters from Kinsella to Peter Fallon, 24 June 1980, and 12 August 1980, regarding the publication of a poem with Gallery Press. Thomas Kinsella Papers, Woodruff Library, Emory University, box 24, folder 1.

38 See Thomas Kinsella Papers, Woodruff Library, Emory University, box 29, folder 10.

39 Ibid. See Dillon Johnston, 'The Anthology Wars', *Times Literary Supplement*, 13 September 1991, 26, in which Peppercanisters 14 and 15 are listed under 'Dublin: Dedalus; distributed in the UK by Manchester: Password.'

40 Thomas Kinsella Papers, Woodruff Library, Emory University, box 22, folder 22.

41 Ibid., box 24, folder 20.

42 Thomas Kinsella, *Poems from Centre City* (Dublin, 1990), 19.

43 See W. Kurth (ed.), *The Complete Woodcuts of Albrecht Dürer* (New York, 1963), plate 172: 'Nude Woman with the Zodiac. Single sheet with the Prognosticon of the Astronomer Stabius for the year 1503–04', 25.

44 Kurth, *The Complete Woodcuts of Albrecht Dürer*, plate 93.

45 R.W. Emerson, *The Complete Works of Ralph Waldo Emerson*, Centenary Edition, 12 vols. (Boston and New York, Houghton Mifflin and Company, 1903–1904; reprinted New York, AMS Press, 1968), Volume 3: Essays, Second Series, 179.

46 Courtney Davis, *Celtic Ornament: Art of the Scribe* (London, 1996), 13, 81, 92–3.

47 Klaus Holitzka, *Mandalas of the Celts* (New York, 1996).
48 Oliver Goldsmith, *The Works of Oliver Goldsmith* (Edinburgh, n.d.).
49 Thomas Kinsella, colophon to *Littlebody (*Dublin, 2000).
50 O'Driscoll, 'Interview', 59.

10: A POET'S JOURNEY HOME

1   The editions referred to in this essay are: *No Continuing City* (Dublin, 1969), and *Poems 1963–1983* (London, 1991).
2   Edna Longley, MS review of *No Continuing City*, Michael Longley Papers, Special Collections Division, Robert W. Woodruff Library, Emory University (hereafter Emory).
3   Letter to Paul Muldoon, 17 July 1972, Paul Muldoon Papers, Emory.
4   Notes for a poetry reading, Longley Papers, Emory.
5   Letter to Harry Chambers, prospective publisher of *Secret Marriages*, 24 August 1967, Longley Papers, Emory.
6   From draft of 'Circe', Longley Papers, Emory.
7   W. H. Auden, *The Enchafed Flood or the Romantic Iconography of the Sea* (New York, 1950), 7, 17.
8   Introduction to *Secret Marriages – Nine Short Poems* (Phoenix Pamphlet Poets, 1968), 2.
9   Edna Longley, MS review of *No Continuing City*, Longley Papers, Emory.
10 Notes for a poetry reading, Longley Papers, Emory.
11 Rainer Maria Rilke, *Letters to a Young Poet*, in *Sonnets to Orpheus with Letters to a Young Poet*, ed. and trans. Stephen Cohn (Manchester, 2000), 174.
12 Stephen Regan, *Philip Larkin* (London, 1992), 19.
13 Lecture on Sextus Propertius, Longley Papers, Emory.
14 The 'Domestic Sonnets' have not been published; they are in the Longley Papers at Emory.
15 A letter from Longley in response to the rejection of *No Continuing City* by Ian Parsons at Chatto & Windus, 8 December 1966, Longley Papers, Emory.
16 Lecture on Sextus Propertius, Longley Papers, Emory.
17 Lecture, 'The Embarrassed Imagination', Longley Papers, Emory.
18 Robert Skelton, *The Poet's Calling* (Heinemann, 1975), 35.
19 Found on a back of a draft of 'Freeze-up', Longley Papers, Emory.
20 'At home', 22 June 1962, Longley Papers, Emory.
21 Gaston Bachelard, *The Poetics of Space*, trans. Maria Jolas (Toronto, 1969), 6–7.
22 Draft of 'Gathering Mushrooms', Longley Papers, Emory.
23 'Orpheus and Eurydice', Longley Papers, Emory.
24 Michael Longley, introduction to *Secret Marriages,* 2.
25 'Ossian in the land of eternal youth', Longley Papers, Emory.
26 Longley Papers, Emory.
27 A comment of Longley's found on a draft of 'Emily Dickinson' – 'A poet is obsessed with words – they constitute his element', Longley Papers, Emory.
28 Lecture on Sextus Propertius, Longley Papers, Emory.
29 Correspondence between Longley and Mahon, Longley Papers, Emory.
30 'This Room', Longley Papers, Emory.

31 Letter to Edna Broderick, 30 March 1964, Longley Papers, Emory.

32 Louis MacNeice, II from 'Trilogy for X', *Selected Poems*, edited by Michael Longley (London, 1988), 73.

33 Lecture on poetic rhyme and rhythm, Longley Papers, Emory.

34 Ibid.

35 Letter to Ian Parsons at Chatto & Windus who rejected *No Continuing City*, Longley Papers, Emory.

36 Lecture, 'The Embarrassed Imagination', Longley Papers, Emory.

37 The publisher comments that 'there are too many inversions, clichés and irrelevant rhymes' and that some of the material is 'intrusive, much too weighty', Longley Papers, Emory.

38 Lecture on Sextus Propertius, Longley Papers, Emory.

39 Lecture, 'The Embarrassed Imagination', Longley Papers, Emory.

40 Letter to Ian Parsons, Longley Papers, Emory.

41 Notes for a poetry reading, Longley Papers, Emory.

42 'Our Great Indoors', Longley Papers, Emory.

43 Bachelard, *The Poetics of Space*, 7.

44 R. S. Thomas, introduction to *A Choice of George Herbert's Verse* (London, 1967), 14.

45 Blake, quoted in Skelton, *The Poet's Calling*, 11.

46 Louis MacNeice, 'Western Landscape', *Selected Poems*, 108.

47 Longley Papers, Emory.

48 *The Paris Review Interview*, (ed.) George Plimpton, *Writers at Work* (London, 1987), 166.

49 Douglas Dunn, 'Longley's Metric', in *The Poetry of Michael Longley* (ed.) Alan. J. Peacock and Kathleen Devine (Gerrard's Cross, 2000), 18.

50 Michael Longley, introduction to Louis MacNeice, *Selected Poems* (London, 1988), xix.

51 Lecture on Sextus Propertius, Longley Papers, Emory.

52 Ibid.

53 'Green Places: Some Nature Poems for Crawfordsburn Country Park', Longley Papers, Emory.

54 'Bach', Longley Papers, Emory.

55 'Comparison', Longley Papers, Emory.

56 Philip Larkin, 'Lines on a Young Lady's Photograph Album', *Collected Poems* (London, 1988), 73.

57 Larkin, 'Absences', *Collected Poems*, 49.

58 Longley Papers, Emory.

59 Ibid.

60 Bachelard, *The Poetics of Space*, 38.

61 'Today and Yesterday in Northern Ireland: Winter', radio script, November 1970, Longley Papers, Emory.

62 Longley Papers, Emory.

63 Ibid. (This poem is pared down appropriately from a very ornate stanza).

64 Longley, interview with Robert Johnstone, 'The Longley Tapes', *The Honest Ulsterman*, 78 (summer 1985), 16.

65 Lecture on poetic rhyme and rhythm, Longley Papers, Emory.

66 Longley Papers, Emory.

67 Philip Larkin, 'Absences', *Collected Poems*, 49.

68   'Dr Johnson's Journey to the Hebrides', radio script, RTE, broadcast 29 September 1974, Longley Papers, Emory.

69   Louis MacNeice, 'The Hebrides: A Tripper's Community', *Selected Prose*, (ed.) Alan Heuser (Oxford, 1990), 24.

11: Seamus Heaney and the Book as Expressive Form

1   Seamus Heaney and Derek Mahon, *in their element* (Belfast, 1977), unpaginated introduction.

2   W. B. Yeats, *The Wind Among the Reeds* (London, 1899).

3   W. B. Yeats, *The Secret Rose* (London, 1897).

4   D. F. McKenzie, *Bibliography and the Sociology of Texts*, rev. edn. (Cambridge, 1999).

5   D. F. McKenzie, 'Typography and Meaning: The Case of William Congreve', in Giles Barber and Bernhard Fabian (eds), *The Book and Book Trade in Eighteenth-Century Europe* (Hamburg, 1981), 81–126, (82).

6   Seamus Heaney with Noel Connor, *Gravities: A Collection of Poems and Drawings* (Newcastle upon Tyne, 1979); Seamus Heaney with Felim Egan, *Towards a Collaboration* (Enniskillen, 1986); Seamus Heaney, *Ugolino* (Dublin, 1979).

7   Seamus Heaney, *Field Work* (London, 1979).

8   Rachel Giese is an American photographer who is also author of *The Donegal Pictures* (Wake Forest, 1987). She has collaborated with Heaney on other projects (under the name Rachel Brown) including Cathal Ó Searcaigh, *Na Piopai Crafoige*/The Clay Pipes, trans. Seamus Heaney (Louisville, Kentucky, 1995).

9   Seamus Heaney, *Sweeney's Flight* (London, 1992), vii, hereafter referred to in references as *SF*.

10   Seamus Heaney, *Sweeney Astray* (London, 1984), unpaginated introduction, hereafter referred to in references as *SA*.

11   Jerome McGann, *The Textual Condition* (Princeton, 1991), 15.

12   W. B. Yeats, *Responsibilities: Poems and a Play* (Dundrum, 1914).

13   Robert Pogue Harrison, *Forests: The Shadow of Civilization* (Chicago, 1992), ix.

14   Heaney writes about the addition of this poem in his preface to *Sweeney's Flight*: 'The volume begins, however, with a poem which evolved from my experience of translating *Buile Suibhne* in the first place. "The King of the Ditchbacks" is a triptych, of which the first part was written a year or two before I thought of undertaking the work at all. In retrospect, it seems as if Sweeney had already arrived and was presenting his visiting card: the "trespasser" moving behind the hedges was simply biding his time' (*SF* viii).

15   Seamus Heaney, *Preoccupations* (London: 1980), 185–6.

16   Although I am suggesting that the tree and pagan symbols are being used in opposition to the traditional Christian symbols, it should be observed that the relationship is a more complex one and that paganism and Christianity share some elements of tree worship. Schama argues that instances exist in which nature symbolism acted as an interface between pagan and Christian worship: 'many of the shrewder proselytizers grafted Christian theology on to pre-existing pagan cults of nature. In Ireland, for example, Lisa Bitel has discovered that monastic cells and hermitages were established on the ancient woodland pagan altars called *bili*. The

idea was to graft, rather than uproot' (Simon Schama, *Landscape and Memory* (London: 1995), 216). See also Schama's account of the tree of St Boniface and the verdant cross (Schama, 217–26).

17 Barrell writes of Clare's 'The Lane', 'Thus the syntax offers us a very urgent sense of the lane's progress through the landscape – the accelerated reading-speed proposed by the syntax invites us to experience the wandering of the lane as restless, as it winds from the open countryside, through the dark tree-tunnel, and out into the open again, and the freedom ("freely") of the fields... This sentence-structure produces an intriguingly ambiguous account of the lane's progress, and of the different parts of the landscape it wanders through.' *Poetry, Language and Politics* (Manchester, 1988), 121.

18 Seamus Heaney, *The Redress of Poetry* (London, 1995), 67.

19 Ibid.

20 McKenzie, *Bibliography and the Sociology of Texts* (Cambridge, 1999), 25.

21 McGann, *The Textual Condition*, xx.

22 Ibid., 27.

12: LIGHT ENOUGH AND TIME

1 For a brief history of this institutional collecting, see 'The Growth of Emory's Modern Irish Collection', in Ronald Schuchard and Stephen Enniss, *Gazette of the Grolier Club*, new series, no. 50 (1999), 35–55.

2 B. L. Reid, *The Man from New York: John Quinn and His Friends* (Oxford, 1968).

3 SUNY Buffalo purchased a collection of John Montague's papers in 1992. The University of Tulsa holds the Richard Murphy Papers, and Boston College recently added the archive of Nuala Ní Dhomhnaill.

4 Ciaran Carson, 'An Evening of Irish Poetry with Ciaran Carson and Michael Longley', audio tape, 23 February 1995, University Archives, Robert W. Woodruff Library, Emory University (hereafter Emory).

5 For an extended discussion of Mahon's revisions, see Peter Denman, 'Know the One? Insolent Ontology and Mahon's Revisions', *Irish University Review*, 24 (spring/summer 1994), 27–37.

6 Derek Mahon, *Collected Poems* (Gallery Books, 1999).

7 Derek Mahon, 'The Art of Poetry, LXXXII,' *The Paris Review*, 154 (spring 2000), 175.

8 Derek Mahon, 'An Interview with Derek Mahon', interview with Terence Brown, *Poetry Ireland Review*, 14 (1985), 13–14.

9 It was preceded by *The Gust the Whirlwind and the Flaw*, by John Cowles, editor of Erato Publishing.

10 Derek Mahon to Michael Longley, [c. autumn 1966], Derek Mahon Papers, Emory.

11 Derek Mahon, 'Derek Mahon Interviewed', interview with William Scammell, *Poetry Review*, 81 (summer 1991), 5.

12 While the book that Mahon wrote to Longley about did not materialise, Jim Randall did publish Thomas Kinsella's *Tear* in pamphlet form just a few years later, in 1969.

13 Derek Mahon to Michael Longley, [c. autumn 1966], Derek Mahon Papers, Emory.

14 Ibid.

15 Ibid.

16 Ibid.

17   At the time, Kinsella was serving as an editor for Dolmen. The two presses were also linked by a distribution agreement allowing OUP to distribute Dolmen titles outside Ireland.

18   Derek Mahon to Frank Ormsby, 18 October [1977], Frank Ormsby Papers, Emory.

19   Derek Mahon, *The Sea in Winter* (Old Deerfield, Mass./Dublin: Deerfield Press/Gallery Press, 1979), 5.

20   Mahon, *Sea in Winter,* 5.

21   Derek Mahon to Peter Fallon, 3 September [*c.* 1981–83], Peter Fallon/Gallery Press Collection, Emory.

22   Ibid., [*c.* 1982].

23   Derek Mahon, 'An Evening of Irish Poetry with Derek Mahon', audio tape, University Archives, Emory, 29 January 1996.

24   *Poems, 1962–1978* had first been published in 1979. The second printing followed in 1986 by which time many of the poems had been revised. Mahon's own working copy of the collection shows evidence of numerous corrections as well as later revisions to individual poems.

25   Derek Mahon to Jacky Simms, 5 March 1987, Peter Fallon/Gallery Press Collection, Emory.

26   Derek Mahon to Peter Fallon, 5 June 1987, Peter Fallon/Gallery Press Collection, Emory.

27   Jacky Simms to Derek Mahon, 29 May 1987, Peter Fallon/Gallery Press Collection, Emory.

28   Denman, 'Know the One?', 30.

29   Derek Mahon to Jacky Simms, 5 Mar 1987, Peter Fallon/Gallery Press Collection, Emory.

30   Derek Mahon, *The Yellow Book* (Gallery, 1997), 12.

31   Ibid, 29.

32   Mahon, 'Derek Mahon Interviewed', 6.

33   Derek Mahon to Maureen Cairnduff, 10 March 1999, Derek Mahon Papers, Emory.

34   Mahon, *Sea in Winter*, [7].

35   Mahon, *Collected Poems*, 41.

13: BLACKSTAFF PRESS: PUBLISHING 'A LOCAL ROW'

1   Patrick Kavanagh, *The Complete Poems* (ed.) Peter Kavanagh (New York, 1984), 238.

2   Patrick Kavanagh, 'The Parish and the Universe', *Collected Pruse* (London, 1967), 282, 283.

3   Personal communication.

14: THE WORLD OF IRISH UNIVERSITY PRESS

1   John O'Meara, formerly Professor of Latin at University College Dublin, and an advisor to IUP from 1971, writes about the Press in 'On the Fringe of Letters', *Irish University Review*, 27 (1997), 310–24 (317–19).

2   Thomas Turley to HMSO, 21 July 1967, archives of the Irish University Press at the

Four Courts Press.

3   Mark Matthews, archives of the Irish University Press at the Four Courts Press.

4   *Choice*, March 1974.

5   Receiver's report (1974), archives of the Irish University Press at the Four Courts Press.

Index